Employment Relations and National Culture

NEW HORIZONS IN INSTITUTIONAL AND EVOLUTIONARY ECONOMICS

General Editor: Geoffrey M. Hodgson
Research Professor, University of Hertfordshire Business School, UK

Economics today is at a crossroads. New ideas and approaches are challenging the largely static and equilibrium-oriented models that used to dominate mainstream economics. The study of economic institutions – long neglected in the economics textbooks – has returned to the forefront of theoretical and empirical investigation.

This challenging and interdisciplinary series publishes leading works at the forefront of institutional and evolutionary theory and focuses on cutting-edge analyses of modern socio-economic systems. The aim is to understand both the institutional structures of modern economies and the processes of economic evolution and development. Contributions will be from all forms of evolutionary and institutional economics, as well as from Post-Keynesian, Austrian and other schools. The overriding aim is to understand the processes of institutional transformation and economic change.

Employment Relations and National Culture

Continuity and Change in the Age of Globalization

Ferrie Pot

Assistant Professor of Economic Organization, Erasmus University Rotterdam, The Netherlands

NEW HORIZONS IN INSTITUTIONAL AND EVOLUTIONARY ECONOMICS

Edward Elgar
Cheltenham, UK • Northampton, MA, USA

Published by
Edward Elgar Publishing Limited
Glensanda House
Montpellier Parade
Cheltenham
Glos GL50 1UA
UK

Edward Elgar Publishing, Inc.
136 West Street
Suite 202
Northampton
Massachusetts 01060
USA

A catalogue record for this book
is available from the British Library

Library of Congress Cataloguing in Publication Data

Pot, Ferrie, 1969–
Employment relations and national culture: continuity and change in the age of globalization / Ferrie Pot.
(New horizons in institutional and evolutionary economics)
Includes bibliographical references and index.
1. Comparative industrial relations. 2. Industrial relations—Cross-cultural studies. 3. Foreign trade and employment. 4. International trade—Social aspects. 5. Industrial relations—United States—Case studies. 6. Industrial relations—Netherlands—Case studies. I. Title. II. Series.

HD6971 .P67 2000
306.3'4—dc21 99–087376

ISBN 1 84064 229 7

Printed and bound in Great Britain by Bookcraft (Bath) Ltd.

Contents

List of Tables

List of Figures

Acknowledgments

This book originates from a joint research program of the Roosevelt Study Center and the Tinbergen Institute of the Erasmus University Rotterdam that has been supported by a number of Dutch and American corporations. The aim of the overall research program has been to identify differences and similarities between the business cultures of the Netherlands and the United States. As a Ph.D. candidate, I was given the opportunity to work on this research program and I chose to focus my efforts on the cultural differences with respect to the management of labour. Although I realize that I can impossibly be complete, I want to thank all those people who have helped me to make my effort a successful one.

I want to start thanking the initiators of the research program, which are Cees van Minnen of the Roosevelt Study Center and Huib Vleesenbeek of the Erasmus University. During the research project, Cees acted as a great organizer and an indispensable integrator of academic and corporate interests. Huib, who was the intellectual father of my sub-project, unfortunately passed away during this research project. In the belief that the end result of the project would have pleased him, I am happy to remember him.

Next, I want to thank my inspirators; those people who gave me the intellectual energy to end this book successfully. At the first place, I want to mention Jaap Paauwe and John Groenewegen. Jaap, who took over the supervisory job of Huib Vleesenbeek in the course of the project, was a major guide in the trouble waters of empirical research through his deep own experience in empirical business research. John, who was my teacher as an undergraduate, continued to be a major source of inspiration. Situated on the same floor of the Erasmus University, he was always there for all sorts of questions, whether they were small or big, smart or stupid, academic or personal. Second, out of all the academics whose publications and presentations have stimulated me, I especially want to mention the organizers of the summer courses of the European Association for Evolutionary and Political Economy, Geoff Hodgson and Tony Lawson. Their summer courses were, besides great places to spend the summer, highly inspiring events.

The next group of people to whom I want to express my gratitude is the group of representatives of the corporations and institutions who supported the research project. They are, in random order, mr. J.C. de Boer (General Electric), mr. M. van Buren (Fluor Daniel), mr. M.A. Stoffels (Vebego International), mr. H.P. van Heel (Branche Technologie Centrum Chemische Industrie), mr. S.W.W. Lubsen (Heineken), mr. J.W. Schipper (Philip Morris), mr. L.M. van der Mandele (Arthur D. Little), mr. A. Bosman (Esso), mr. M. Westerlaken (Dow Benelux), mr. R. Ruules (Dow Benelux), mr. A.J. Coster (VB Deloitte & Touche), mr. H.H.F. Wijffels (Rabobank), mr. G. van der Scheer (Province of Zeeland) and mr. L.A. Geelhoed (Ministry of General Affairs). These people enabled me to write this book, not only by donating financial means, but primarily by opening the gates of the various companies.

The group of people who most deeply deserve my gratitude are the informants of the various companies where I conducted my empirical research. Although I had little to offer them, they received me in their offices and gave me their time during their busy work schedules. Their willingness to cooperate was at the basis of this study. Special thanks go to the contact persons of the four companies that I visited most often, both in the Netherlands and in the United States: General Electric Plastics, Dow Chemical, DSM and Akzo Nobel. In random order, I want to mention Aadje van 't Riet, Joop de Rooy, Randy Price, John Meijs, Amy Parrish, Francois Vissers, Mike Hanley, Ruud Klaassen, Mike Vatalaro, Gerard van Harten, Marinus Follon and Steve Wilson.

Finally, I want to thank some people who do not classify in the above categories. Lee Dyer who hosted me for several months at the School of Industrial and Labor Relations of Cornell University in Ithaca. Joris Meijaard, my closest colleague whose similar research experiences made me feel less lonely. Wilma Speijer, the secretary of the department of Economic Organization, who was always ready for assistance. Last, but certainly not least, I need to thank Gülbahar Tezel. Without her support and assistance this book would not have been published, in any case not in its current form.

1. Cultural embeddedness of the employment relationship

INTRODUCTION

Since the dramatic developments in the former Soviet Union and the East European countries at the end of the 1980s, capitalism has established itself as the dominant mode of economic organization in the modern world. Capitalism has overcome the debate between communist ideologists and proponents of free markets.

Nevertheless, this landslide victory has not calmed down discussions on the superior form of economic organization, for capitalism is not a homogeneous form of economic organization. Historically, alternative models of capitalist economic organization have developed across culturally diverse nation states, each with its own strengths and weaknesses (Clegg et al., 1990; Streeck, 1992; Guillén, 1994; Groenewegen, 1997). For example, Sakakibara (1993) and Dore (1997) describe the distinct Japanese model of market economics. The Anglo-Saxon model of capitalism is extensively examined by Lazonick (1997). Albert (1990) presents a popular account of the Rhineland model, while Whitley (1992) and Min Chen (1995) describe the particularity of East Asian economic models.

This book addresses the question of how important these differences are and will continue to be. The last decade has witnessed an increasingly political, cultural and economic interdependence among nation states. These fundamental developments characterizing the modern world order are captured by the notion of 'globalization'. The process of globalization has added new fuel to the debate around the unity or diversity of capitalism, for, as the argument goes, culturally based differences will vanish as obsolete national economic practices are sanctioned by the iron hand of the global market. Allegedly, a single capitalist system organized on the basis of a universal logic is emerging in which differences between national systems of economic organization are only a matter of consumer taste or a symbol of cultural style.

Of all the factors of production, labour is the one that is most society-bound and instilled with cultural meaning. Analysis of developments in the realm of the management of labour can shed light on the intensity of the global pressures towards convergence. This book explores the proneness of capitalist organization to global convergence with regard to the employment relationship. The question is posed whether there is a universal logic to organize the employment relationship to which corporations are forced to adjust.

CULTURAL DIVERSITY

The starting-point of the book is the current diversity of employment practices across culturally diverse nation states. This initial assumption is documented extensively at the societal as well as the corporate level. Consider first the evidence for the cultural embeddedness of the organization of the employment relationship at the societal level. Various disciplines in the social sciences have contributed to the identification of nation-specific features of the employment relationship. In a seminal work in the study of industrial relations, Dunlop (1958) introduced the concept of a 'national industrial relations system'. Drawing on this framework, Bean (1985) and Poole (1986) collected evidence on the broad variety of national systems of industrial relations. In the realm of management and organization studies, Whitley (1997) developed the concept of 'national work system' to capture the manner in which employment relations are socially regulated. Using a Marxist perspective, Edwards (1994) employed the concept of a 'national regime of labour regulation' to grasp the distinct approach to labour management that unifies employers within a single country. In the domain of the sociology of work, a group of French researchers demonstrated a 'societal effect' on the organization of work (Maurice et al., 1986). Finally, out of a collaborative research effort of an economist and a political scientist, the concept of a 'social system of production' was born (Hollingsworth and Boyer, 1997).

If one turns the attention away from the societal level of analysis to the level of the private firm, one enters the realm of personnel management or, as the discipline is more recently called, 'human resource management'. Numerous studies have demonstrated the diversity of corporate human resource management practices across culturally diverse nation states. Although the issues that are dealt with by management are similar across nation states, national differences have been observed in the way they are handled. In the early 1990s, three edited books that demonstrated the diversity of employment relations across Europe appeared (Pieper, 1990; Brewster and Tyson, 1992; Kirkbride, 1994). Furthermore, two comparative surveys on corporate human resource management practices on, respectively, a European and a world scale were conducted (Brewster and Hegewisch, 1994; Towers Perrin, 1992). Finally, Begin (1997) developed the concept of a 'human resource system' to model the systematic differences of corporate employment practices across six major developed nations.

THE CONVERGENCE/DIVERGENCE DEBATE

Proponents of the convergence postulate and adherents of the divergence thesis have debated the persistence of cultural diversity of economic organization. The former group views diversity as a temporary state of affairs and notes a tendency of societies to grow more alike. The latter maintains the existence of cultural variety as a continuing aspect of socioeconomic reality. In the postwar literature, the convergence thesis has been formulated in a wide variety of forms (Kerr, 1983; Boyer, 1996). With regard to the organization of the employment relationship, the case for convergence has passed through two distinct stages (Smith and Meiksins, 1995).

The first case for convergence of the employment relationship was advanced by Kerr et al. (1960), who proposed a 'logic of industrialization' that entailed the adoption over time, across capitalist and communist societies alike, of the same social, political and economic structures. The unifying effect of technology was thought to underlie the logic of industrialization. The more closely social arrangements were tied to technology, the more uniform they were held to be from one society to another. Theorists of the so-called 'contingency school' explored this perspective in organizational theory. It was argued that firm structure is largely free from cultural influence, because it is determined by external contingencies, such as size and technology (Pugh, 1981). The postulate of the culture-free thesis invoked an inverse reaction among researchers who emphasized the persistence of significant cultural differences of economic organization. Various studies appeared that found diversity among organizations across nations that could not be explained by reference to technology (Dore, 1973; Gallie, 1978; Maurice et al., 1980; Sorge and Warner, 1986). Most importantly, these studies demonstrated that, unlike the common assumption of the convergence thesis, organizations cannot be separated into a distinct technological and cultural sphere (Sorge, 1983). Human actors are not guided by either economic or social motives. Instead, actors' economic preferences are socially constructed in distinct national environments yielding different ways in which they relate to each other and to their firms.

Although the evidence seemed to favour a cultural viewpoint, the convergence thesis has been reformulated during the 1980s. Rather than imposing some technological constraint on the organization of the employment relationship, the new case for convergence draws on the process of economic globalization. Owing to the globalization of the economic realm, formerly 'national economies' are unleashed from the influence of national institutions. In semi-popular business literature, new prophets of globalization discovered 'forces' smashing national borders, creating a global market that national interventions were helpless to resist (Ohmae, 1990). This progressive erosion of sovereignty of nation states has cast increasing doubt on the persistence of nation-specific institutions as barriers against global convergence. However, since the universal standard of competitiveness has remained undefined, the direction of convergence is disputed. Three options can be considered. From the neoliberal perspective, it is suggested that, in order to survive and to sustain affluence in the new world order, national governments need to restrict their economic policies to the enforcement of an optimal functioning of markets (Friedman, 1982). According to this view, the United States is showing the other countries the way (The Economist, 1996).[1] At the organizational level, this trend was reflected by the advice given to employers to introduce more market mechanisms in the employment relationship: people are nothing but human 'resources' that should be managed according to economic principles. Dore (1986) proposes a reverse convergence thesis that originates in the Japanese model of economic organization. According to his proposition, market mechanisms should be softened by long-term relationships between firms and employees based on trust and solidarity to enable skill and knowledge development. A third convergence thesis suggests the reconfiguration of existing models of economic organization by a process of cross-fertilization. Pushed by competitive pressures, 'nations' will correct the flaws in their systems by adopting global 'best practices' (Groenewegen, 1997).

However, institutionalist writers once again challenge the convergence thesis. Although the altered nature of the global economy is acknowledged, Hollingsworth and Streeck (1994) identify eight reasons why convergence may fail to occur. Pre-eminent among these is the argument that the evolution of an institutional configuration is path-dependent. The number of developmental trajectories of a national system is limited, because it is conditioned by its historically grown structure (Hollingsworth, 1997). Moreover, it is argued that efficiency is a multidimensional concept. There are alternative standards of good economic performance that cannot be optimized by a single institutional configuration. Each model of capitalism possesses its own relative strengths and weaknesses (Streeck, 1992). In the same vein, the evidence for convergence at the organizational level is far from conclusive. Although the American model of human resource management has found worldwide appeal, various studies observe continuing diversity in corporate human resource management practices (Sparrow et al., 1994; Brewster et al., 1994). It is argued that the American origins of the original human resource management model inhibit its adoption in the distinct cultural contexts of European countries (Brewster, 1995).

THE IMPACT OF NATIONAL CULTURE

It is true that the continuing process of globalization compels those actors that are involved in the organization of the employment relationship, such as employers, union representatives or state officials, to adapt. However, to assess the direction of this process of adaptation, one needs to consider to what extent the process of globalization constrains the room for manoeuvre of the actors who are involved in shaping the employment relationship. Does the trend of globalization leave these actors with no other choice than to implement a universal model of 'best practice', or do these actors have sufficient strategic choice to enable them to adjust the employment relationship in a manner that is more in line with their cultural predisposition?

The literature on globalization is not conclusive in this respect. The notion of globalization captures various social processes that potentially give rise to global convergence of employment relations. Yet the degree to which these processes can constrain employment relations is not established. Although international competition has intensified in recent years, it is not true that national borders have lost their relevance to multinational firms. Divergent conditions in the home country of international firms remain an enduring source of competitive advantage (Porter, 1990). Moreover, the idea that global diffusion of microelectronic technology will end up in similar employment practices across nation states is contestable. It can be argued that the specific use of microelectronics is likely to be shaped in accordance with the cultural predisposition of the actors that use the technology (Sorge and Streeck, 1988). Likewise, the adoption of best-practice management methods is unlikely to account for global convergence. Although the Japanese model of lean production has been adopted outside the Japanese cultural context (Kenney and Florida, 1993), its global diffusion faces strong competition by other best-practice models with different cultural roots, such as flexible specialization, sociotechnical system design and diversified quality production (Berggren, 1992; Dankbaar, 1997). Finally, it is not at all clear how the power balance between employers and employees will develop in the near future. Although the process of globalization seems to strengthen the position of capital over labour, there are no indications that the new balance of power will favour employers to a similar extent across different national contexts (Boyer, 1997).

Clearly, the employment relationship is under the homogenizing pressure of various global trends. Nevertheless, it remains unclear whether these trends are sufficiently constraining to justify the convergence thesis. The literature on globalization identifies elements that oppose the global pressures for change. National culture appears as the primary source of institutional resistance withstanding the unifying impact of various global trends. While various global trends induce firms to change the employment relationship in accordance with a global standard, national culture preserves the existing diversity. However, the claim for continued divergence is seriously weakened by the vague treatment of the concept of culture. National culture is commonly introduced as a residual variable, a 'concept for the lazy' that only enters theory in the case that cross-national differences cannot be explained by more tangible variables. This failing to open the black box of culture weakens the plausibility of the divergence claim. Insight into the causal processes by which elements in the realm of national culture affect changes in employment relations is indispensable.

This book contributes to the convergence/divergence debate by studying the relation between national culture and the employment relationship. For this purpose, the notion of culture is carefully defined. Based on the structuration theory of Anthony Giddens, national culture is substantiated as a country-specific set of rules that structures human action. Members of the country's population unconsciously reproduce these cultural rules by acting in accordance with them. Furthermore, the book contains an empirical cross-cultural study that includes the Netherlands and the United States. The comparison of developments in the employment relationship between these two countries throws light on some of the causal processes by which national culture continues to affect employment relations. The main mechanism by which national culture exerts its influence on the management of labour appears to be the design of the procedure by which management realizes changes in a firm's employment practices. It is demonstrated that the procedure by which changes in the employment relationship are realized in, respectively, the Dutch and the American context is fundamentally different. Consequently, the outcomes of the change processes differ fundamentally. It is shown that the differences in the design of the change procedure reflect the cultural context of the Netherlands and the United States. In other words, in shaping the change processes, the actors have acted in accordance with, respectively, the Dutch and American cultural 'rules'. In so doing, the actors have, unconsciously, reproduced the specific cultural rules of each country. This continuous reproduction of cultural rules that guide the design of the change procedure is revealed as the major mechanism that ensures the continuing divergence of employment relations across the world.

In sum, this book offers confirmation of the intuition that actors respond to global challenges in ways that are in accordance with their cultural inclinations. It is not denied that there are globally common features in the nature and evolution of the employment relationship; global trends operate as triggers of change in the employment relationship. However, the ultimate effects of globalization are nation-specific. National culture shapes the process whereby global trends are institutionalized in a particular country. The book therefore challenges the widespread belief that global trends will lead to the homogenization of the employment relationship.

STRUCTURE OF THE BOOK

This book is composed of two parts. The first part (Chapters 2, 3 and 4) elaborates on the core theoretical concepts that are referred to in the book. These are the 'employment relationship', 'globalization' and 'national culture'. The second part (Chapters 5 and 6) concentrates on actual developments in the real world. An empirical analysis considers the effects of globalization on the employment relationship in, respectively, the United States and the Netherlands. A schematic overview of the study is shown in Figure 1.1.

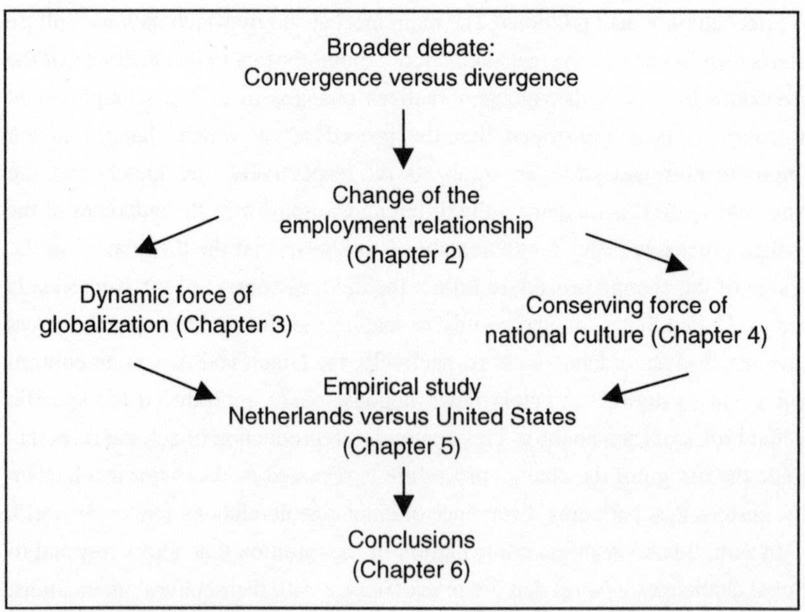

Figure 1.1 Overview of the book

The employment relationship is the first building block of the conceptual framework. In Chapter 2, the employment relationship is analysed at the level of the firm, for the firm is considered as the major actor in shaping the employment relationship and the one that is most exposed to the process of globalization. Accordingly, initiatives to change the organization of the employment relationship originate, most likely, within the management of the firm. The analysis of the literature on the theory of the firm identifies the major variables that affect the organization of the employment relationship. The analysis results in a theoretical framework that encompasses, on the one hand, variables that induce firms to adjust the employment relationship and, on the other hand, variables that mediate such a change process.

The notion of globalization is central in Chapter 3. Globalization is an umbrella concept. It refers to a set of mechanisms by which the organization of the employment relationship becomes more homogeneous across different cultural regions of the world. Five mechanisms are distinguished that might account for such homogenization: international competition, microelectronic technology, management methods, power balance between capital owners and labour, and individual value attributes. The current societal trends in the realm of each mechanism are examined to establish whether the claim of global convergence can be justified. The extent to which firms are actually exposed to pressures that apply in a similar way, irrespective of national borders, all over the world is analysed.

Chapter 4 takes up the challenge to conceptualize the notion of national culture. Culture is often treated as a black box – a residual variable that enters into explanations when more tangible variables are insufficient to explain cross-national differences. To prevent such an abuse, culture needs to be carefully defined. To meet the task of defining the notion of culture, Chapter 4 dwells upon the methodological perspective of the book. It contrasts two perspectives that focus on the relationship between the individual and the society, namely Bhaskar's critical realism and Giddens' structuration theory. In the end, a concept of 'work-related national culture' is presented that is based on Anthony Giddens' structuration theory. This theoretical perspective is adopted since it overcomes the traditional shortcomings of individualistic and holistic stances towards culture without compromising on the knowledgeability of the individual.

Chapter 5 reports on an empirical study that applies the theoretical framework. It presents a cross-cultural comparison of change processes of the employment relationship at the level of the firm. The Netherlands and the United

States are chosen as the subjects of this cross-cultural comparison. These countries are taken to be exemplars of, respectively, the Rhineland and the Anglo-Saxon model of capitalism. The comparative analysis is conducted in two parts. First, the Dutch and the American work-related cultures are substantiated by the construction of ideal types. Second, data on actual change processes of the employment relationship at four matched samples of American and Dutch production plants are presented.

The final chapter weaves the threads together. The empirical findings are discussed in terms of the theoretical framework. At first sight, the empirical findings suggest that similar development paths irrespective of the cultural context are followed in both the Netherlands and the United States. In recent years, most companies have entertained notions such as 'downsizing', 'delayering', 'empowerment' and 'total quality management'. This observation might indicate a clear trend towards global uniformity. However, a more detailed scrutiny of these seemingly common developments reveals a number of differentiating aspects. The responses of, respectively, Dutch and American firms to the challenges of globalization appear to differ in fundamental respects. To account for this outcome, an explanation is given that refers to the procedure by which the change processes are realized. The different design of the change procedure resulting from different culturally based preferences of the relevant actors explains the continuing divergence of employment practices.

NOTE

1. The idea that the United States has a leading role in the development towards global convergence has a long history. As early as 1901, Wilfred Scawen Blunt published a treatise titled 'The Americanization of the world' that referred to the erosion of local cultures by cosmopolitan influences (Spybey, 1996). Accordingly, some understand 'globalization' and 'Americanization' as synonyms.

2. The employment relationship: mechanisms of change

INTRODUCTION

Abundant evidence confirms the observation that the employment relationship is differently organized across culturally diverse nation states. Nevertheless, the persistence of this cultural diversity is debated. While some authors announce that cultural differences will vanish in the continuing process of globalization, others predict the preservation of cultural diversity and national peculiarities.

The contribution of this book to the convergence/divergence debate starts with an analysis of the theory of the firm, for the firm is the major actor that shapes the employment relationship. A shift in the organization of the employment relationship is most likely to be initiated by the firm. Accordingly, the mechanisms that induce firms to adjust their labour management practices need to be identified to assess the direction in which the employment relationship will evolve. This chapter provides a conceptual framework by which the development of the employment relationship can be understood. The starting-point of the conceptual framework is the notion of the firm. Before one can understand the behaviour of the firm with regard to the employment relationship, one needs to have a clear view on the nature of the firm.

Where would one look for a theoretical elaboration of the firm? A non-economist would take it for granted that the economic discipline has a highly developed theory of the firm. After all, firms are the engines of growth of modern capitalist economies. However, the non-economist is bound to be disappointed. The standard neoclassical theory of the firm has an extremely rudimentary conception of the firm. According to this theory, which is presented in most modern-day microeconomic textbooks, the firm is a set of feasible production plans. It represents a manager who maximizes the owner's welfare by buying and selling inputs and outputs in a spot market. Clearly, such a perspective is a caricature of the modern firm and has some very clear weaknesses. It does not explain how production is organized within a firm or how conflicts of interests between the firm's various participants – owners, managers and workers – are resolved.

In this chapter, the search for a theoretical foundation of the behaviour of the firm is taken beyond the realm of mainstream economics. What is a firm? Why do firms exist? This chapter does not pretend to be a systematic survey of the theory of the firm; rather, it serves to highlight some of the most important ideas on the issue. Six theories of the firm and their associated perspectives on the organization of the employment relationship are presented. The various theories are classified into two groups. The first section will address the so-called 'efficiency branch' of the firm that entails three theories of the firm: agency theory, transaction cost theory and competence theory. The common denominator that unifies these theories is the efficiency postulate. The pursuit of efficiency is the primary driver of firm behaviour and, consequently, the organization of the employment relationship. However, the efficiency thesis is not left without criticism; on the sidelines of the literature on the firm, one can find several theoretical traditions that raise doubt about its validity. The second section draws attention to three alternative perspectives of the firm. Successively, attention is given to the radical school of political economy, the new institutionalism in organizational analysis and the neoinstitutionalism in economics. Alternative mechanisms that drive the organization of the employment relationship, such as power, social legitimization and ceremonial values, are suggested. The third section draws the threads together. Based on a pluralist perspective, a framework that integrates the various theoretical viewpoints is presented.

EFFICIENCY BRANCH OF ORGANIZATION

The efficiency branch of organization contains a number of rival theories that explain the nature of the firm. Their common denominator is the adoption of economic efficiency at the roots of their explanation. The firm exists because of its superior economic efficiency vis-à-vis other modes of organization. This view is extended to the behaviour of firms. Firm behaviour, including the organization of the employment relationship, is guided by the pursuit of efficient outcomes.

Two alternative perspectives of the firm that adhere to the efficiency thesis can be distinguished (Foss, 1993; Hodgson, 1996). The first perspective is labelled the 'contractual view' of the firm and focuses on the costs of contracting. The second perspective is referred to as the 'competence perspective' and emphasizes productive capabilities.

The contractual perspective originates with Ronald Coase's classic contribution, 'The nature of the firm', published in 1937: 'Coase's contribution is seminal for many reasons, but certainly for calling attention to the absence of a theory of the existence of the firm' (Demsetz, 1993, p.159). Coase (1937) is one of the first attempts to rationalize the existence of firms. He rejected the, by then, prevailing explanation of the firm that was based on Adam Smith's division of labour argument, for specialized production can be regulated by the price mechanism of the market without the need for any formal organization. Therefore, Coase asked the question: why do firms, 'these islands of conscious power' which eliminate market transactions, exist? Why are not all economic agents independent traders who are coordinated by the price mechanism? The answer that Coase brings forth is that there is a cost of using the price mechanism. Markets do not function without costs, because transaction costs are involved. Accordingly, firms will arise when the costs of the market become excessive in comparison with the costs of internal organization of the firm. In his words, 'the operation of a market costs something and by forming an organization and allowing some authority (an 'entrepreneur') to direct the resources, certain marketing costs are saved' (Coase, 1937, p.22).

The so-called 'competence perspective' of the firm provides the major alternative to the contractual view. The competence perspective is not a homogeneous body of work, but a collective label for a variety of different theories. The common feature of this theoretical branch is the acknowledgment of the importance of 'firm-specific assets that are knowledge-related, intangible, hard to trade and shared among the agents of the firm' (Foss, 1996a). The firm should essentially be viewed as a 'repository of such firm-specific competencies'. Edith Penrose is recognized as the primary antecedent of this theoretical approach to the firm: 'It may with much justice be said that what Ronald Coase is to the contractual approach, Penrose is to the competence perspective' (ibid., p.3). Penrose (1959) emphasized the importance of excess firm resources to explain the growth process of the individual firm. Lack of managerial talent is argued to be the primary bottleneck to a firm's growth. The gradual routinization of tasks over time, however, allows the manager to direct attention to new activities and to expand the organization. Implicit in Penrose's depiction of the growth process is the perspective of a firm as a repository of competencies that have accumulated over time. In her view, 'a firm is more than an administrative unit; it is also a collection of productive resources' (Penrose, 1959, p.24).

The contractual view of the firm has been further developed by agency theory (Alchian and Demsetz, 1972) and transaction cost economics (Williamson, 1975, 1985). These contributions are elaborated below, with a discussion of recent developments in the field of strategic management that are based on the competence perspective of the firm ending the present section.

Agency Theory

Generally, agency theory focuses on contractual relationships between principals and agents. In a principal–agent relationship, the agent is employed by the principal to perform some service on his behalf. The concern of the principal is to ensure that the agent acts in his best interests. The challenge in the agency relationship arises whenever the principal cannot perfectly and without costs monitor the actions of the agent. Then problems of inducement and enforcement come to the fore, problems which should be solved by appropriate design of the contractual relationship.

Alchian and Demsetz (1972) applied the reasoning of agency theory to the firm and derived a theoretical explanation for the existence of the firm. They do not deny the transaction cost argument of Coase, but they dispatch his insight as a tautology and 'difficult to disagree with'. For them, it is obvious that the competitive advantage of organizing resources within the firm improves if the costs of transacting across the market increase. Instead, Alchian and Demsetz take another path to account for the existence of the firm. They challenge the meaning Coase attaches to a firm. According to Coase, the distinguishing mark of the firm is the supersession of the price mechanism by hierarchical authority, or 'conscious power'. Alchian and Demzetz reject this distinction between markets and firms. In their view, the employment contract cannot be distinguished from an ordinary market contract: 'It is common to see the firm characterized by the power to settle issues by fiat, by authority, or by disciplinary action superior to that available in the conventional market. This is delusion. The firm does not own all its inputs. It has no power of fiat, no authority, no disciplinary action any different in the slightest degree from ordinary market contracting between any two people' (Alchian and Demsetz, 1972, p.777). Alchian and Demsetz assert that both markets and firms are coordinated by contracts that are essentially the same. The relationship between a boss and an employee is no different from the relation between a grocer and a customer. Nevertheless, the organizational structures of markets and firms are not similar. In what sense, then, does a firm relationship deviate from a market relationship, according to Alchian and Demsetz?

The firm arises, according to Alchian and Demsetz, as a rational response to the efficiency gains of team production. Productivity can be enhanced if people are organized in cooperative team production. Alchian and Demsetz assert that rather than by linking individual efforts across impersonal markets, teams of input owners can produce more in cooperation with one another than separately. However, they state that, in the case of team production, individual productivity can no longer be measured adequately. This difficulty in identifying individual efforts creates the potential for shirking among the team members.[1] The effects of shirking might nullify the increased productivity of team organization. Accordingly, the efficiency effect of team production can only be sustained if member shirking can be reduced. At this point, the firm enters the world of Alchian and Demsetz.

Alchian and Demsetz propose to mitigate the shirking problem by the introduction of a monitor who ensures the full devotion of the team members. However, the problem of individual shirking is not solved unless the monitor can be withheld from shirking himself. The key to team productivity is to ensure that the monitor has incentives to do his job efficiently. In other words, the monitor also needs to be monitored. The monitoring problem is most efficiently solved, Alchian and Demsetz argue, if the monitor is provided with the net earnings of the team production (as 'residual claimant') and if he can adjust the contracts with the team members in accordance with their individual productivity (as 'central contractor'). The monitor with such features is the central contracting agent or the 'classical firm'.[2]

All rational team members favour the instalment of the classical firm, for all team members are better off if the shirking problem is mitigated. Because of its efficiency, Alchian and Demsetz assume that the firm emerges spontaneously from the contracting behaviours of rational economic actors whenever the net value of team production (including monitoring costs) exceeds the net value of bilateral market exchange among independent input owners. Thus the hierarchical employment relationship inherent to the classical firm is not one of authority and dominance, but solely a voluntary contractual relationship. In essence, the classical firm is 'the centralized contractual agent in a team productive process – not some superior authoritarian directive or disciplinary power' (ibid., p.776). The central agent is called the firm's owner and the employer. In this view, the employer is not a buyer of labour capacity on the labour market; to the contrary, the employer 'sells' his capability to monitor efficiently to employees. Employees hire the employer because he supports them in ascertaining good input combinations of team activity.

Implications for the employment relationship

The Alchian–Demsetz perspective on the firm has a number of normative implications for the employment relationship. The reward system is of central concern, for their logic implies that the primary function of firm management is to monitor the efforts of the employees and to adapt rewards to their marginal productivity. In their view, the competitive advantage of firms originates from having more efficient monitoring systems: 'Efficient production with heterogeneous resources is a result not of having better resources but in knowing more accurately the relative productive performances of those resources (...) greater accuracy of knowledge of the potential and actual productive actions of inputs rather having high productivity resources makes a firm profitable' (Alchian and Demsetz, 1972, p.790). Management should be given the role of residual claimant. It should receive proper incentives through profit-sharing mechanisms, such as bonuses and options, to maximize the value added of team production. Furthermore, the employment contract should allow for flexible rewards that are in line with the marginal productivity of the individual employee. Performance appraisal becomes a key practice of personnel management.[3]

Holmstrom and Milgrom (1991) infer implications for job design from the analysis of multi-task jobs. First, they argue that each task should be made the responsibility of just one agent (the principle of unity of responsibility). Moreover, activities should be grouped into hard-to-monitor and easy-to-monitor jobs or skilled and unskilled jobs. In this way, the central monitor can give strong incentives for tasks that are easily monitored without fearing that the employee will neglect those tasks that are harder to measure. With regard to the management of the human resource flow, Alchian and Demsetz identify certain efficiency gains for internal labour market mechanisms. Internal labour markets economize on monitoring costs since information on incumbent employees can be ascertained more accurately than on people outside the firm. However, lifetime employment arrangements cannot be taken for granted, for the employee and the employer are equally free to terminate the contractual relationship. The firm is just a nexus of contracts without 'social responsibility'. Accordingly, the quest for employee participation is not rooted in motives of social responsibility. Employee participation exists because it economizes on monitoring costs. A higher degree of loyalty reduces the incentive to shirk of the team members.

Transaction Cost Theory

Oliver Williamson is widely acknowledged to have diffused Coase's transaction cost argument to a broad audience (Williamson, 1975, 1985). The theoretical framework of his transaction cost economics builds on the major insight of Coase: 'activities are internally organized whenever the costs of managing that activity within the firm are lower than the transaction costs that are involved with market coordination'. Williamson's response to the two major criticisms of Alchian and Demsetz (1972) on the argument of Coase clarifies his position.

First, Alchian and Demsetz assert that the market and the firm are two sides of the same coin. They maintain the view that the firm is no different from the market in contractual respects. Williamson, in contrast, ensures the distinction between an employment contract and a market (or sales) contract. The firm is different from the market, because coordination in an authority relationship is not accomplished through 'price', but by means of 'fiat'. The employment contract entails an agreement concerning the worker's willingness to accept the employer's authority in exchange for a wage. In this way, the employer can direct the worker to specific actions that the worker must perform. Moreover, the firm is 'its own court of ultimate appeal' (Williamson, 1996). Firms have to solve internal problems by themselves, for they are denied access to public courts to resolve intra-firm disputes (in contrast to inter-firm disputes).

Second, Alchian and Demsetz object to the tautological nature of Coase's transaction cost argument as it fails to specify 'the circumstances under which the cost of "managing" resources is low relative to the cost of allocating resources through market transactions' (Alchian and Demsetz, 1972, p.784). Without proper definition of the concept of transaction costs, almost everything can be rationalized by invoking suitably specified transaction costs. Williamson responds to this criticism by defining the concept of transaction costs. For this purpose, the transaction is taken as the basic unit of analysis. Williamson identifies three principal dimensions that determine the magnitude of the transaction costs: 'frequency', 'uncertainty' and 'asset specificity'. The main inferences of transaction cost economics are based on the dimension 'asset specificity': 'Asset specificity is the big locomotive to which transaction cost economics owes much of its predictive content. Absent this condition, the world of contract is vastly specified; enter asset specificity, and non standard contracting practices quickly appear' (Williamson, 1985, p.56).[4] However, the role of asset specificity for the magnitude of transaction costs becomes crucial only in conjunction with two critical assumptions with regard to human behaviour. The fiction of a perfectly rational economic man is replaced by the notion of 'bounded rationality'. Although actors are 'intendedly rational', limits on human cognitive competencies prevent actors foreseeing all future contingencies that come along with uncertain transactions. The second behavioural assumption is that human agents are given to opportunism: that is, 'a deep condition of self-interest seeking that contemplates guile'.

Within this framework of behavioural assumptions and transaction attributes, Williamson links the transaction with an appropriate mode of coordination mechanism: in his own terms, 'aligning transactions with governance structures in a discriminating way' (Williamson, 1993, p.90). To do so, Williamson compares the magnitude of transaction costs under alternative governance structures.[5] The main case to which transaction cost economics subscribes is 'efficient organization' or 'economizing on transaction costs'. That is, a governance structure is selected if it minimizes transaction costs.[6] Table 2.1 depicts the main conjectures of Williamson.

The earlier question can now be answered. Why do firms exist? Given bounded rationality and opportunism, a transaction that involves a high degree of asset specificity is more efficiently coordinated (that is, with lower transaction costs) by internal governance than by means of the market mechanism. Thus, according to Williamson, the existence of asset specificity in an imperfect environment provides the rationale for the existence of the firm.[7] Coordination of transactions that involve little asset specificity can be left to the market

Table 2.1 Attributes of the contracting process

Bounded rationality	Opportunism	Asset specificity	Implied contracting process
–	+	+	Planning
+	–	+	Promise
+	+	–	Market competition
+	+	+	Internal governance

Source: Williamson (1985).

mechanism without facing increased transaction costs. 'Given bounded rationality and opportunism, the study of economic organization needs to make allowance for both. The following imperative is therefore proposed: organize economic activity so as to economise on bounded rationality while simultaneously safeguarding the transactions in question against the hazards of opportunism' (Williamson, 1993, p.93).

Implications for the employment relationship

The essential elements of the transaction cost framework are outlined above. Some implications for the organization of the employment relationship are outlined by Williamson et al. (1975), who apply the transaction cost framework to the transaction of idiosyncratic labour. The notion of 'idiosyncratic labour' resembles the notion of asset specificity. It refers to firm-specific skills of workers that are indispensable for productive performance. Clearly, such firm-specific skills are not freely available on the external labour market, but they have to be acquired by experience and by learning-by-doing. General classroom education is inadequate to disclose certain job details. Therefore, on-the-job training is considered to be essential for the effective communication of task-specific knowledge. However, the success of on-the-job training is conditional on the information disclosure attitudes of incumbent employees.[8] Here Williamson et al. (1975) locate the root of potential opportunistic behaviour: 'Both individually and as a group, incumbents are in possession of a valuable resource (knowledge) and can be expected to fully and candidly reveal it only in exchange for value (...) The danger is that incumbent employees will hoard information to their personnel advantage and engage in a series of bilateral monopolistic exchanges with the management to the detriment of both the firm and other employees as well' (Williamson et al., 1975, p.63). The existence of idiosyncratic tasks might result in increased transaction costs when incumbent employees pursue the value of their specific skills. Williamson et al. (1975) analyse the properties of various governance structures to coordinate the transaction of idiosyncratic labour. They conclude that an internal labour market structure will provide optimal outcomes in terms of transaction costs minimization. Internal labour markets evade opportunities for opportunistic bargaining by individual employees through the instalment of a reward system that attaches wage rates to jobs rather than to workers. Moreover, recognition of individual performance is accomplished through an internal promotion system. Higher-level positions are filled by 'promotions from within' so that the interests of the workers are tied to the firm. Furthermore, by making a cooperative attitude a criterion for further promotion, consummate cooperation among employees is stimulated.

Competence Theory

The so-called 'competence perspective' of the firm provides the main alternative to the contractual view. The competence view of the firm is not a homogeneous body of theory; rather it is a collection of contributions that emphasize the Penrosean view of the firm as a repository of specific competencies (Foss, 1996a; Knudsen, 1996). In recent years, the competence perspective of the firm has gained increasing influence in the field of strategic management.

A primary mission of the strategic management discipline is to analyse the diversity of performance among firms and to identify the origins of competitive advantage of successful firms. Traditional industrial organization theories that dominated the field of strategic management until the early 1980s emphasize industry structure (concentration, barriers to entry and so on) rather than internal features of firms to account for profitability (see for example Porter, 1980). In other words, the traditional approach focused primarily on the analysis of environmental opportunities and threats to the neglect of internal strengths and weaknesses of individual firms (Foss et al., 1995). However, the empirical observation that profit rates are more dispersed within industries than among industries has shifted attention towards firm-specific factors to explain differential firm performance.

Prahalad and Hamel (1990) are acknowledged as introducing the competence-based view of the firm to a large audience in the field of strategic management

(Wernerfelt, 1995). Their aim was to make normative suggestions to corporate managers on how to run a business successfully. On the basis of case studies of successful firms they inferred the notion of 'core competencies' as an essential ingredient for a firm's sustained competitive advantage. Earlier, Teece (1988) introduced core competencies as 'sets of differentiated technological skills, complementary assets and routines that provide the basis for a firm's competitive capacities in a particular business'. In the strategic management literature this notion of core competence has been variously described as 'firm-specific resources' (Wernerfelt, 1984; Conner, 1991), 'strategic assets' (Amit and Schoemaker, 1993) or 'dynamic capabilities' (Teece and Pisano, 1994; Foss, 1996b). Notwithstanding differences in emphasis among the various labels, they entail a similar perspective of the firm. Firms are seen as essentially heterogeneous. Firms do not have at their disposal similar resources, assets and/or capabilities, which provides firms with different productive possibilities and abilities to attract 'Ricardian rents'.[9]

Essential to the competence-based view is the identification of those dimensions of firm-specific resources that result in sustained competitive advantage. Several authors have tackled this question (Reed and DeFillipi, 1990; Barney, 1991; Amit and Schoemaker, 1993; Peteraf, 1993). Their contributions boil down to essentially one key source of sustained competitive advantage: 'imperfect imitability or tradability'. Resources are 'strategic' if they are valuable (advantage) and scarcely available (firm heterogeneity). However, valuable and rare resources result only in sustained competitive advantage if competitors that do not possess them cannot obtain them by imitation or trade. Barney (1991) provides three reasons to account for imperfect imitability and tradability of firm resources: path dependency, causal ambiguity and social complexity. First, certain resources cannot be developed from scratch, but are derived from unique historical conditions. A firm's ability to acquire and exploit certain resources depends upon the historical path that the firm has followed. Second, causal ambiguity or tacit knowledge exists when the link between the resources controlled by a firm and a firm's sustained competitive advantage is poorly understood or cannot be codified. Under such conditions, imitating firms cannot know the actions they should take in order to duplicate the strategies of firms with a sustained competitive advantage. A third reason to account for imperfect imitable resources is their complex social origin. Examples are interpersonal relations, corporate culture and a firm's reputation. Consequently, firms without the right attributes cannot engage in systematic efforts to imitate them.

The essence of the firm in the competence-based approach can now be clarified in contrast with the contractual view of the firm. The main contrast between these perspectives resides in their conception of the nature of competencies. In the contractual perspective of the firm, competencies are treated as a tradable entity. Competencies, such as technological artefacts or individual skills, can be traded across the boundaries of the firm. Conditional upon the level of transaction costs, competencies are internalized in the firm rather than coordinated by the market. The resource-based view replaces this 'thin conception of competence'. Instead, it conceives competencies as 'idiosyncratic knowledge capital to perform activities that resides within firms rather than individuals' (Foss, 1996a). At the root of the competence perspective is the acknowledgment of the tacit nature of competencies, for the tacit nature inhibits contractability and, therefore, tradability across markets. Accordingly, the market is not transcended by the firm in response to transaction cost considerations, but because of the intrinsic nature of competencies. 'The very essence of capabilities/competences is that they cannot be readily assembled through markets (...) entrepreneurial activity cannot lead to the immediate replication of unique organizational skills through simply entering a market and piecing the parts together overnight' (Teece and Pisano, 1994, p.540).[10]

Implications for the employment relationship

The competence perspective of the firm lays the foundation for a high status of the personnel management function in firms, for people are regarded as the carriers of much of the organization-specific knowledge (Wright et al., 1994; Kamoche, 1996). The competence-based view suggests that the role of personnel management is to contribute to sustained competitive advantage of a firm by facilitating the development of competencies that are both firm-specific and hard to imitate. Normative implications for human resource management practices are advanced by distinguishing between 'competence enhancing human resource systems' and 'competence destroying human resource systems' (Lado and Wilson, 1994). It should be noted that the implications for human resource management are not exhausted with recruitment and training of individual employees. The notion of 'competence' is characteristic of the organization as a whole and does not refer simply to the sum of knowledge and skills of individual employees.

In the area of work organization, the competence-based view has adopted a critical stance towards traditional organizational designs in which jobs are described in terms of individual tasks (Lawler, 1994). Instead, it is held that job descriptions should indicate required skill levels. 'Blocks of skills that are needed by the organization, rather than jobs, are the basic unit of analysis' (Lawler, 1994, p.9). Furthermore, the competence-based view suggests the instalment of work teams to support competence building. Teams prevent the potential erosion of competencies by employee turnover (Nordhaug and Gronhaug, 1994). Finally, Foss (1996a) draws attention to the 'perils of outsourcing'. If the path-dependency of competence building is acknowledged, extensive outsourcing leads to a loss of ability to upgrade competencies.

With regard to the management of the human resource flow, the competence-based view warns against excessive turnover. Firm-specific competencies cannot be bought on the external labour market, but need to be built over longer periods. The virtues of an internal labour market structure as a mechanism to foster learning are stressed as it creates long-term commitment from both the firm and its employees. A stable relationship induces greater investments in firm-specific human capital by both parties (Lado and Wilson, 1994). With respect to the reward system, a competence-based perspective of the firm should stimulate the enhancement of employees' skill level. Skill-based pay appears to be a good fit (Lawler, 1994). However, according to Teece and Pisano (1994), the use of 'high-powered' individual incentives should be avoided. They perceive the essence of firm organization as a 'domain of unleveraged or low-powered incentives' which fosters collaborative activities that are essential to competence building.

ALTERNATIVE MECHANISMS OF CHANGE

The previous section examined three distinct theories of the firm that share a common perspective on the essence of the firm. All theories support the assumption that the firm is an efficient solution to the failures of the market. On the one hand, the contractual perspective derives the existence of the firm from contractual hazards that are involved with pure market contracting. The firm is an efficient solution in response to cost-raising factors that are involved with formulating and monitoring contracts. On the other hand, competence theory argues that markets are unable to generate and coordinate certain kinds of capabilities. It is the firm which breeds and exploits efficiency-enhancing, firm-specific competencies.

Although the efficiency thesis seems plausible in a competitive business environment, it is challenged by various other schools of thought. In these views, the behaviour of the firm is not driven by the continuous striving for efficiency, but alternative mechanisms guide the actions of the firm. This section looks at three alternative explanatory mechanisms to account for the behaviour of firms: power, social legitimization and shared norms and values. First, we explore the school of radical political economy that focuses on the power balance between capital owners and labourers. Next, attention will be paid to the so-called 'new institutional school in organizational analysis'. This school, with a 'distinct sociological flavour', emphasizes social legitimization as a driver of firm behaviour. Finally, the tradition of neoinstitutional economics is examined in which the pattern of shared norms and values is given a crucial role.

Power

A number of theoretical approaches have proposed the concept of power as a fundamental mechanism to account for firm behaviour.[11] For the purpose of understanding the employment relationship, the scope of this section will be restricted to the power of capital over labour. Radical political economy conceives the capitalist firm primarily in terms of power relations.[12] The power of capital over labour guides the behaviour of the firm at the expense of its efficiency (Marginson, 1993). Three fundamental ideas characterize the radical position (Rebitzer, 1993). The first idea refers to the political structure of the firm. Radical authors challenge the postulate that the capitalist firm is an institution that originates from the mutual interest of both workers and employers; rather the firm incorporates a conflict of interest between parties that is resolved by the exercise of power. Second, radical authors assert that work organizations other than the capitalist firm are feasible and can be more efficient. It cannot be claimed that the ubiquity of the capitalist firm in the actual world reflects its efficiency. The third idea advanced by the radical school is that existing organizational forms are the contingent result of particular historical developments. Below, the three objections to the efficiency postulate are examined in further detail.

The radical analysis of the firm starts with the acknowledgment of its political structure. Essentially, the radical approach objects to the view that the capitalist firm accommodates a consensus over goals.[13] It challenges the assumption of the efficiency branch that the firm is a rational instrument for pursuing the common goals of both workers and employers. Instead, the work setting is seen as a 'contested terrain' with various parties vying for control and for a greater share of the created value (Edwards, 1979). The firm incorporates an inherent conflict between workers and employers. Workers are motivated by the need to attain an adequate standard of living and to exert control over the pace and content of work. Employers are motivated by acquisition of profit that necessitates cost minimization and control over the production process.[14] According to the radical viewpoint, the capitalist firm is primarily an institution for solving the conflict of interest to the advantage of the employer. Rather than a rational system for performing work in the most efficient manner, the firm is viewed as a power system designed to maximize control and profits in favour of the capital owners. The capitalist firm operates in the interests of the capitalist owner because it combines an incompletely specified employment contract with a system in which employers appropriate the final returns. The employment contract leaves the employer with the right (within limits) to direct workers to tasks and to specify effort levels after the contract terms are agreed. When additional value is generated because the value of actual work performed exceeds the price of labour inputs, it will only benefit the employer. By securing greater effort from workers, employers can increase output and revenues while the costs of labour inputs remain unchanged. Consequently, a strengthening of the authority relation results in more output from the same capacity of labour purchased. In this view, prevalent forms of work organization are not based on considerations of efficiency, but 'employers select that means of work organization consistent with the objectives of maximizing their own return and maintaining or strengthening their own authority' (Marginson, 1993, p.142). Accordingly, attempts of firms to improve human relations by means of participative structures are questioned. Such initiatives are perceived as new bureaucratic control mechanisms or 'psychological tools' to disguise the fundamental exploitative nature of organizations.[15]

The power argument of the radical approach is supported by the assertion that the capitalist firm is relatively inefficient. Radical authors contend that more efficient forms of work organization than the capitalist firm are feasible. Superior efficiency is claimed for firms that are more democratically run, such as labour-managed firms or workers' cooperatives (Ben-Ner et al., 1996). Nevertheless, the dispersion of such alternative modes of work organization is prevented as capital owners hold to their power. The efficiency branch rejects this claim by reference to the selective attributes of the market environment. Entrenched power interests can delay the displacement of less efficient modes of work organization, but 'later if not sooner, inefficiency in a commercial sector invites its own demise' (Williamson, 1994, p.87). Authors in the efficiency tradition take the limited spread of worker-managed firms as proof of the inferior efficiency of this organizational form. 'The fact that this system [of worker participation] seldom arises out of voluntary arrangements among individuals strongly suggests that codetermination or industrial democracy is less efficient than the alternatives which grow up and survive in a competitive environment' (Jensen and Meckling, 1979, cited in Hodgson, 1993, p.200). Radical economists object to the efficient selection argument, on two grounds. One concerns the issue of appropriation and technical efficiency. The second refers to the path-dependent nature of historical development. Below, each argument is briefly examined.

Radical economists criticize the selection argument because it conflates efficiency with profit maximization. Radical authors have demonstrated that profit maximization does not necessarily result in increased efficiency. They did so by introducing the concept of technological efficiency. An increase in technological efficiency refers to an increase in output for given inputs. It is argued that a more profitable production system may be less efficient in technological terms: 'the social function of hierarchical work organization is not technical efficiency, but accumulation' (Marglin, 1974, p.62). The inferiority of the capitalist firm in terms of technical inefficiency is rooted in the unspecified employment contract, for in such a contract with a fixed wage level, employers gain more profits by extracting more labour effort from a given workforce. This course of action stimulates the profit level. Nevertheless, the outcome in terms of technological efficiency remains indeterminate, because outputs as well as labour inputs have increased. Conventional efficiency arguments refer only to cost minimization and increased profits to the neglect of technological efficiency and considerations of appropriation. Marglin (1974) applies this thesis to the emergence of the factory system. He argues that the early machine-powered factories arose because they assured individual capitalists of access to rents and authority over their labour force. 'The key to the success of the factory, as well as its aspiration, was the substitution of capitalist for workers' control of the production process; discipline and supervision could and did reduce costs without being technologically superior' (Marglin, 1974, p.62).

A further argument in defence of the worker-managed firm against objections from the efficient selection thesis refers to the institutional context in which firms operate. The capital market is of particular importance. It is argued that capital markets tend to penalize democratically run firms. Equity is provided on less favourable rights to worker-managed firms because voting or other supervisory rights are not available (Putterman, 1993). Furthermore, capitalist firms are preferred by stockholders as they are less risk-averse than worker-owners (Rebitzer, 1993). Bowles and Gintis (1976) show that the education system in the United States has been fashioned to reflect the dominant capitalist mode of work organization. Levine and Tyson (1990) note other environmental issues. They show that productivity benefits of employee participation are maximized when jobs are secured. However, employment stability is more expensive in an environment where other employers do not offer comparable policies. Finally, the path-dependent nature of technology is emphasized. Historical studies demonstrate that the supplanting of craft-based production by the factory system is better explained by considerations of control rather than efficiency (Marglin, 1974; Piore and Sabel, 1984). Nevertheless, once the technological path of the factory system had been selected, the direction of technical change was determined to a large extent.

To sum up, the radical view holds that the historical evolution of the firm reflects a series of choices by employers over technology and work organization which serve the aim of maximizing their own private return. It cannot be presumed that these choices are either technologically or organizationally more efficient.

Social Legitimization

A second alternative mechanism to account for firm behaviour is provided by the so-called 'new institutionalism in organizational analysis', a school that exhibits a 'distinct sociological flavour' (DiMaggio and Powell, 1991).[16] Traditionally, sociological approaches are critical of economic perspectives of firms that emphasize rationality and efficiency. Rather than efficiency, the new institutionalism in organizational analysis advances social legitimization or conformism as the critical mechanisms that explain firm behaviour: 'Today, however, structural change in organizations seems less and less driven by competition or by the need for efficiency. Instead, we contend, bureaucratization and other forms of organizational change occur as the result of processes that make organizations more similar without necessarily making them more efficient' (DiMaggio and Powell, 1983, p.63).[17]

The roots of the new institutionalism in organizational analysis can be traced to the 'old' institutionalist work of Selznick. In the writings of Selznick, attention was focused on the non-rational features of organizational behaviour. Organizations have formal structures that are consciously designed to attain certain goals. However, Selznick asserts that these formal structures can 'never succeed in conquering the nonrational dimensions of organizational behaviour' (Selznick, 1948, p.25). The non-rational features of organizations originate from (1) the individuals who do not act merely in accordance with their formal roles, and (2) the informal organizational structures that link the individuals with one another outside the formal system. In the work of old institutionalists, attention is directed away from the formal structures and procedures towards mechanisms such as informal structures (coalitions and cliques), ideologies and cooptation. Informal interaction is highlighted to illustrate in what way the rational mission of the organization is subverted by parochial interests. The 'new' institutionalism departs from the 'old' programme in at least two significant ways (DiMaggio and Powell, 1991; Dobbin, 1994). First, the new institutionalism shares with the old that environmental constraints inhibit organizational rationality, but it has identified different sorts of constraint. Second, the new institutionalism does not only pay attention to environmental aspects that inhibit organizational rationality; it questions the notion of rationality itself. Below, each aspect is considered in more detail.

The old institutionalism version focused on interest conflicts between organizational participants. The 'new' version plays down the importance of interest conflicts within firms. Instead, it emphasizes the common understandings of social reality within and among organizations. These common understandings of social reality in general are considered to be rational and necessary. Organizations must incorporate them to avoid illegitimacy: 'Many of the positions, policies, programs and procedures of modern organizations are enforced by public opinion, by the views of important constituents, by knowledge legitimated through the educational system, by social prestige, by the laws and by the definitions of negligence and prudence used by the courts' (Meyer and Rowan, 1977, p.44). These common understandings or 'highly rationalized myths' exert an 'enormous impact' on organizational behaviour.[18] Such myths define organizational issues and specify the means for coping rationally with each of them. Importantly, the 'startling homogeneity of organizational forms and practice' should be understood as the outcome of the diffusion of such rationalized myths among organizations. DiMaggio and Powell (1983) capture this process of homogenization by the notion of 'isomorphism'. Three kinds of isomorphic processes are distinguished: (1) coercive isomorphism, (2) mimetic isomorphism and (3) normative isomorphism. 'Coercive isomorphism' results from both formal and informal pressures that are exerted on organizations. Such pressures can originate from other organizations, such as quality standards, or from the cultural expectations of society that are reflected in the legal environment. 'Mimetic isomorphism' or 'imitation' occurs if organizations model themselves on other organizations. Uncertainty is an important motive that encourages imitation. Organizations tend to model themselves on similar organizations in their field to enhance their legitimacy. Models may be diffused through employee transfer or by organizations such as consulting firms or employer associations. Consulting firms are thought to be a particularly strong mechanism that pushes organizations towards homogenization: 'Large organizations choose from a relatively small set of major consulting firms, which, like Johnny Appleseeds, spread a few organizational models throughout the land' (ibid., p.70). The third mechanism of isomorphic change of organizations is 'normative' and stems primarily from professionalization. Professionalization is understood as the collective definition of the conditions and methods of work of the members of an occupational group. The behaviour of large organizations is primarily determined by the professional norms of managers and specialized staff. Accordingly, the behaviour of firms cannot be detached from formal educational and professional networks that promulgate normative rules about efficient organizational and professional behaviour.

A second element that distinguishes the 'new' from the 'old' institutional programme relates to the notion of rationality. The criticism of the old institutionalist approach of Selznick on rational conceptions of organizations boils down to their neglect of the informal side of organizational life. The rationality of formal structures and objectives was not challenged. Accordingly, the social world was still divided into the categories of rational and non-rational action. New institutionalists have questioned this dualism: 'In general, we question the utility of arguments about the motivations of actors that suggest a polarity between the rational and the nonrational' (DiMaggio and Powell, 1983, p.81). It is suggested that all rationalized managerial precepts are social inventions. The distinction between rational and non-rational action is false: 'instrumental rationality is just one in a series of constructed meaning systems' (Dobbin, 1994, p.122). This sceptical perspective on organizational rationality applies to non-profit and government agencies as well as commercial and profit-driven private firms. Powell (1991) lists studies that have successfully applied institutional models to the adoption of structural practices by private firms. The studies refer to the spread of the multidivisional firm, accounting practices, personnel policies and corporate philanthropy. They show that the diffusion of particular forms of organizational behaviour is better explained by the pursuit by firms of legitimacy than by reference to efficiency. 'Each of the institutional isomorphic processes can be expected to proceed in the absence of evidence that it increases internal organizational efficiency. To the extent that organizational effectiveness is enhanced, the reason is often that organizations are rewarded for their similarity to other organizations in their fields' (DiMaggio and Powell, 1983, p.73).

In sum, the new institutionalist school in organizational analysis brings forward an alternative view for organizational success and survival. In addition to the pursuit of efficiency, organizational behaviour is driven by the need to conform to the rationalized myths of the social environment: 'Organizations that incorporate societally legitimated rationalized elements in their formal structure maximize their legitimacy and increase their resources and survival capabilities' (Meyer and Rowan, 1977, p.53).[19]

Ceremonial Values

A final school that challenges the thesis that efficiency drives firm behaviour is the neoinstitutional tradition in economic thought.[20] The identification of the neoinstitutionalist school as a distinct school with a well circumscribed theoretical core is problematic (Hodgson, 1994; Samuels, 1995).

Neoinstitutional economics is better described as a collection of works that approach the study of economic issues from a common methodological viewpoint (Wilber and Harrison, 1978).[21] A crucial feature of neoinstitutional economics is the perception of the individual. In opposition to mainstream schools in economic thought, human nature and its preferences are not taken as given and inert. Instead, neoinstitutionalists argue that all human behaviour is socially prescribed and subject to continuing modification during processes of social interaction. Human beings are not driven by universal economic motives, but are shaped by the societal and cultural context in which they have grown up. This view of human actors is prominent in the neoinstitutionalist theory of social and economic change. Further examination of this theory sheds new light on the mechanisms that drive firms to change the employment relationship.

The value system of the society is the centrepiece of the neoinstitutionalist theory of institutional change. Values function as the standard of judgment for actual human behaviour. All behaviour is related to an associated value. Human behaviour is 'patterned' or 'correlated' because it is guided and rationalized by stable values. In this view, a change of values underlies a change of human behaviour and, consequently, the behaviour of firms. Values are not of one kind. The neoinstitutionalist theory of institutional change is founded on the Veblenian dichotomy between ceremonial values and instrumental values (Tool, 1993). The ceremonial value category refers to cultural values that are 'based on legend, inherited beliefs, mores, status and the hierarchical ordering of society' (Gruchy, 1972, p.95). Ceremonially warranted behaviour is backward-looking, resistant to change and seeks to preserve existing class arrangements. Moreover, the latter is not subjected to critical scrutiny, but accepted on the basis of authority. Instrumental values, on the other hand, give rise to behavioural patterns that are based on reflection. Instrumental efficiency is the criterion on which the community judges instrumentally warranted behaviour (Bush, 1987). Such behaviour is characterized as forward-looking and supportive of scientific and technological development.[22] The core of the neoinstitutionalist theory of institutional change is derived from the analysis of the 'clash' between the two polar sites of behaviour. Table 2.2 addresses three possibilities.

'Regressive institutional change' is generated when instrumentally warranted behaviour is supplanted by ceremonially warranted behaviour. In this case, ceremonial dominance is deliberately increased at the expense of instrumental efficiency. Examples of regressive institutional change commonly refer to

Table 2.2 Patterns of institutional change

	Instrumentally feasible	Instrumentally non-feasible
Ceremonially feasible	II Ceremonial encapsulation	I Regressive institutional change
Ceremonially non-feasible	III Progressive institutional change	IV Empty set

Source: Bush (1987).

ideological, religious or nationalistic control of the values of the community. Veblen refers to imbecile institutions: 'history records more frequent and more spectacular instances of the triumph of imbecile institutions over the life and culture than of peoples who have by force of instinctive insight saved themselves out of a desperately precarious institutional situation' (Veblen, 1914, cited in Bush, 1987, p.25).

A second form of institutional change is labelled 'ceremonial encapsulation'. In this case, instrumental efficiency is enhanced by technological innovation that conforms to existing patterns of ceremonial behaviour. Innovations that enhance the efficiency have to meet the standards of ceremonial adequacy if they are to be permitted within the community. 'New knowledge will be incorporated into the institutional structure only to the extent that it can be made ceremonially adequate; that is, only to the extent that the incorporation can be accomplished without upsetting the existing degree of ceremonial dominance embedded in the value structure of the community' (Bush, 1986, cited in Tool, 1993, pp.135–6). Ceremonial encapsulation occurs whenever new knowledge and technology represent no threat to existing patterns of ceremonial behaviour. In those circumstances, the technological innovation can be reconciled with the established ceremonial value pattern.[23]

The stage of ceremonial encapsulation is thought to precede the stage of 'progressive' institutional change. In this case, established ceremonial patterns of behaviour are displaced by increased reliance on instrumental values. Following new innovations, the community becomes habituated to the new standards of instrumental valuing. Learning and the diffusion of the new instrumental values erode the ideological foundations of the former ceremonial practices: 'Eventually, instrumental standards of judgment displace ceremonial standards of judgment in the correlation of behaviour in a range of problem-solving activities not contemplated in the original technological innovation' (Bush, 1987, p.1102).

In sum, the neoinstitutionalist perspective of institutional change contends that the pursuit of efficiency cannot be assumed beforehand. Firms will display a mixture of instrumental and ceremonial behaviour. To understand the employment relationship one needs to know the ceremonial value system of the society in which the firm is embedded. Change of the employment relationship is only possible if it involves a 'minimal dislocation' of the behavioural patterns of the members of the community.

TOWARDS AN INTEGRAL FRAMEWORK

Six perspectives of the firm have been discussed in the foregoing sections. Each perspective suggests a different mechanism that governs the organization of the employment relationship. This section pulls the threads together and discusses the various approaches in combination. First, the crucial differences that separate the various theories are summarized by reference to the instalment of internal labour market principles. Secondly, we examine whether different theories can coexist beside one another on the basis of a theoretical pluralist viewpoint. Finally, we conclude that the various theories can be integrated into a coherent theoretical framework.

Alternative Mechanisms Governing the Employment Relationship

This chapter has discussed six theoretical views of the firm. Each theory suggests a different perspective on the nature of the firm and advances a different perspective on the organization of the employment relationship. Below, the differences that separate the various theoretical viewpoints are explicated by contrasting the way each of them explains the ubiquity of internal labour market mechanisms among modern firms. Internal labour market principles have become widely used tools to organize the employment relationship.[24] To account for this observation, the various theories of the firm propose different explanations.

First, agency theory considers the firm as a monitoring mechanism that enhances the efficiency of team production. The firm arises as a cost-efficient institution that prevents shirking behaviour of employees ('team members'). The firm is considered as the central contractual agent that rewards the team members according to their marginal productivity. To perform this function adequately, the firm needs information on the employees. An internal labour market is explained as an instrument to minimize such information costs, for information on employee performance is more readily available and accessible for incumbent employees than for workers who are recruited on the external labour market.

Second, transaction cost theory regards the firm as a cost-efficient governance structure to coordinate certain transactions. If asset specificity is involved, the transaction costs of the market will rise in order to prevent opportunistic behaviour. In such cases, the transaction can be coordinated against lower costs by internalization within the firm. Accordingly, the logic behind the introduction of internal labour market schemes lies in the reduction of the transaction costs that are involved with idiosyncratic skilled labour. The firm relies on internal labour market mechanisms to prevent the opportunistic abuse of firm-specific skills by employees. Moreover, the development of idiosyncratic skills is stimulated by tying the interests of the workers to their continuous employment within the same firm.

Third, the competence theory views the firm as a source of productive capabilities. By their very nature, these capabilities are firm-specific, in the sense that they are not transferable to other firms. Firm-specific competencies cannot be bought on an external market, but need to be built over longer periods. Internal labour market schemes are stressed as mechanisms to create the long-term commitment among the firm and its employees that is necessary to build firm-specific competencies.

Fourth, radical theory refers to the firm as a power system designed to maximize control and profits in favour of the capital owners. The rise of internal labour markets is perceived as an outcome of the power struggle between capital owners and workers. Two contrasting perspectives with respect to internal labour markets are advanced. Some conceive the internal labour market as a 'baddy', a form of bureaucratic control that is imposed by employers on employees to cultivate loyalty (Edwards, 1979). Others view internal labour markets as a valuable thing for employees that they have extorted from employers by increased bargaining power through 'acting in concert' (Goldberg, 1980).

Fifth, the new institutionalism in organizational analysis maintains that firm behaviour is not guided by rational pressures for more effective performance, but by social pressures to conform to conventional beliefs. Accordingly, the ubiquity of internal labour markets is understood as a method that legitimizes the firm within the wider society. Furthermore, the common background and mindset of professional managers is emphasized. In this view, internal labour markets disperse because firms have installed personnel departments that are populated by like-minded professional managers.

Sixth, institutional economics has emphasized the importance of ceremonial or cultural values for firm behaviour. The leeway for efficient firm behaviour is constrained by its accommodation to existing culturally based beliefs. In this view, the presence of internal labour markets is explained by reference to the cultural context in which the firm is embedded. Firms in individualistic-oriented nations, such as the United States, are expected to rely on external labour markets, while internal labour market arrangements are relatively more widespread among firms in collectivist cultures, such as Japan.

In sum, six distinct theoretical explanations can be put forward to explain the ubiquity of internal labour market mechanisms. Current empirical research has not provided conclusive evidence that allows one to evaluate the theories on the basis of their explanatory power.[25] This is not necessarily a scientific shortcoming. The next section will argue that the various theories can coexist side by side.

Theoretical Pluralism

Reviewing the various perspectives on the nature of the firm, what is the best way to proceed? Does one need to identify which perspective is right and which is wrong? Or can the various perspectives coexist side by side? Theoretical monists and theoretical pluralists answer this question differently. According to theoretical monism, one should search for a single, superior theory. It holds that there exists only one true theory for any set of phenomena. A plurality of theories is tolerated only as a temporary state. The procedures of scientific scrutiny should be so devised that, in the end, only one of these theories survives. In contrast to the theoretical monist perspective is the position of theoretical pluralists. Theoretical pluralism approves of a plurality of theories for a given set of phenomena, not just as a transitory, but as an enduring state.

Below, the pluralist perspective is applied to the various theories of the firm.

The pluralist idea is grounded on the basis that any single theory can only give a partial account of a phenomenon (Groenewegen and Vromen, 1996). The complexity of social phenomena cannot be captured by a single theory. Instead, the combination of several theories can illuminate more aspects of a phenomenon than any of them can do in isolation: 'The leading idea in theoretical pluralism is that our understanding of phenomena can be enhanced if we entertain several theories instead of just one' (ibid., p.371). However, theoretical pluralism cannot accept just any combination of theories. Theories can only coexist if they do not contradict each other. Contradictory statements follow if different theories advance a different central explanatory variable to address the same phenomenon. In such a case, the theoretical accounts cannot be accepted simultaneously, because acceptance of one account implies rejection of the other. Accordingly, two conditions for the application of theoretical pluralism are suggested. First, theories can coexist if they address different issues. Groenewegen and Vromen (ibid., p.373) subscribe to the slogan: 'Different theories for different issues'. Furthermore, rival claims can be considered complementary if each theoretical account is operative under different conditions. Once again in the words of Groenewegen and Vromen (ibid., p.371): 'Different theories under different conditions'. Accordingly, the application of the pluralist perspective to the six identified theories of the firm and, relatedly, the employment relationship, needs clarification on two issues. First, do the various theories address the same set of phenomena? Second, if the theories appear to focus on the same issue, under what conditions is the theory applicable?

Different theories for different issues

A first case in which seemingly contradictory theories can be considered as complementary concerns the contractual versus the competence perspective. The theories apparently focus on the same issue, namely the reason why firms exist. Contractual theories offer an account in terms of cost minimization, while competence theory refers to dynamic aspects of product development. Rather than being mutually exclusive, these claims can be viewed as complementary if one considers that firms are not all of one kind. For example, a distinction can be made between firms which strive for cost leadership and firms that are based on product diversification. On the one hand, firms that pursue cost leadership might be better explained by a contractual theory. On the other hand, firms that follow a strategy of product diversification cannot be understood without a competence perspective of the firm. To understand firms that combine both strategies it makes sense to use both theoretical insights. The two theories in combination shed light on more aspects of the same firm.

A next case of seemingly rival theories that on closer sight appear to focus on different issues refers to the competence theory and the new institutionalism in organizational analysis. Both theories are concerned with the dynamic development of firms, but each theory advances a different mechanism that guides the change process. While efficiency is the crucial impetus for change according to competence theorists, the new institutionalism depicts a firm that implements change in order to enhance its social legitimacy. However, on closer analysis, it appears that the theories are concerned with different issues. The competence perspective focuses on diversity among firms. The new institutionalism in organizational analysis, in contrast, focuses on the similarities among firms: 'we ask, instead, why there is such startling homogeneity of organizational forms and practices, and we seek to explain homogeneity, not variation' (DiMaggio and Powell, 1983, p.64). Accepting the principle 'different theories for different issues', the institutionalist theory can be reconciled with the efficiency branch. The change process of firms proceeds in two stages: efficiency-seeking behaviour explains change efforts of early adopters, while conformism explains the further diffusion of a particular change.

Different theories under different conditions

The subscription to the efficiency thesis constitutes the main ground for the diversity in viewpoints of firm behaviour. Adherents to the efficiency thesis locate the critical impetus for the firm's actions in the pursuit of efficiency advantages. Other theories have advanced alternative mechanisms, such as power, social legitimacy and social values, which are unrelated to efficiency considerations. Under what conditions has the efficiency perspective more explanatory power than the alternative views? To answer this question, one should take a look at the theoretical considerations in defence of the efficiency claim. Following Dow (1987), three arguments are advanced to underlie the efficiency thesis: (1) intentionality, (2) competitive market pressures, and (3) adaptive learning. Below, the three arguments are elaborated in more detail. In this way, the conditions can be identified that make the applicability of the efficiency thesis more, or less, plausible.

A first argument to support the efficiency thesis refers to the intentionality of human action. The efficiency of firm behaviour follows from conscious evaluation by the firm of all alternative modes of behaviour. Prior to undertaking an action, the firm has considered its relative efficiency against other options. The firm chooses the mode of action that is most efficient. Intentionality might offer a good explanation in circumstances where the actors have all the required information at their disposal. Under the condition that the information is not available, the argument must be rejected. For this reason, Williamson (1996) acknowledges that power, rather than efficiency, has more to contribute to the study of the employment relationship than it has to contribute to the study of intermediate product markets and capital markets: 'It is more plausible to assume that parties to a transaction are knowledgeable of transactions between two firms than of transactions between firms and workers (...) That is because of information asymmetries in which firms often enjoy an information advantage in relation to workers' (ibid., p.29).

A second defence of the efficiency thesis refers to competitive market pressures. This argument is based on an evolutionary perspective of the economic process in which more efficient firms replace the less efficient ones (Alchian, 1950; Friedman, 1953). This approach to efficiency focuses on the wider environment in which firms operate rather than the proper motivations of firms. The question whether firms can intentionally pursue efficient outcomes is considered to be irrelevant. Market selection will eliminate inefficient firms. In this view, the efficiency thesis hinges on the presence of market competition as an effective selection mechanism. In other words, the efficiency argument 'relies in a general background way on the efficacy of competition to preserve a sort between more and less efficient modes and to shift resources in favour of the former' (Williamson, 1985, pp.22–3). Williamson (1994) holds that the relevance of the efficiency argument is enhanced if competition is becoming more vigorous. The efficacy of the selection mechanism is increased if politically imposed impediments are removed and disadvantaged parties can no longer 'delay the reckoning'.

The third argument in favour of the efficiency thesis is adaptive learning. The idea is that firms, over time, accumulate experience that provides the basis for successive modifications that enhance efficiency. Indeed, adaptive learning can provide the rationale for the efficiency view of the firm. However, learning cannot be introduced without incorporating the social values into the explanation. Learning is a social experience that cannot be detached from the cultural context in which the learning actor is socialized. Moreover, learning does not start from scratch, but is path-dependent: that is, learning builds upon previous acquired experience. This acknowledgment of path dependency conditions the efficiency claim (Hodgson, 1993), for, in circumstances of path dependency, firms can get locked into a given path of development to the exclusion of other, perhaps more efficient, possibilities. In other words, the path that the firm has traced out in the past strongly restricts the options available to the firm. Accordingly, the applicability of the efficiency-based theories of the firm is disputable in conditions of path dependency. Some have argued that the efficiency argument has more to contribute in explaining the course of developments in the early history of capitalism than it has to modern economic systems. 'Early capitalism operated wit relatively small productive units, and with a more or less intelligible, fairly simple technology (...) they made 'rationality by natural selection' plausible. (...) The very large and often state-linked technical innovations, requiring an enormous infrastructure, so characteristic of later and advanced economies, no longer lend themselves quite so easily to the model. The commitment of resources is so great as frequently to be irreversible' (Gellner, 1992, p.140).

In sum, the theories of the firm that are based on efficiency and those that are not are not mutually exclusive. The question of which theoretical perspective contributes more to the explanation of firm behaviour cannot be answered without taking the conditions in which the firm operates into account. The explanatory strength of arguments based on power, legitimization and shared norms becomes stronger in conditions of path dependency, limited market competition and imperfect information.

Towards an Integral Framework

Six theories of the employment relationship have been discussed in terms of their complementarity or rivalry. The conclusion is that the various theories can coexist, either because they do not focus on the same issues or because their applicability is restricted to different conditions. The exception concerns agency theory and transaction cost economics. These theories address the same issue (the existence of cost-efficient firms) under the same conditions (effective market selection). A theoretical pluralist framework cannot accommodate both theories since they are mutually exclusive. Following the observation of Vromen (1994) that transaction cost economics 'has won the day' in academic circles, agency theory is dropped. Hence the analysis ends up with five theories that are relevant to explaining organizational changes of the employment relationship. The task at hand is to integrate them into a coherent framework that can explain the emergence of new organizational models of employment relations. A schematic attempt is provided by Figure 2.1.[26]

Figure 2.1 distinguishes two stages. The change process starts off with the identification of the pressures that induce firms to modify the existing employment relationship. Six triggering factors are distinguished on the basis of the various theories. First, the efficiency branch emphasizes the need to survive in a competitive market. Increased competition compels firms to remove existing inefficiencies in the organization of the employment relationship. Accordingly, an alteration of the competitive conditions is put forward as a first impetus for change. Furthermore, the transaction cost framework directs attention to the institutional environment. Changes in the institutional environment urge firms to adjust their transaction cost considerations. Accordingly, a shift of government regulation can be advanced as a second triggering force. A third mechanism of change is implied by the competence-based view of the firm. This perspective draws attention to the innovative capabilities of the firm. Accordingly, innovation of production technologies is suggested as a third mechanism that drives the management of labour. A fourth pressure for change is derived from the power-based view of the firm. In this tradition, changes in the employment relationship result from a shift in the power balance between employees and capital owners. A fifth trigger for change is based on the notion of normative isomorphism advanced by the new institutionalist theory in organizational analysis. Rationalized myths in the form of new ideas on personal management that proliferate among professional managers and consultancy firms constitute a powerful force to change the employment relationship. Finally, the neoinstitutional school in economics suggests a sixth trigger for change. A change in the ceremonial value orientation of the actors enables the introduction of new labour management practices.

The second stage is concerned with the process by which firms search and select new organizational models of the employment relationship. Three forces have an impact on this process. The power-based perspective gives a decisive role to the endowment of power among the participants in the change process. When alternative models can be chosen, the division of power mediates the selection process. The acknowledgment of path dependency by the competence perspective provides the ground for a second set of factors that intervene in the search and selection process. Path dependency restricts the search process for new models to the experience that the firm has built up in the past. In other words, the historical path that has led to the existing employment relationship in a firm restricts the options that are available to the firm. Finally, institutional economics suggests a major role for ceremonial values, for ceremonial values constrain and guide the search for alternative models of the employment relationship. New efficient models for organizing the employment relationship need to be in accordance with the prevailing values of the community.

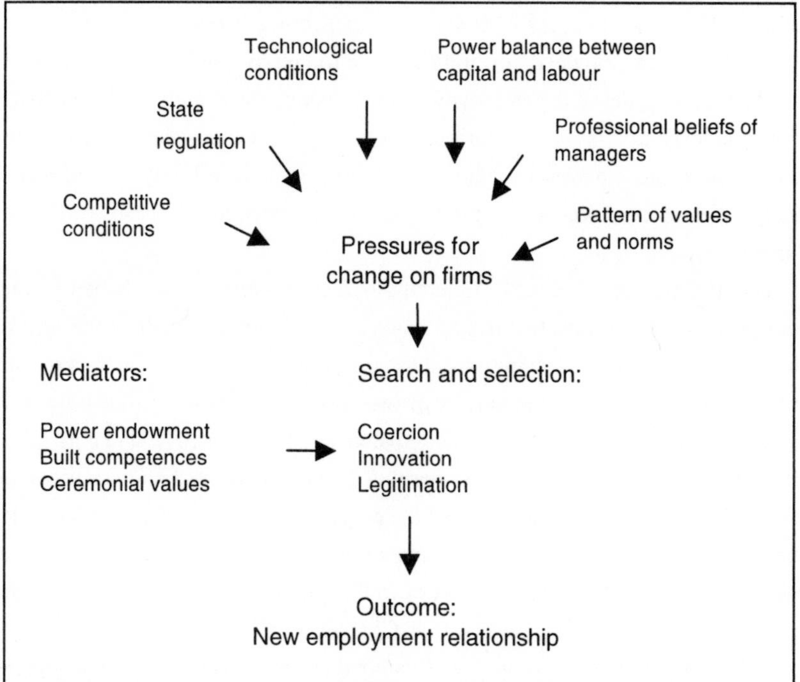

Figure 2.1 Selection of a new model of the employment relationship

CONCLUSIONS

This book studies the convergence/divergence thesis with respect to the evolution of the employment relationship. Are the various modes of organizing the employment relationship that can be observed across different national economic systems converging to a single universal model under the homogenizing pressure of globalization? This chapter contributes to answering this question by identifying the factors that shape the change process of the employment relationship at the level of the firm. Based on the analysis of the theoretical literature on the firm, an integral framework is created. The framework, as depicted in Figure 2.1, distinguishes between elements that trigger the search for change and elements that mediate the search process. With respect to the triggering forces, a universal organizational model of the employment relationship will only develop if firms across the world face the same triggers for change. The claim of cross-national convergence needs reference to pressures of a global nature. However, even if firms are forced by similar global pressures to adapt their model of the employment relationship, one cannot safely conclude that convergence is near. Various mediating and constraining elements codetermine the outcomes of the change process. Accordingly, the ultimate occurrence of convergence is dependent on the strength of these mediating forces.

The dynamic development of the employment relationship is shaped by the interplay between forces that trigger change and forces that mediate the search process for new forms of employment relations. In this book, the analysis of this interplay is simplified to the inquiry of two 'forces'.[27] Figure 2.2 illustrates the conceptual scheme that underlies the remainder of this book. The dynamic force of globalization encompasses the various global trends that induce firms to change their organizational model of the employment relationship. Opposed to the force of globalization is the force of national culture. National culture mediates between the global pressures and the national environment. The nature of this force is essentially conservative. Chapter 3 will elaborate on the concept of globalization, while the concept of national culture is the focus of Chapter 4.

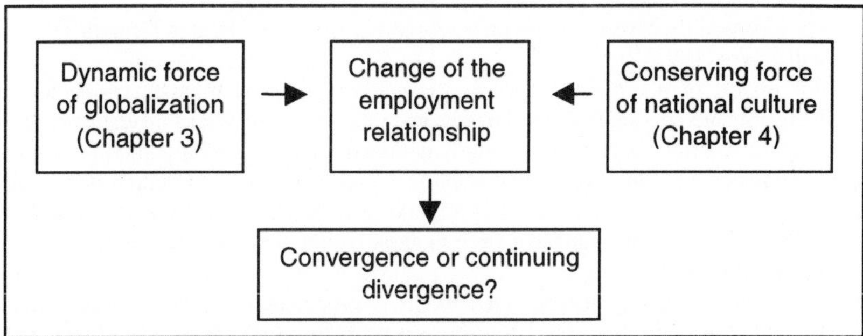

Figure 2.2 Conceptual scheme of the volume

NOTES

1. Shirking can be understood as free-riding behaviour of the team members and follows from the assumption of utility-maximizing individuals. For each individual, the fact that other team members benefit from his productive efforts is external to his decision calculus, and he therefore chooses more leisure than is desirable for the team.
2. The classical firm is endowed with the following special contractual rights: (1) to be the residual claimant, (2) to observe input behaviour, (3) to be the central party who writes down all contracts with inputs, (4) to alter the membership of the team, (5) to sell his rights.
3. Holmstrom and Milgrom (1991) reject the argument for flexible pay structures in the case of multi-task jobs. In that case, optimal incentives are provided by a fixed wage contract independent of measured performance, for incentive pay does not only motivate hard work; it also misdirects the allocation of the agents' attention among their various duties.
4. Asset specificity is defined as the degree to which an asset can be deployed to alternative uses without sacrifice of productive value (Williamson, 1993, p.94). Klein et al. (1978) introduced the concept into transaction cost economics under the label of 'appropriable quasi rents of specialized assets'. The relevance of asset specificity arises as it gives rise to small-numbers bargaining. That is, only a limited number of users owe value to the employment of a specific asset. Accordingly, the bargaining position of an owner of a specific asset is weak relative to that of the user.
5. Williamson employs the notion of governance structure to denote how a transaction is coordinated. The wide variety of governance structures is conceptualized as a continuum, with the spot market and the hierarchy or firm as two polar forms.
6. Williamson recognizes that it is the sum of production costs and transaction costs that is relevant. However, his main conjectures are based on the magnitude of transaction costs. Production costs are little emphasized, as technology is taken as given and not a matter of deliberate choice of the firm.

7. Criticisms of the heavy reliance on asset specificity can be found in Demsetz (1993) and Coase (1993).
8. An important distinction concerns perfunctory and consummate cooperation. Consummate cooperation involves the exercise of initiative and ingenuity by the employee. Efforts are not purposefully withheld. Perfunctory cooperation refers to compliance with directives and discipline in accordance with minimum standards.
9. Ricardian rents result from a firm's superior productive factors that are limited in supply. They are distinguished from monopoly rents that originate from a firm's market power.
10. However, it is acknowledged that distinctive competencies and capabilities might be traded through the market for business units or corporate control (Teece and Pisano, 1994).
11. Game-theoretic approaches use the concept of power in a strategic sense; that is, power is exercised by firms against competitors in the industry. Traditional theories of industrial organization explain power in terms of market share which allow firms to set prices above average costs. Political theories of organization relate power to the positions of the various players in the firm. Relatedly, the behavioural theory of the firm advances the thesis that firm behaviour is guided by a political contest within the firm. Furthermore, power is proposed by theories of resource dependency. Dependence is taken to be the obverse of power.
12. Two features define the capitalist firm: first, it has installed employment contracts and, second, it possesses the property rights of the produced outcomes. The latter condition distinguishes the capitalist firm from other types of firms, such as public firms or worker cooperatives (Hodgson, 1997).
13. Alchian and Demsetz (1972) argue that the firm is installed by the initiative of workers themselves. Workers, to prevent shirking, hire managers. According to Williamson (1975), workers voluntarily cede authority to management in return for a guaranteed wage and security of employment.
14. Edwards (1979) distinguishes three kinds of control mechanisms to strengthen managerial authority. First, 'simple control' refers to the control of subordinates by supervisors. Second, 'technical control' emanates from the physical and technological aspects of production such as the design of machines and the architecture of the work floor. Third, 'bureaucratic control' is embedded in the social and organizational structure of the firm, such as job categories, work rules, promotion procedures, discipline, wage scales and definitions of responsibilities. It is argued that, as firms grow in size and complexity, they shift from hierarchical to bureaucratic control systems.
15. Barker (1993) comments that the implementation of self-managing teams introduces a fourth control mechanism in the workplace, namely 'concertive control' that refers to the need to conform to the values, norms and rules that are created by the team. Furthermore, the control perspective questions the diffusion of human resource management principles among firms. It is argued that the widespread adoption of human resource management principles reflects managerial attempts to change employees' norms and values in order to reconstruct the motivation to work and relegitimize managerial authority in the employment relationship (Keenoy, 1990).
16. The 'new institutionalism in organizational analysis' should be distinguished from the 'new institutionalism' in economics. The latter school is confined to the economics discipline and encompasses theoretical approaches such as transaction

cost theory and agency theory.

17. Scott (1987) notes that the institutional approach to organizations is far from homogeneous.
18. They are 'myths' because they are widely held beliefs that cannot be objectively tested. They are 'rationalized' because their truth is not disputed: they are true because they are believed to be true.
19. Hannah and Freeman (1989) have incorporated this institutionalist view within an evolutionary model to explain differential rates of survival and mortality of firms. In contrast to the efficient selection argument, they contend that selection is not based solely on profits, but on a broader 'fit' of the organization with specific environmental characteristics. 'Selection processes are multidimensional (...) efficiency in production and marketing, broadly defined, is only one of the relevant dimensions' (ibid., p.37). In addition to competition, Hannah and Freeman propose legitimization as a selective mechanism. Firms are not selected just on the basis of profits, but also on the basis of reliability and accountability: 'selection within organizational populations tends to eliminate organizations with low reliability and accountability' (ibid., p.74). In order to survive, efficiency is not enough. Firms have to conform to social norms over time if they want to prosper.
20. The neoinstitutional branch of economics has a long tradition in economic thought and includes writers such as Veblen, Commons, Mitchell, Myrdal, Polyani and Galbraith. Various precepts, such as 'old', 'American' or 'neo', are employed to specify the school of institutional economics. The important point to note is the distinction from the branch labelled as 'new institutionalist economics' that includes approaches such as agency theory and transaction cost economics (see Rutherford, 1994).
21. Wilber and Harrison (1978) characterize the methodological perspective of institutionalist economists as 'holist', 'systematic' and 'evolutionary'.
22. The set of all behaviour is formed by the subsets of ceremonial behaviour and instrumental behaviour and behaviour having both ceremonial and instrumental significance. Generally, the members of a culture believe that their ceremonial values are instrumentally efficient. Accordingly, institutionalists believe that ceremonial values dominate instrumental ones. This 'ceremonial dominance' is not a constant, but varies across cultures and time.
23. Two different forms of ceremonial encapsulation are distinguished: 'past-binding' and 'future-binding'. The resistance to technological innovation is 'past-binding' when it is rooted in the desire to protect the status quo. The community attempts to minimize the impact of technological advances on established habits. 'Future-binding' encapsulation occurs when the vested interests actively promote new science and technology, but effectively control its outcomes. Among alternative technological trajectories, they select the path that preserves the ceremonial values that are favourable to their survival.
24. The notion of the internal labour market originates with Doeringer and Piore (1971), who define an internal labour market as an 'administrative unit, such as manufacturing plants, within which the pricing and allocation of labour is governed by a set of administrative rules and procedures'. Among the key features of internal labour markets are hierarchical structuring of jobs into job ladders representing a progression in knowledge or skills; wage rates attached to job ladders; restricted entry to lower hierarchical levels; and higher hierarchical positions filled by

promotion from within.

25. For example, Pfeffer and Cohen (1984) employed data from a sample of about 300 large organizations in the San Francisco Bay area to test alternative explanations of internal labour markets. Degree of specificity of skills as measured by extensiveness of employer training provided support for the transaction cost argument. But the impact of unionization provided support for a radical interpretation. In addition, Pfeffer and Cohen reported that the development of internal labour markets was associated with the existence of a personnel department, a finding that supports the institutional interpretation.
26. The presented framework draws heavily on Campbell and Lindberg (1991). For ease of presentation, it is abstracted from feedback mechanisms of the firm towards the institutional environment (lobbying, technological innovation), competitive conditions (takeovers) and individual attributes (psychological indoctrination).
27. The use of the notion of 'force' should not be misunderstood. The notion is used only as a metaphor rather than as a real force that transcends the free will of people, as in natural sciences. This methodological issue will be extensively discussed in Chapter 4.

3. Globalization of the employment relationship

INTRODUCTION

This book has started from the observation that the employment relationship is differently organized across nation states with diverse cultural backgrounds. Few people will deny this. However, it is questioned whether these cultural particularities are enduring. What will happen if the protective shields around national economies are removed? Can cultural differences survive if national economies are exposed to foreign economic competition, or will the employment organization be pushed towards a single model based on the universal criterion of economic efficiency? Underlying this question of convergence versus divergence is the awareness, shared among both scholars and policy makers, that the world economy has entered a new phase, the era of globalization, in which the removal of national protective shields is thought to have become reality.

The objective of this chapter is to examine the potential effects of globalization on the organization of the employment relationship. The question first needs clarity on the nature of globalization. Waters (1995) opposes a globalized world to a world characterized by cultural differences: 'In a globalized world there will be a single society and culture occupying the planet (...) territoriality will disappear as an organising principle for social and cultural life'. According to Waters, globalization is the 'social process in which the constraints of geography on social and cultural arrangement recede' (ibid., p.3). In this view, globalization is an umbrella notion to capture a number of mechanisms in the sphere of the economy, polity and culture that are united by their unifying impact on the organization of the world. If this conception of globalization is applied to the organization of the employment relationship, one can define globalization as 'the set of mechanisms by which the organization of the employment relationship becomes more homogeneous across different cultural regions of the world'.[1]

This chapter will substantiate this conception of the relationship between globalization and the employment relationship with the use of the six 'triggers for change' that were identified in Chapter 2. In that chapter it was concluded that the firm is induced to adapt the employment relationship if changes occur in the competitive conditions, state regulation, technology, professional beliefs, power balance and value attributes of actors. A necessary condition for global convergence of the employment relationship is the simultaneous operation of one (or more) of these mechanisms irrespective of national borders. Can a global mechanism be identified with sufficient power to justify the convergence thesis with respect to the management of labour?

The following sections critically analyse whether this necessary condition for global convergence has been satisfied. Recent societal developments in the area of the six 'triggers of change' are examined. For each mechanism, arguments in favour of global convergence are balanced by arguments in defence of continued cultural diversity. The first section analyses two mechanisms, 'competitive pressure' and 'state regulation', in the context of the increasing degree of interdependence between national economies. The second section examines the mechanism 'technological development' by reviewing the impact of information technology on the management of labour. The third section examines the mechanism 'professional beliefs' by analysing recent developments in the labour management literature. The fourth section is concerned with the shifting 'power balance' between capital and labour. The fifth section examines the impact of altered individual value attributes on the organization of the employment relationship. A final brief section concludes.

ECONOMIC GLOBALIZATION

Competitive pressure and state regulation are two mechanisms that affect the organization of the employment relationship. It is widely argued that fundamental changes in the international economy, captured under the label of 'economic globalization', have affected the nature of these mechanisms. Economic globalization has increased competitive pressures. At the same time, it has marginalized the role of national governments in economic affairs (Daniels and Lever, 1996). Hirst and Thompson (1996) characterize these developments as the transition from an 'international economy' to a 'globalized economy'. In an 'international economy', the principal entities are still national economies. Although trade and investment interconnect national economies, the international economic sphere remains relatively separated from domestic economic affairs, leaving scope for national considerations. In contrast, in a globalized economy distinct national economies have lost their autonomy as they are subsumed in a global system by all kinds of international processes and transactions.

This section will discuss the relation between 'economic globalization' and the organization of the employment relationship. The trend towards a globalized economy refers primarily to capital, since national borders still largely bind labour. The principal capital flows linking national economies are monetary flows related to international trade and foreign direct investment (FDI). Below, recent global developments within both categories are examined. The section concludes with some critical observations that weaken the claim that economic globalization is a reality.

The Rise of International Trade

A first aspect of the globalizing economy is concerned with the extent of international trade, traditionally the principal mechanism linking national economies. For centuries people have traded goods and services across nations on the basis of comparative advantages. However, contemporary trade patterns are argued to be exceptional with regard to the magnitude of imports and exports. Driven by a variety of factors – liberalization of markets and changes in production, telecommunications and transport technologies – the growth of world trade has consistently outstripped that of world production since the early 1970s (OECD, 1997). Figure 3.1 shows the index of world exports between 1957 and 1997. It reveals that the volume of exports has increased by a factor of three since the early 1970s: 'This increase surely reveals a trend to globalization rather than a minor structural change in international trade' (Bairoch, 1996, p.174).[2]

A direct consequence of the rise of international trade for the organization of employment relations can be derived from traditional economic analysis. More intensive international trade enhances the number of suppliers in non-domestic industries. In this way, increased international competition leads to further rationalization of production and work organization, since firms are impelled to

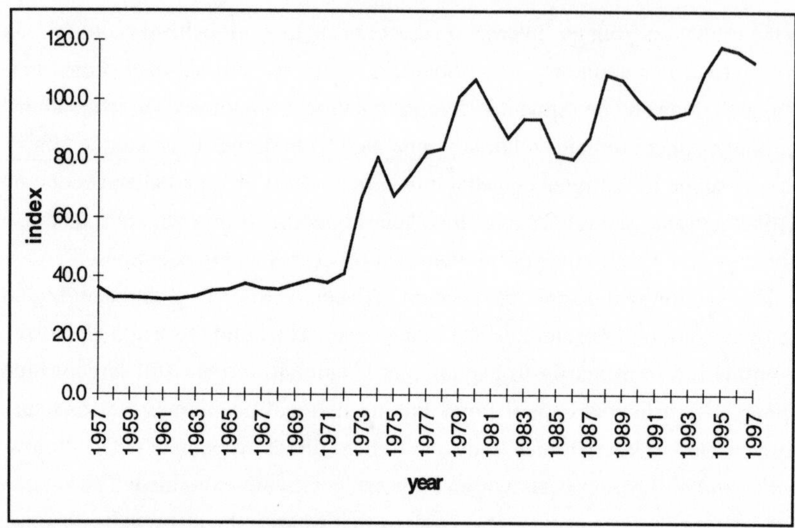

Source: IFS database.

Figure 3.1 Index of world exports 1957-97

reduce costs by removing slack and inefficiencies. Indirectly, intensified international competition affects the organization of the employment relationship by changing government regulation. In contrast to product markets, which have moved beyond national borders, the governance of labour markets has remained at the national level. Labour institutions and labour market regulation, such as employment rules, pay, working conditions, social security and occupational health and safety, are still largely determined at national level. Consequently, an international competitive framework in which suppliers produce under different conditions is installed. As a consequence, national governments face corporate pressure to adopt labour market regulation: 'Enterprises are pressing the state to introduce policies favourable to their freedom of action in the field of labour market regulation. They want lower labour standards in the name of competitiveness' (Petrella, 1996, p.75). Proponents of free market theories welcome such pressure for a rational world freed from 'obsolete' national public intervention (Ohmae, 1990). Others have expressed the fear that the loss of national autonomy will throw national systems of labour institutions into international competition, leading to 'destructive social conflict' (Sengenberger and Wilkinson, 1995).

The Rise of Foreign Direct Investment

The expansion of international trade occurred primarily during the 1970s. In the 1980s, growth rates stagnated and balanced the global growth of gross domestic product (GDP). Ever since, international trade growth has been surpassed by the growth of foreign direct investment (FDI), giving rise to the claim that 'the growth and structure of international direct investment is the best documented measure of globalization' (Vickery, 1996, p.96). In the period 1983–89, the average annual growth rate of world exports was 9.3 per cent, while during the same period FDI grew by 28.9 per cent (Petrella, 1996). Figure 3.2 shows the evolution of FDI outflows from Western developed countries. It reveals the spectacular growth of FDI between 1985 and 1990.[3] Since the early 1990s, there has been a slowdown in the growth of FDI, but investment flows experienced a growth rate of 40 per cent in 1995, setting a new FDI flow record (UNCTAD, 1996).

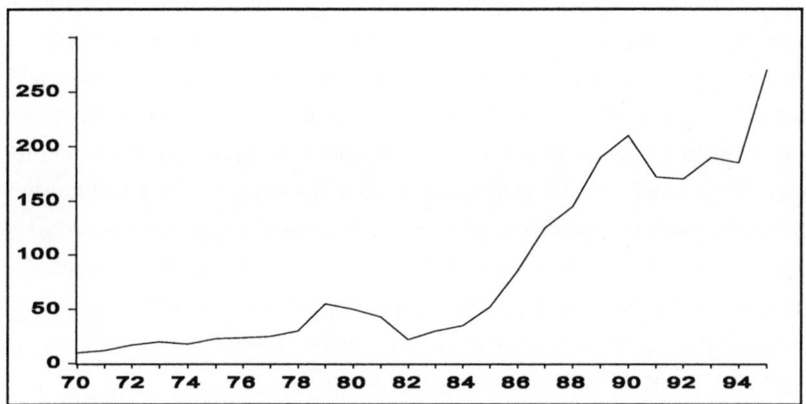

Source: IMF (1997).

Figure 3.2 FDI outflows (billions of US dollars)

The increase of foreign direct investment in the globalizing economy is reflected by the emergence of the transnational corporation as the key global actor. Hirst and Thompson (1996) distinguish the transnational corporation (TNC) from the traditional 'multinational corporation' (MNC). While the latter operates from a particular predominant national location, the TNC represents genuine 'footloose' capital. Without any specific national identification of its internationalized management, the TNC will locate and relocate its establishments anywhere in the globe to obtain either the most secure or the highest returns on investment. The TNC will serve global markets through global operations. National commitment will disappear: 'Before national identity, before local affiliation, before German ego or Italian ego or Japanese ego – before any of this comes the commitment to a single, unified global mission (...) Country of origin does not matter. Location of headquarters does not matter. The products for which you are responsible and the company that you serve have become denationalized' (Ohmae, 1990, p.94).

The analysis of the economic bargaining position of transnational corporations vis-à-vis other players in the field of labour relations has implications for the employment relationship. The TNC, as a unitary global actor, is endowed with a number of advantages in its confrontations with states and collective labour, because the latter are poorly coordinated across national borders. Jones (1995) characterizes the strategy of TNCs as the principle of 'divide and rule'. In direct negotiations, a TNC can often threaten to relocate its operations in another country. Moreover, the TNC retains unique knowledge of the strategic importance of its operations in any country. Consequently, according to Petrella (1996), a new alliance has developed between enterprises and national governments in which the enterprise has privatized the role of the state. Most states have adopted a combination of strategies of national research and development programmes, tax breaks and commercial measures in exchange for socioeconomic development: 'In the process, they are carrying out a massive transfer of collective public resources to private enterprises, mostly multinational corporations, in order to enable them to remain competitive in the so-called "fight for survival" at the world level' (ibid., p.76).

Likewise, the economic bargaining power of organized labour versus TNCs has declined at both the firm and the national level. At the firm level, transnational firms have shifted from administrative towards performance control mechanisms (Marginson et al., 1995). Among TNCs a growing use is observed of performance comparisons between operations across different countries, enabling the exertion of coercive pressure on local workforces to improve performance. At the national level, collective labour organizations face pressure as globally mobile capital selects those locations with the best deal in terms of labour costs and supply ('regime shopping'). Advanced countries can still be attractive locations when highly skilled labour is required, but the trend of the global mobility of capital and the relative national rigidity of labour favours those advanced countries with the most tractable labour forces and the lowest social overheads: 'Social democratic strategies of enhancement of working conditions would thus only be viable if they assured the competitive advantage of the labour force, without constraining management prerogatives, and at no more overall cost in taxation than the average for the advanced world' (Hirst and Thompson, 1996, p.12).

Economic Globalization: a Myth?

Although the thesis of economic globalization has been put forward with strong conviction and supported by impressive statistics, it must not go uncriticized. A number of caveats weaken the claim of the emergence of globalized economies.

A first criticism concerns the limited historical scope of the economic globalization thesis. Critics claim that the current level of international dependence is not unprecedented in history (Bairoch, 1996; Hirst and Thompson, 1996). If trade is related to GDP, it appears that a similar period of economic openness occurred before the First World War. Table 3.1 reveals that the highest rate of exports in Western economies was reached almost everywhere just before the First World War.[4] It took until the 1970s to achieve similar levels of economic interdependence.[5] For the United States, the openness of the turn of the century was only surpassed during the 1980s: 'Thus, even for the country where the process of globalization seems the most obvious, the process is not a new one' (Bairoch, 1996, p.180).

A further comment on the globalization thesis concerns the geographical concentration of trade and FDI patterns in the 'triad' of Western Europe, Japan and North America. 'Today's globalization is a truncated globalization: "triadization" is a more correct definition of the current situation' (Petrella, 1996, p.77). Petrella illustrates the phenomenon of 'triadization' by reference to the geographical pattern of inter-firm alliances. Out of the 4200 inter-firm strategic cooperation agreements that were signed by enterprises during the 1980s, 92 per cent were closed between enterprises from Japan, Western Europe and North America.

Table 3.1 Exports of merchandise as a percentage of GDP

	Western developed countries	United States	Western Europe	Japan
1890	11.7	6.7	14.9	5.1
1913	12.9	6.4	18.3	12.6
1929	9.8	5.0	14.5	13.6
1938	6.2	3.7	7.1	13.0
1950	7.8	3.8	13.4	6.8
1970	10.2	4.0	17.4	9.7
1992	14.3	7.5	21.7	8.8

Source: Bairoch (1996).

A final critique of the alleged transition to a global economy concerns the conversion of MNCs into TNCs. Hirst and Thompson (1996) argue that genuine transnational companies are still rare. In terms of both sales and manufacturing assets, most MNCs rely upon their 'home base' as the centre for their economic activities. Likewise, Wade (1996) calls global corporations 'national firms with international operations' (NFIOs). He asserts that MNCs have most of their assets and employees in the home country. Moreover, the home nation is also the centre for MNCs shareowners, top management and R&D activities. In sum, it is argued that the number of MNCs without any preferences for a particular country is tiny: the importance of the home nation for international competitiveness, as documented by Porter (1990), seems to have kept its validity.

TECHNOLOGICAL CHANGE

Technology is the third mechanism that affects the organization of the employment relationship. The view that technology is an important factor shaping the relationship between workers and management can be traced back to Marx. Technology constituted the 'Unterbau' which narrowly prescribed the whole superstructure of society. A more recent technological determinist view of societal development was proposed in the form of the 'logic of industrialization' (Kerr et al., 1973). In this view, other parts of society have to change in order to meet the requirements of the industrial system of production and distribution. Cross-national differences in employment relations are expected to vanish as production technology will diffuse globally: 'social arrangements will be most uniform from one society to another when they are most closely tied to technology: they can be more diverse the further removed they are from technology' (Kerr et al., 1973, p.17).

This section considers the so-called 'neo-Schumpeterian school in economics' that has advanced a modern technological determinist view of society in general, and the employment relationship in particular. According to the neo-Schumpeterians, the diffusion of microelectronic technology is at the root of the current transformation of work organizations. In the second part of this section the claim of technological determinism will be challenged. On a number of theoretical grounds the claim that technology has causal primacy above the wider socioinstitutional context is opposed.

The Neo-Schumpeterian Approach

The neo-Schumpeterian approach starts from Schumpeter's reworking of Kondratiev's notion of long waves in economic growth patterns (Amin, 1994). Kondratiev focused attention on a particular regularity in the development of capitalist economies. Cycles of economic growth and stagnation appeared to occur at intervals of 40 to 60 years. Schumpeter explained these long-term fluctuations in the growth of the economy by reference to radical innovations. In his view, business cycles reflect long-term changes in the technological base of the economy. Neo-Schumpeterian scholars have refined Schumpeter's original formulations and have applied the framework to the widespread introduction of microelectronic technology (Perez, 1985; Freeman and Perez, 1988).

The neo-Schumpeterian conceptualization of the world consists of two subsystems, a 'technoeconomic' subsystem and a 'socioinstitutional' framework. The technoeconomic subsystem refers to the 'dominant technological style' that characterizes the organization of production in the economy as a whole. It encompasses the dominant products, production processes and management methods. The occurrence of upswings and downswings in the business cycles is explained by, respectively, the 'match' or 'mismatch' between the technoeconomic paradigm and the socioinstitutional framework. A match between a stable technoeconomic paradigm and the socioinstitutional environment results in a 'climate of confidence' stimulating private investment decisions, resulting in a period of economic growth. However, a distortion of the prevailing match is brought about by renewed technological innovation, for the accommodation of social behaviour and institutions to the new requirements of the technoeconomic sphere requires time. A downswing in the business cycle results.

Freeman and Perez (1988) use the label 'Kondratiev wave' to denote a period of domination of a certain technoeconomic paradigm. Each Kondratiev wave is based on a certain 'key factor', that is, a particular production input with superior technical and economic features. In the history of capitalism 'cotton', 'pig iron', 'coal', 'transport', 'steel' and 'energy (oil)' have been identified as the key factors giving rise to four separate Kondratiev waves. Each wave corresponds to a specific type of work organization (see Table 3.2).

Table 3.2 Some characteristics of long waves

Wave	Description	Key factor	Organization of firms
First Kondratiev 1770s–1830s	Early mechanization	Cotton/Pig iron	Individual entrepreneurs
Second Kondratiev 1830s–1890s	Steam power and railway	Coal/Transport	Small firms
Third Kondratiev 1890s–1930s	Electrical and heavy engineering	Steel	Giant firms
Fourth Kondratiev 1930s–1980s	Fordist mass-production	Energy (oil)	Oligopolistic competition
Fifth Kondratiev 1980s– ?	Information and communication	Chips (microelectronics)	Networks of large and small firms

Source: Freeman and Perez (1988).

Freeman and Perez hold that the world is currently witnessing a transition from the fourth to the fifth Kondratiev wave. The fourth Kondratiev, Fordist mass-production, emerged after the Second World War and was based on low-cost oil and energy-intensive materials.[6] Its ideal type of production organization was the continuous flow assembly line to turn out massive quantities of standardized goods. However, Perez and Freeman question the viability of the Fordist system of mass-production. The application of microelectronic technology is leading to higher productivity and profitability in almost every industry. 'Today, with cheap micro-electronics widely available, with prices expected to fall still further and with related new developments in computers and telecommunications, it is no longer "common sense" to continue along the (now expensive) path of energy and materials-intensive inflexible mass-production' (ibid., p.60).

A new technoeconomic paradigm based on microelectronics brings with it a restructuring of the entire socioinstitutional system. The use of microelectronic technology needs to be supported by the production system. Perez (1985) characterizes the new productive system by two key terms: 'information intensity' and 'flexibility'. In contrast with the Fordist paradigm, the new paradigm supports information intensity rather than energy and materials intensity. Moreover, mass-production of standardized goods is being replaced by flexible low-volume production of diversified goods. Computerized production facilities can carry out a range of operations and change their specification with the minimum of cost and delay. Perez (1985) relates this paradigm shift to emerging concepts for production and work organization. Organizational 'best practice' is based on the integration of information channels between design, production and marketing. Furthermore, flatter control systems bringing decision and action closer together enable more flexible and rapid responses to changing market demands. Finally, computerized production systems yield their optimal results when they are accompanied by the introduction of teamwork and polyvalent workers (Ozaki, 1992).

In sum, the neo-Schumpeterian approach offers a perspective to understand contemporary changes in the organization of the employment relationship as a response to the technoeconomic paradigm based on microelectronics. New labour management initiatives, such as flexible working times, teamwork and retraining systems, are interpreted as products of the search for socioinstitutional adjustment. Although socioinstitutional developments are not fully determined and may differ across national settings, it is clear that the socioinstitutional factors are perceived as subordinate to the technoeconomic: 'we can tinker at the edges, but basically the force of the technological trajectory drives society forward and establishes the limits within which we are free to choose' (Peláez and Holloway, 1991, p.138).

Against Microelectronic Determinism

The technological determinist view of the neo-Schumpeterian school has been criticized on three levels. First, the subordination of the socioinstitutional context to developments in the realm of production technology is challenged. Second, the attribution of the breakdown of the Fordist mode of production to the diffusion of microelectronic technology is questioned. Finally, the introduction of microelectronics does not determine work organization: microelectronic technology can be compatible with different forms of work organizations. These three criticisms will be discussed below.

Technological determinism is first criticized for its technocratic view on technological development. The 'social shaping' approach rejects the view that technology develops along an implacable trajectory. Instead, technological development is shaped by social considerations concerning gender, race, class and professional groups. In the words of Piore and Sabel (1984, p.5): 'Industrial technology does not grow out of a self-contained logic of scientific or technical necessity (...) Machines are as much a mirror as the motor of social development.' This approach opens up a more political understanding of technology. It shows that the course of technology is not predetermined, but that the whole technological process, from invention to implementation, is full of choices, conflicts and negotiations. For example, Piore and Sabel (1984) claim that reference to the alleged superior efficiency of mass-production cannot account for its diffusion. Instead, mass-production spread as a result of a number of deliberate choices and active policy decisions at the level of industrial companies, unions and politics. 'From the views of late-twentieth-century scholarship (...) even the successes of mass-production seem less the outcome of mechanization than of an interplay of social and political forces' (ibid., p.20). It is argued that under somewhat different historical conditions modern economic life could have been dominated by a combination of craft skill and flexible equipment.[7]

A second critique of neo-Schumpeterian technological determinism concerns the attribution of the breakdown of the Fordist mode of production to the emergence of microelectronic technology. Boyer (1988) advances alternative explanations for the transition of Fordism towards 'post-Fordism' without relapsing into technological determinism. He describes various tendencies that have led to the structural crisis of Fordism that were unrelated to new technological opportunities. First, Fordist production systems faced increasing problems in balancing output with demand, both quantitatively and qualitatively. Second, the expansion of mass-production led to increasing internationalization of economic flows, which made national economic management (including oligopolistic pricing) increasingly difficult. Third, the indexation of nominal wages to consumer prices generated a wage/price/profit spiral that culminated in high inflation.

A final issue facing the neo-Schumpeterian approach is concerned with the univocal relationship between microelectronic technology and work organization. Critics have emphasized the relative openness of microelectronic applications and, consequently, the significance of strategic choice (Jaikumar, 1986; Sorge and Streeck, 1988). It is argued that 'technology does not determine manufacturing policy, but rather offers options from which management, trade unions and industrial policy makers can select' (Sorge and Streeck, 1988, p.28). Sorge and Streeck distinguish four general manufacturing strategies based on the degree of standardization and the production volume (see Table 3.3).

Table 3.3 Classification of manufacturing strategies

	Standardized price competitive products	Customized quality competitive products
Low volume	1. Specialized component production	2. Craft production
High volume	3. Mass-production (Fordism)	4. Diversified quality production

Source: Sorge and Streeck (1988).

According to Sorge and Streeck, new microelectronic technology offers opportunities for performance improvement whatever the firm's manufacturing strategy. Microelectronics can rationalize the traditional system of mass-production by cutting labour, extending the separation of planning and execution, and intensifying the control of management over labour (cell 3) as well as being able to lower the costs of customized high-quality production applied by small specialist producers (cell 2). However, most importantly, new microelectronic technology may erode the distinction between mass- and specialist production. The flexibility of microelectronic equipment enables firms to combine a high degree of variety and quality in large-batch production (cell 4). In sum, 'new technology, since it may improve firms' survival chances in any of our four types of production, does not as such determine manufacturing policy. If at all, it seems to extend rather than to narrow down the range of available choices' (ibid., p.31).

NEW MANAGEMENT METHODS

The worldwide dispersion of similar management and organization methods can be postulated as a fourth mechanism for effectuating global convergence of the organization of the employment relationship. Although the creative act of developing new management models is best understood as an attempt to increase efficiency, the new institutional school in organizational analysis has argued that the dispersion of management models across different companies cannot be understood without reference to isomorphic pressures on professional management.[8]

This section will analyse whether present-day changes in the organization of the employment relationship can be understood as the dispersion of a particular management method. A multitude of management methods can be nominated as potential sources of global convergence. Management literature abounds with new, superior ways to manage the company. Concepts such as 'total quality management', 'benchmarking', 'customer focus', 'business process re-engineering', 'empowerment', 'delayering' and 'the learning organization' have become standard notions in the vocabulary of the modern professional manager (Crainer, 1997). These recent developments in the management literature cannot be dismissed as 'hypes' and 'fads' (Eccles and Nohria, 1992; Hilmer and Donaldson, 1996). Instead, it can be argued that these new methods fit a new consensus among professional managers on the most efficient organization of the company that is captured by the model of 'lean production' (Womack et al., 1990).

The 'lean production' model is among the most influential new concepts that have guided modern management thinking about the organization of the employment relationship: 'Lean production is the most widely used of the competing organizing concepts for post-modern times. (...) Lean production has been taken up by journalists, industry executives and policy makers who are otherwise not followers of intellectual fashion' (Williams et al., 1992, p.321). Lean production has its origins in Japan and can be considered as a product of the reorientation of American management towards Japanese organization methods in response to the loss of American market share in international markets to Japanese corporations (Deming, 1986; Dertouzos et al., 1989; Locke, 1996). The first part of this section will present the lean production model of the firm and its impact on employment relations. Although lean production is presented as a universal medicine for impoverished productivity, strong arguments can be given to reject the option of global convergence along the lines of this model. The second part of the section considers the major objections.

Lean Production

The concept of lean production originates in the Japanese motor car industry. Postwar Japanese industrial entrepreneurs visited the United States to scrutinize the American production system that was characterized, in those days, by mass-production and Tayloristic work organizations. The owner of the Toyota Motor Company observed possibilities for improving the production system. With the assistance of a talented production engineer, Taiichi Ohno, Toyota developed out of the Taylorist system a production system that was many times more efficient. This system was called the 'Toyota Production System', also known as 'Ohnoism' or 'Toyotism'. 'Lean production' is the most recent label and the one that has worldwide appeal (Womack et al., 1990). The term emphasizes the limited use of resources in comparison to mass-production: 'half the human effort in the factory, half the investments in tools, half the engineering hours to develop a new product in half the time. Also it requires keeping far less than half the needed inventory on site, results in many fewer defects, and produces a greater and ever growing variety of products' (ibid., p.13). The impressive performance improvement of lean production has resulted from a combination of innovations within the production organization, supply chain management, product development and customer interaction. Below, the major consequences of lean production for employment relations are derived from a closer analysis of the production organization.[9]

Central to lean production is the just-in-time (JIT) production system.[10] The basic idea of JIT is to eliminate inventories by matching quantities of production with real customer demand. Lean production has ensured a close match between demand and production in versatile demand conditions by producing in small lot sizes. Shortened set-up times of machinery have prevented the loss of scale economies. A further reduction of inventories is accomplished by eliminating stocks at different assembly operations. Instead, a continuous flow of parts and components is moved in the direction of production, where they arrive just in time to be used ('zero buffer principle'). The major drawback of the system is its vulnerability to failures in availability and quality of the different parts and components. The whole system can get stuck if one small production part is unavailable or does not satisfy quality standards. To avoid such production jams, lean production makes extensive use of microelectronic technology to accompany the production flow with information flows. Moreover, to prevent defective parts disrupting JIT, lean production contains an explicit emphasis on quality ('zero defect principle'). Quality control is handled both automatically ('autonomation') and manually ('kaizen'). Kaizen refers to a particular system of continuous improvement that emphasizes the role of the production worker. Lean production limits the role of quality control departments because quality inspectors do not add any value to the product. Instead, workers themselves are encouraged to take responsibility for the quality of their own work: individual workers are given the means and authority to stop the production process whenever they identify problems that cannot immediately be fixed. Furthermore, workers are assigned a role in so-called 'quality circles': groups of employees from several hierarchical layers that trace production problems to their ultimate cause and devise long-term solutions.[11]

Womack et al. (1990) mention two key organizational features of the 'truly' lean production organization that affect the role of the production workers. First, a maximum number of tasks and responsibilities are transferred to workers on the production floor. Second, a system for detecting defects is installed that quickly traces every problem, once discovered, to its ultimate cause. With this objective the lean production model suggests a form of work organization that in many respects is the opposite of Taylorism. Important organizational changes are required, including a reduced division of labour at the workplace, flat hierarchical structures, decentralization of authority and responsibility, breaking up of narrow job territories, broader job classifications, workers' understanding of the entire production process, and a more qualified and better trained labour force (Sengenberger, 1993).

Womack et al. (1990) present lean production as a universal model that is not confined to the automobile industry and the Japanese cultural context. Instead, each manufacturer across the globe that wishes to survive is advised to implement the principles of lean production. 'In the end, we believe, lean production will supplant both mass-production and the remaining outposts of craft production in all areas of industrial endeavor to become the standard global production system of the twenty-first century' (ibid., p.278). The following part of this section will critically evaluate this claim of global applicability.

Objections to Lean Production

The assertion that lean production provides a new organizational blueprint leading to global convergence of work organization is criticized on three grounds. First, the long-term acceptance of lean production organization methods by workers is questioned. Various commentators have depicted lean production as a 'double-edged sword' combining superior productive performance with strongly adverse consequences for working conditions on the shop floor. Second, lean production is not the sole new organization paradigm; it faces 'competition' from alternative paradigms offering more humanly fulfilling opportunities for workers. Third, the universal claim of the lean production model is opposed on the grounds of its Japanese cultural background. It is questioned whether lean production can be introduced in a Western cultural environment.

The consequences of lean production for the quality of working life has been a source of extensive debate (Sengenberger, 1993). Dohse et al. (1985) distinguish between a 'human relations' and a 'production control' view of lean production (or Toyotism). The human relations approach considers lean production profitable to both employers and employees: while it raises productive performance, it also provides the worker with a more challenging work environment. Lean production is presented as a break with the Taylorist division between intellectual and manual labour as workers' knowledge is taken seriously in the process of continuous improvement. Moreover, to encourage workers' commitment to company objectives, they are provided with broad training and extensive job security. In contrast, the production control approach presents a less optimistic picture of lean production. Based on ethnographic research on shop-floor relations, it is argued that lean production is a more advanced form of Taylorism that has aggravated rather than improved the quality of work.[12] Lean production has not changed the Taylorist system, but it has intensified the repetitious, specialized and standardized character of work by the systematic removal of all slack in the form of buffer stocks, manning and working times (Williams et al., 1992).[13] The main innovation of lean production has been to overcome workers' resistance to further rationalization of production and to draw on shop-floor knowledge to this end: 'Toyotism is not different from Fordism in its goal but in the way in which the goal is to be achieved. (:...) Toyotism is, therefore, not an alternative to Taylorism but rather a solution to its classic problem of the resistance of the workers to placing their knowledge of production in the service of rationalization' (Dohse et al., 1985, p.128).

Lean production has thus been criticized for its roots in Taylorism. Other organizational researchers have searched for a more humanly fulfilling model of work organization. They have resisted the idea of global convergence along the lines of lean production by proposing the concept of 'sociotechnical systems design' (STSD) as a real alternative (Dankbaar, 1997). STSD was originally developed in the British mining industry and has subsequently evolved from 'classical STSD' to the stage of 'modern STSD' (Eijnatten, 1993).[14] Some of the best known experiments with STSD were undertaken in the car industry by Volvo plants in Kalmar and Uddevalla in Sweden (Berggren, 1992).[15] On the surface, STSD and lean production seem to have a lot in common. Both approaches emphasize the need for multi-skilling, teamwork and job rotation. However, on closer scrutiny fundamental differences between the two approaches appear. Eijnatten (1993) distinguishes them in seven aspects (see Table 3.4). STSD is built on the recognition that the low quality of work of Taylorism, caused by fragmentation and standardization of jobs, cannot be challenged if the basic technology and work structure are not adapted. Therefore the sociotechnical approach is based on the need to design novel production processes enabling workers to perform holistic work tasks (Berggren, 1992). In this system, a high skill level of workers is essential and supported by the reward system. In contrast, lean production retains short, standardized work cycles. In that case, 'multi-skilling' is better interpreted as 'multi-tasking' as workers are alternating between similarly repetitive operations. Likewise, the concept of 'teamwork' holds a different meaning in each perspective. The Japanese notion of 'teamwork' refers to a sense of responsibility for the whole enterprise and to improvement activities outside production work (Dankbaar, 1997). Doing operational work in teams, as proposed by the STSD, is not implied.[16] Finally, the approaches hold a different assumption with regard to the nature of the employment relationship. Lean production hides the conflict of interest between employee and firm and encourages a convergence of viewpoints ('the company as a community against its competitors'). In contrast, STSD, acknowledging opposite interests, has proposed a democratic dialogue between firm and employees to overcome them.

Table 3.4 Modern STSD and lean production

	Modern STSD	Lean production
1. Ultimate goals of the enterprise	Quality of work, organization and labour relations	Quality of organization
2. Typical production structure	Dock structure (whole task domain) with long and changeable cycle time	Conventionally paced conveyor belt with short and fixed cycle time
3. Degree of standardization	Low, standardization through memory built up in workers' heads	High for both products and processes
4. Preferred type of renumeration	Fixed, on the basis of skills and personal development	Variable, depends on actual plant performance
5. Typical form of control structure	Self-managing teams performing whole tasks (leaderless groups)	Work teams with small operational tasks controlled by strong leader
6. Basic source of motivation	Continuous personal development and participation in decision making	Pay-based moral/ psychological contract
7. Source of commitment	Democratic dialogue with respect to collective interests	Enforced commitment to some anonymous collective interest

Source: Eijnatten (1993).

A third objection to global convergence along the lines of lean production refers to its Japanese origins. Observers of Japanese production systems argue that the historical development of lean production cannot be understood without reference to the specific institutional configuration of Japan. Commonly, lean production, or 'Toyotism', is differentiated from 'Japanization' or 'Nipponism'. The former refers to a set of organizational techniques, while the latter entails a broader picture of the Japanese system of industrial relations (Wood, 1991; Durand, 1997).[17] A major question concerns the possibility of transfer of lean production as a management technique to other societal contexts without the adoption of those institutional arrangements that have accompanied its development in Japan (Elger and Smith, 1994). Kenney and Florida (1993) answer this question positively. Using the experience of Japanese transplants in the United States, they conclude: 'the Japanese system (...) consists of organizational practices whose fundamental "genetic code" can be successfully inserted into another society and can then begin to successfully reproduce in the new environment. In this sense, the system is independent of Japanese culture and society' (p.8). However, they consider the labour movement in Europe and America the most important potential barrier to further diffusion of the Japanese production system. Here they agree with Dohse et al. (1985), who argued against the cross-cultural transfer of the Japanese organizational model, because 'it is rooted in a system of labor relations that for a number of reasons is unacceptable for trade unions in Europe and the United States' (Dohse et al., 1985, p.117).[18] However, Durand (1997) doubts the ability of European and American unions to resist the introduction of the broader framework of Japanese employment relations. According to him, the undermining of the ability of unions to make radical claims and the diffusion of new ways of managing employees are indications that 'the Nipponisation of employment relations in Europe and the United States is well under way' (Durand, 1997, p.138).

SHIFTING CAPITAL–LABOUR POWER BALANCE

The distribution of power between capital and labour is advanced as a fifth mechanism operating on the organization of the employment relationship. Since the 1970s, a shift in this power distribution has been observed (Hirsch, 1991). After the Second World War, a particular successful compromise between capital and labour in terms of productivity growth and social stability, the so-called Fordist era or the 'Golden Age', settled (Boyer, 1995; Lipietz, 1995).[19] However, in the early 1970s, the Fordist consensus broke down, for various reasons, and a new search for a stable capital–labour relationship was initiated.[20]

This section presents various interpretations of the capital–labour relationship that will characterize the post-Fordist era.[21] Three alternative trajectories are proposed: a single path in which Fordism is continued on the basis of new technology and automation; a dual path in which labour is split into a core group and a peripheral group; and a pluriformity of paths based on distinct social and cultural conditions. The three scenarios are described in more detail below.

Neo-Fordism

A first scenario for the future of capital–labour relationships is referred to as 'neo-Fordism', a term that implies continuity with the 'old' Fordist mode of regulation. Neo-Fordism goes beyond Fordism, but does not negate its fundamental principles. Instead, neo-Fordism represents a further refinement of Fordist or Taylorist principles.

Aglietta (1979) is among the first to have employed the concept of neo-Fordism. To him, it denotes a new regime of economic growth that can sustain the hegemony of the United States in world economic affairs. Among its components are the internationalization of production activities and the application of Fordist methods of production to non-Fordist product areas such as services. Above all, neo-Fordism involves a new stage in the evolution of the capital–labour relationship based on the emergence of new automatic control equipment. Automatic technology is not conceived as neutral machinery, but as shaped by capitalism ('just as it shapes every other system of productive forces', ibid., p.123). Aglietta argues that the introduction of automated production control has divided the production process in a new, more rigorous, way. Automatic control enables the complete centralization of production programming decisions within the engineering department, while it eliminates the need for skilled production workers. It has deepened the division of mental labour between production workers and skilled engineers, to the benefit of the capitalist class. 'The capitalist class then has simply to make sure of the essential factor: total domination of programming centres, research methods, and processing of information, and total submission of the highly skilled personnel responsible for them' (ibid., p.127).

Furthermore, control takes on a different form in the neo-Fordist employment relationship. Personal supervision is replaced by direct control of the production process by means of information systems: 'Control is both more abstract and more rigorous. The workers are no longer subjected to a constraint of personal obedience, but rather to the collective constraint of the production process' (ibid., p.128). The introduction of new management methods, such as job rotation, job enrichment and autonomous workgroups, should be interpreted in this light.[22] Autonomous groups are not autonomous at all, but constrained by detailed production programmes and subjected to the information centre of the enterprise: 'The principle of automatic control completely removes the manufacturing process from the workers' vigilance or influence' (ibid., p.129).

Dual Trajectories

The neo-Fordist perspective on the emerging capital–labour relationship presents a single trajectory of a reinforced Taylorism that extends managerial control to the 'intellectual capacities' of the employees. Others have disputed the viability of the neo-Fordist pathway, for neo-Fordism combines two incompatible objectives, employee commitment and managerial control. On logical grounds, Lipietz (1995) doubts that collective involvement of workers will emerge if the objectives of the firm and the employees do not coincide. Accordingly, a choice needs to be made between workers' involvement and managerial control or flexibility. This choice can be made at national, industrial and company level.

Lipietz (1995) discusses the choice between flexibility and involvement at national level. He argues that national systems of capital–labour relations need to support either one of these dimensions. He proposes two 'privileged lines of evolution' of capital–labour relations that he labels respectively as 'neo-Taylorism' and 'Kalmarism' to replace the Fordist compromise. The neo-Taylorist pathway involves external labour market flexibility and renounces negotiated workers' involvement. This option is likely to be followed in countries where individualistic ideologies prevail and the working population is divided, as in the United States. The alternative pathway, Kalmarism, refers to external rigidity and negotiated involvement of the workers at the societal level.[23] This paradigm can prevail when the labour movement is strong and takes into account the interests of the whole wage-earning population, as in the continental European countries.

Similar dual pathways of capital–labour relations have been developed at industrial and firm level. The Japanese system of industrial relations provides an example of such a dual pathway at industrial level: many of its industries consist of core firms that provide lifetime employment for their employees, and small, peripheral subcontractors that stick to flexible employment relations (Lazonick, 1995). Atkinson (1987) applies this hybrid model to the single firm. His model of the flexible firm divides employees into two groups. The first group consists of a core group of employees who perform the central activities of the firm. These employees tend to be male and well trained, and are provided with full-time contracts for unlimited duration. The second group of workers carries out routine activities requiring skills that are readily available on the external labour market. These peripheral workers are often female, receive little training and have shorter job tenures.

National Specific Variants

Robert Boyer (1995, 1997) presents a third perspective on the post-Fordist relationship between capital and labour. His view acknowledges that capital and labour are embedded in specific social and cultural contexts. He denies that a homogeneous Fordist model of capital–labour relations was ever established. Among advanced capitalist countries, a wide diversity of Fordist capital–labour configurations have been observed. Fordism must be considered as an ideal type model that has found alternative applications in different national circumstances.[24]

Likewise, Boyer does not expect the emergence of a unique post-Fordist relationship between capital and labour. Instead, his picture contains a variety of national strategies in response to the demise of the Fordist compromise: 'every nation would grope in the search for a new capital–labour relation which would make national political and cultural heritage coherent with the new trends in lifestyle, technology and finance' (Boyer, 1995, p.50). Boyer identifies six alternative developmental paths of the wage relationship that are based on two strategic choices (see Figure 3.3). The first issue (horizontal axis) refers to the use of new information technology in restructuring the work organization. Two options are open: deepening scientific management principles by using electronic equipment that strengthens control over blue- and white-collar workers, or reversing the previous trend of scientific management by using electronic equipment to enhance workers' skill level and autonomy in the workplace. The second dimension (vertical axis) refers to the distribution of the dividends. Three strategies are available: the market mechanism, negotiation between stakeholders at the firm level (micro-corporatism), and negotiation between stakeholders at a national level (social democratic compromise).

Having identified six alternative forms of employment relations, Boyer relates each form to individual nation states on the basis of their current regulatory scheme of industrial relations. He arrives at the following prospective views. Countries such as the United States and Canada, with decentralized systems of

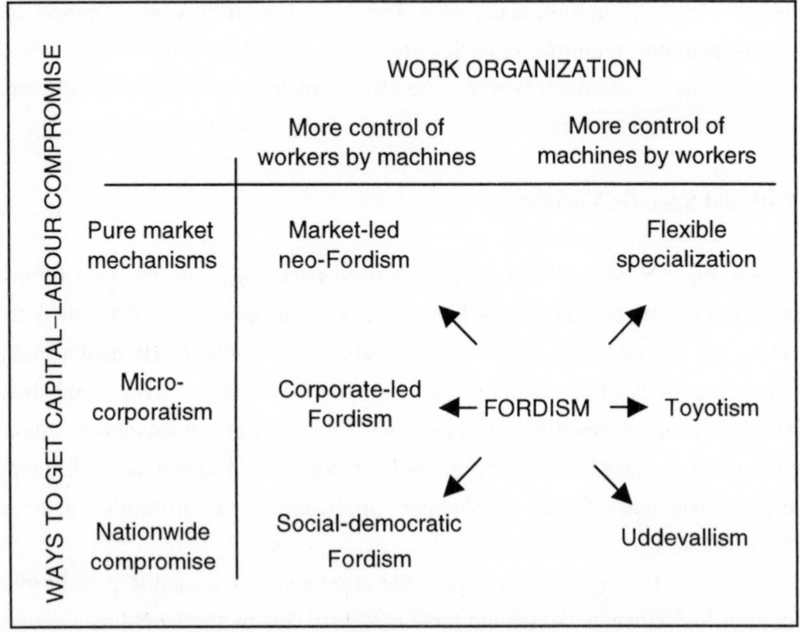

Source: Boyer (1995).

Figure 3.3 Alternative capital–labour relations

wage bargaining and low incentives to invest in labour-saving technical change, are expected to develop in the direction of 'market-led neo-Fordism'. Japan is advanced as the prime example of a Toyotist capital–labour relationship, while social-democratic countries, such as Sweden and Germany, are thought to develop in the direction of the Uddevallist model. Most other countries of the European Community are still qualified as 'hybrid', as they combine features of market-oriented and social-democratic strategies.

VALUE SHIFT: FROM MATERIALISM TO POST-MATERIALISM

The final mechanism for understanding contemporary global changes of the employment relationship relates to shifting individual preferences. Inglehart (1990) documents a value change during the 1970s and 1980s across advanced industrial societies from 'materialism' towards 'post-materialism'. Among Western nations he discerns a growing emphasis on quality of life, individual growth and self-expression, while adherence to physical sustenance, safety and traditional moral and social norms is in decline.[25] Inglehart's hypothesis is confirmed by Ester et al. (1994). In the view of these researchers, the rising level of 'individualization' in both Europe and North America reflects the emergence of a post-materialist value system. 'Self-actualization' and 'personal happiness' have become the core of value development and norm selection.

This section considers the implications of the emerging post-materialist value system for the organization of the employment relationship. Two mechanisms are proposed that relate individual values to the employment relationship. First, individuals will express their value orientation in their consumption behaviour, which, in a competitive market environment, needs to be taken into account by producers. Second, individuals will display their value orientations in negotiation with employers on the terms of employment. Both mechanisms are discussed in more detail below. The final section addresses some arguments to counter the claim that the employment relationship is converging on the basis of post-materialist values.

Shifting Consumer Tastes

The link between changing customer tastes and the organization of the employment relationship was elaborated by Piore and Sabel (1984) and culminated in the 'flexible specialization thesis'. In this view, models of craft production will underlie the organization of the employment relationship in the coming decades. Mass-production is a memory of the past as consumer-goods markets have been saturated and customers increasingly demand more diversity.

Piore and Sabel (1984) assert that flexible specialization, a craft-based model of production organization, is likely to replace mass-production as the dominant production paradigm. Central to their argument is the concept of 'industrial divide', that 'brief moment when the path of technological development itself is at issue' (ibid., p.5). Two alternative production technologies figure in an industrial divide: mass-production and craft production. While the former involves the use of product-specific machinery and semi-skilled workers producing large quantities of standardized goods, the latter is based on general-purpose machines and skilled workers producing a variety of customized goods.

The first industrial divide, occurring at the turn of the twentieth century, was decided in favour of mass-production technologies, but not, as noted by Piore and Sabel, because mass-production was technologically superior. Instead, the structure of market demand is accorded decisive influence: 'Industrial technology does not grow out of a self-contained logic of scientific or technical necessity: which technologies develop and which languish depends crucially on the structure of the markets for the technologies' products' (ibid., p.5). Logically, the adoption of mass-production techniques has become more widespread in the United States, where 'ancestral diversity of tastes has been erased by transplantation to the New World', than in France, where 'tastes and markets differed from region to region' (ibid., p.40).

Similarly, market demand factors are also thought to be at the root of the break-up of mass markets that gave rise to the 'second industrial divide' in the early 1970s. Although Piore and Sabel pay ample attention to supply-side factors, they consider the saturation of consumer-goods markets as 'the most consequential and long-term postwar development' (ibid., p.184). The second industrial divide involves a renewed choice between mass-production, this time sustained by an international Keynesian regulatory framework, and craft production embedded in the institutional structure of flexible specialization.[26] Although Piore and Sabel are careful to stress that there is no inherent logic for determining the outcome of the second industrial divide, their analysis of contemporary market developments tends to point the future in the direction of flexible specialization.[27] There is a strong hint that the availability of flexible, multi-purpose machines, together with the growth in markets for better quality, non-standardized products, will tip the balance in favour of flexible specialization as the dominant industrial paradigm (Amin, 1994).[28] More bluntly formulated: 'the experience of labour is entirely subordinate to the supreme market. The core worker produces designer goods for the core New-Timer citizen' (Pollert, 1991, p.30).

Shifting Employee Preferences

A second mechanism for relating the rise of post-materialist values to changes in the realm of the employment relationship builds on the alteration of the needs of the employee. The expectations of the individual employee with regard to working life are affected by a shift in value orientation. Employers need to take account of employee preferences if they want to attract workers and to keep them motivated to direct their efforts in the interest of the firm.

A characterization of the 'new' employee and effective managerial responses can be found in modern handbooks of human resource management.[29] For example, Beer et al. (1984) denote two aspects of the workforce inducing firms to reconsider the employment relationship. In the first place, the 'new employee' has less acceptance of authority. In response, as suggested by Beer, firms need to re-examine the amount of 'voice' and participation that they afford to their employees. Secondly, the new employee demonstrates a greater concern with career and life satisfaction. Accordingly, it is recommended that firms drop traditional assumptions about career paths. Career paths need to become more closely matched with individual expectations. Moreover, firms need to take employee lifestyle into account in transferring and scheduling work.

Some Counter-Evidence

The combination of a post-materialist value orientation leading to diversified consumer tastes and shifted workers' preferences with the organization of the employment relationship predicts a trend towards improved quality of work and a strengthening of the position of the individual worker. Global convergence in this direction can be postulated if value orientations across nations are becoming more similar, along the lines of post-materialism. This section argues that such a conclusion is premature: three arguments are presented to undermine the claim of convergence along post-materialist lines.

A first argument challenges the alleged convergence of values across advanced economies along the lines of post-materialism. Recent cross-cultural value studies (Inglehart, 1990; Ester et al., 1994) do indeed indicate similar shifts in value orientation among advanced societies; nevertheless, these studies show that substantial differences in value patterns between national populations continue to exist. Although in both Western Europe and the United States the percentage of people that adhere to post-materialist values is growing, differences between societies in terms of proportions of people supporting these values remain. 'No total homogenization of systems of meaning and expression has occurred, nor does it appear likely that there will be anytime soon' (Ester et al., 1994).

A second argument challenges the alleged consumption preferences of the new post-materialist individual. Essential to the flexible specialization thesis is the claim that consumer tastes have increasingly become more diffuse and diversified. However, Ritzer (1993) reaches an utterly opposite conclusion. He advances the McDonaldization thesis, in which a growing uniformity of customer behaviour is emphasized. Rather than consumer tastes diversifying, 'McDonaldized' consumers are guided by a preference for 'efficiency', 'calculability', 'predictability' and 'control'. The American fast-food industry confirms most obviously Ritzer's thesis. However, he asserts that the main characteristics of McDonaldization affect virtually every other aspect of society in the United States, as well as the rest of the world: 'McDonaldization has shown every sign of being an inexorable process by sweeping through seemingly impervious institutions and parts of the world' (ibid., p.1). With regard to the employment relationship, he suggests an intensification of Taylor's scientific management principles. The drive for 'efficiency' and 'calculability' has rehabilitated the use of time and motion studies to design 'just-in-time' production organizations. Standardization and formalization by the use of 'scripts' and 'procedures' enhance 'predictability' and 'control'.

Finally, the proposed relation between the dominance of quality of work issues found in human resource management handbooks and the shift of employee preferences is called into question. Abrahamson (1997) argues that normative rhetoric, including the emphasis on human relations and corporate culture, has recurred at frequent intervals throughout the history of professional personnel management. He presents evidence that the prevalence of normative rhetoric correlates with the peaks of economic business cycles, rising labour union activity and high voluntary turnover rates of employees. Employee values do not appear to be a major explanatory factor.

CONCLUSIONS

The aim of this chapter was to infer the potential impact of 'globalization' on the organization of the employment relationship across culturally diverse nation states. The widely heard claim that globalization is pushing firms to adjust their employment relations in the direction of a global uniform standard has been critically evaluated by taking a close look at six mechanisms. A necessary condition for convergence to occur is the operation of at least one mechanism irrespective of national borders. The global developments in the domain of each mechanism were reviewed to inquire whether this condition for global convergence of employment relations is satisfied.

It appears that the organization of the employment relationship has indeed faced strong pressures to change. Intensified international competition has urged firms to further rationalize employment relations; the use of microelectronic technology has entailed different work organization and skill demands; new managerial 'best practices' have been developed, awaiting adoption by management across the world; the Fordist capital–labour compromise has collapsed and a renewed 'choice' between flexibility and commitment needs to be made; and finally, the value systems of people in advanced economies have shifted towards individual goals, such as self-actualization and personal happiness. Notwithstanding the multitude of pressures on the employment relationship, a consensus, in broad lines, can be discerned about the direction of the development of employment relations. A firm eager to survive in an increasingly competitive business environment needs to develop more flexible employment relations in both qualitative and quantitative terms. Such a firm produces, with the use of microelectronic technology, a broad variety of products to satisfy the post-materialist customer. Furthermore, the firm is strongly advised to breed commitment among its individualized core workers to unlock their intellectual capacities for the goal of continuous quality improvement.

However, there is no consensus on which mechanism is the driving force behind the changes. For example, various mechanisms may account for the increase of product variety that has occurred over the last decades. Is this due to a change in consumer behaviour based on the rise of post-materialist values? Or is increased product variety due to exacerbated competition among producers or the emergence of the microelectronics-based production technologies? Moreover, there is a great deal of confusion about the nature of change from the worker's perspective. Does the introduction of microelectronic technology liberate the workplace by providing workers with more autonomy, training and job security, or is the worker increasingly a replaceable 'resource' submitted to enhanced managerial control?

Finally, although sufficient evidence for the presence of global forces exists, the question whether these global pressures push the organization of the employment relationship towards convergence across culturally diverse nation states is still before the judge, for the operation of mechanisms with a global scope represents only a necessary condition, not a sufficient one. The analysis of the global forces makes clear that each of them leaves room for strategic choice to the actors that are involved in the organization of the employment relationship, such as employers, union representatives or state officials. The global forces are not constraining enough to justify the convergence thesis. Indeed, substantial evidence is presented to take the claim seriously that the introduction of microelectronic technology, the diffusion of new management methods and the shift in capital–labour relations do not follow a universal imperative, but that these recent developments are embedded in a broader system of societal institutions. It appears that the actors who shape the employment relationship can respond to the global forces in accordance with their cultural inclinations. Elements in the realm of national culture are thus advanced as primary mechanisms that preserve the existing cultural diversity. Empirical study is required for an ultimate verdict.

NOTES

1. Petrella (1996) employs a similar umbrella notion to capture globalization. He identifies seven spheres of globalization in contemporary societies: globalization of finances and ownership, globalization of markets, strategies and competition, globalization of technology and knowledge, globalization of modes of life and consumption patterns, globalization of regulatory capabilities and governance, globalization as the political unification of the world, and globalization of perception and consciousness.
2. Geographical analysis of world trade patterns shows that the largest rise of export shares has occurred in Japan and the newly industrialized economies in Asia (Vickery, 1996). The share of the newly industrialized Asian economies in world trade has risen steadily, from less than 8 per cent in the early 1970s to almost 20 per cent in 1995 (OECD, 1997).
3. Important changes in regional composition of FDI flows have occurred (OECD, 1997). With respect to FDI outflows, in which the OECD countries account for more than 96 per cent of the world FDI flows, the importance of the United States as a capital investor has decreased at the expense of Japan and other major OECD countries. The share of the United States in the total of world FDI outflows decreased from 53.2 percent in 1975 to 23 per cent in 1985 and recovered in 1993 to the level of 31 per cent. As a destination for foreign investments, the position of OECD countries is less dominant. Since 1975, the share of non-OECD countries in total world FDI inflow has remained stable at around 35 per cent. However, a major

shift of FDI flows has occurred in the direction of Asia, whose share of world inward FDI has increased from 5.9 per cent in 1975 to 25.6 per cent in 1993 (OECD, 1997). Moreover, Eastern Europe has emerged as a main destination of capital investment. UNCTAD (1996) reports a share of 5 per cent of world inflows in 1995, compared with only 1 per cent in 1991.

4. Obviously, the current period differs from the pre-1913 level in the product composition of international trade that has shifted from primary to manufactured goods.
5. Bairoch (1996) arrives at a similar conclusion using the measure of foreign direct investment. The relative importance of FDI stocks of Western developed countries in the early 1990s equalled figures from 1913. The importance of globalization of FDI is further questioned by analysing it as a proportion of net domestic business investment. Wade (1996) assesses the typical order of magnitude over the 1980s as between 5 and 15 per cent: 'Domestic investment by domestic capital easily dominates both direct investment overseas and foreign investment at home' (Wade, 1996, p.70).
6. The concept 'Fordism' refers to Henry Ford, who put the Taylorist principles of work organization into actual practice. Nowadays, Fordism is understood in two ways: first, as a distinctive organization of the labour process, it refers to the use of dedicated machinery operated by semi-skilled labour to produce long runs of standardized goods (mass-production); second, as a certain macroeconomic regime, 'Fordism' refers to the virtuous circle of capital accumulation based on the balanced growth between mass-production and mass-consumption.
7. The validity of this claim is doubted by Williams et al. (1987) as Piore and Sabel do not provide any comparative productivity figures to analyse the potential of, respectively, craft and mass-production productivity at the end of the nineteenth century.
8. Examples of 'isomorphic' pressures on management to adopt similar management methods across the world are global consulting firms, international business schools, management gurus, mass-media business publications, 'benchmarking' or 'best practice sharing' among multinational companies, global quality standards (ISO) or quality contests (for example, Baldridge and Deming awards).
9. Dankbaar (1997) summarizes the lean production organization by means of six principles: just-in-time logistics, group technology in components production, autonomation, responsibility for quality of production, self-inspection and multi-skilling, and economies of cooperation.
10. At the Toyota factories, the just-in-time system is given the label 'Kanban'.
11. The success of continuous improvement processes relies on the commitment of workers to contributing their knowledge to perfect the production process. Essential to the lean production model are management methods to mobilize workers' initiative. Kenney and Florida (1993) identify the ability to harness workers' intelligence and knowledge of production as the most distinctive achievement of the Japanese organizational techniques. Therefore they propose calling the Japanese work organization 'innovation-mediated production' to highlight the integration of innovation and production or intellectual and physical labour.
12. See, for example, Rinehart et al. (1997).
13. Time and motion studies 'with stop-watch and all' are common practice for employee groups ('quality circles') in Japanese plants (Dankbaar, 1997).

14. A specific variant of sociotechnical systems design developed in the Netherlands is called 'Integral Organization Renewal' (Sitter et al., 1997).
15. Womack et al. (1990) belittle the STSD experiments at the Uddevalla plant as a step backwards in history. They perceive STSD as a resurgence of craft production that is unable to compete with mass- and lean production.
16. Dankbaar (1997) notes that the use of teamwork in connection with lean production has led to confusion. Originally, teamwork was not a part of Japanese organization methods. He understands the emphasis on teamwork in connection with lean production as a proof of the impact of STSD on organizational thinking in the United States.
17. Durand (1997) identifies five general traits of the broader system of Japanese industrial relations: a merit-based promotion system linked to individual evaluation creating keen competition for promotion within the company; a wage structure in which a substantial part of the wage level is variable and dependent on supervisory evaluation of the individual worker; lifetime employment which is protected by segmentation of the labour market in permanent and temporary workers and allows for training investments in permanent workers; 'enforced consensus' between companies and employees to meet production fluctuations by means of overtime resulting in a high number of working hours per employee; a coercive social environment, reflected among others by close relations between management and company unions, leaving little room for employees to object to the terms of employment.
18. The argument that the choice between lean production and STSD depends on the strength of the position of labour in the production system is confirmed by the observation that Volvo's experiments with STSD started when labour supply for the car industry in Sweden was tight (Berggren, 1992). Likewise, Toyota is said to have improved the quality of work of its lean production system as it increasingly faces labour market shortages (Dankbaar, 1997).
19. Boyer (1995) describes four pillars of the Fordist capital–labour relationship: (1) a deep division of labour to allow mass-production of standardized goods; (2) a compromise to share productivity gains through higher wages; (3) collective bargaining to spread wage increases from leading sectors to secondary sectors and civil servants; and (4) redistribution of income by means of welfare provisions.
20. The four basic features of the Fordist labour regime find themselves in a state of flux (Boyer, 1995): (1) mass-production is thought to be being replaced by flexible production methods; (2) the indexation of wage to productivity has been under challenge; (3) the wage hierarchy is destabilized by decentralization of bargaining and segmentation of labour markets; and (4) the welfare state is meeting increasing pressure to cut budgets.
21. The main source of reference is the so-called 'French regulation school' (for reviews, see Nielsen, 1991; Amin, 1994; Jessop, 1995).
22. Durand (1997) applies the neo-Fordist interpretation of the emerging capital–labour relationship to the diffusion of Japanese management methods. He perceives the Japanese organizational techniques as 'refinements' or 'reinforcements' of Fordism. He characterizes 'just-in-time' production systems as 'hyper-Fordist'. Moreover, participatory programmes, such as total quality management, have not overthrown rigid hierarchical structures. Instead, they have been used as 'ideological' projects to encourage a convergence of interests between management and employees.

23. The term 'Kalmarism' refers to a car factory of Volvo located in Kalmar (Sweden) that has implemented a work organization designed on the basis of the lessons from the sociotechnical school (see Berggren, 1992).
24. Boyer (1995) distinguishes seven types of Fordism among the OECD countries: corporatist Fordism (Austria), state-led Fordism (France), hybrid Fordism (Japan), democratic Fordism (Sweden), flexible Fordism (Germany), flawed Fordism (United Kingdom) and genuine Fordism (United States).
25. To account for this value shift, Inglehart (1990) postulates a combination of a 'scarcity' and a 'socialization' hypothesis: an individual's basic priorities reflect the socioeconomic conditions that prevailed during his or her pre-adult years. Therefore a shift towards post-materialist values in the last two decades is understood as a reaction to the increase in prosperity that was effectuated during the post-Second World War decades.
26. The success of flexible specialization depends on its ability to sustain innovation by balancing cooperation and competition among productive units. Piore and Sabel (1984) mention two institutional settings performing this function: 'industrial districts' of geographically localized networks of small and medium-sized firms and large decentralized companies with relatively autonomous productive units.
27. According to Piore and Sabel (1984) the rise of flexible specialization opens up long-term prospects for improvements in the conditions of working life. In contrast to mass-production, flexible specialization is predicated on collaboration, solidarity and communitarianism. It puts a premium on craft skills and revitalizes the role of the individual worker as his intellectual participation in the work process is enhanced.
28. Note that Piore and Sabel (1984) do not believe that increased consumer preference for diversity is caused by a rise in post-materialist values. Rather, they suggest that consumers' tastes are socially constructed by the products that are offered by the market. In markets with overcapacity, quality and diversity have become key factors for competitiveness. Faced with increased diversity in the shops, consumers will become less satisfied with standardized products.
29. The gradual replacement of 'personnel management' by the idea of 'human resource management' in the 1980s can be understood as a response to new perspectives on employee preferences. While personnel management emphasizes the collective nature of employees, human resource management starts from the employee as an individual (Storey, 1995).

4. The concept of culture

INTRODUCTION

To recapitulate, the central research object of this study concerns the national organization of the employment relationship. A starting position of the study is that the employment relationship has been differently organized across culturally diverse nation states. Numerous studies have demonstrated the variety among employment relations that could not be explained by reference to universal variables. Commonly, it is left to variables in the domain of national culture to account for such cross-national differences. However, the persistence of such culturally based differences is increasingly disputed as it is widely believed that the globalization of economic processes will press economic systems to adopt a universal logic based on economic efficiency. A contrary argument is that, although global pressures for change can indeed be identified, adaptation will be culturally mediated. That is, different cultures will find different solutions to similar challenges posed by globalization. Empirical study should settle the debate. Such empirical study cannot refrain from the study of national culture, for national culture is thought to play a crucial role in shaping the organization of the employment relationship.

The examination of the relationship between national culture and the development of national patterns of employment relations necessitates a clarification of the notion of culture. To prevent its widespread abuse as a residual variable that enters into explanations when cross-national differences cannot be explained by more tangible variables, this chapter takes up the challenge to define and conceptualize the notion of culture. This exercise should be a deliberate process, for conceptualization determines a substantial part of the research method. What culture is held to be influences the manner in which it is investigated. Furthermore, the adoption of a particular concept of culture cannot be detached from certain basic assumptions about the nature of society. The view one holds about the nature of society will largely determine how culture as a social phenomenon is conceptualized.

This chapter will pay significant attention to the philosophical and methodological foundation that underlies the proposed concept of culture. Two major debates in the social sciences guide the exploration. First, the ontological conception of culture is discussed along the lines of the debate between individualism and holism. What is the ultimate nature of culture? Is culture a social structure that affects human agency from the outside, or is culture internal to the minds of human beings? A second debate concentrates on the question of how culture can become known and introduces the opposite perspectives of positivism and hermeneutics. How can scientists acquire knowledge of culture? Should culture be studied from the outside, like natural objects, or is culture concerned with meaning that can only be penetrated by immersion in a certain culture? The first section elaborates on both debates. It clarifies the terms of discussion by examining four theoretical approaches to the study of culture in organization studies.

After the shortcomings of both individualist and holistic approaches are pointed out, the main part of the chapter is devoted to the search for an alternative approach to studying culture. Two alternative conceptions of society are examined. The second section examines Roy Bhaskar's 'transformational model of social activity', while the third section focuses on Anthony Giddens' structuration theory. Both new directions in the study of society propose to overcome the dichotomy of the individual and society by conceptualizing them as a duality in which the individual presupposes society and vice versa. In other words, the lines of separation between the individual and society are blurred; they are regarded as two sides of the same coin. Notwithstanding substantial similarities, a crucial ontological difference separates the two approaches. The fourth section demonstrates that Bhaskar's adherence to a naturalist philosophy, transcendental realism, inhibits him from breaking away from a holistic conception of culture. It makes clear that Giddens' perspective offers a more promising way out of the traditional debate between agency and social structure. The chapter concludes with a proposal to conceptualize culture on the basis of Giddens' structuration theory.

FOUR APPROACHES TO STUDYING CULTURE

A search in the literature for a theoretical foundation for the notion of culture brings forth a multitude of different approaches, concepts and definitions. The study of Kroeber and Kluckhohn (1952) is significant in this regard. The authors listed 164 distinct uses of the concept of culture in academic studies.[1] Almost 50 years later, many more definitions and perspectives have been added to this list. Attempts to reconcile the different viewpoints and to find consensus have not been successful. Consequently, great efforts have been devoted to reviewing the concept of culture, both within the boundaries of one discipline and across the various branches that constitute the social sciences.[2] Schneider and Bonjean (1973) and Alexander and Seidman (1990) look at the use of culture across the whole of the social sciences. DiMaggio (1990), Jackson (1993) and Jones (1995) examine the culture concept within the economic discipline. DiMaggio (1994) provides an overview of cultural studies in the field of economic sociology. The use of culture in sociology is analysed by Münch and Smelser (1992), Dirks et al. (1994) and Crane (1994). Psychology's use of culture is reviewed by Segall (1986, 1990). Finally, Eckstein (1988, 1996) and Demertzis (1986) review the concept of culture in political studies.

In this section, the discussion is confined to the use of culture in the field of management and organization theory. In this field of research, the concept is reviewed by, among others, Child (1981), Smircich (1983), Allaire and Firsirotu (1984), Roberts and Boyacigiller (1984), Reichers and Schneider (1990), Sackmann (1991), Alvesson (1993), Gordon Redding (1994) and Tayeb (1988, 1994). Despite the diversity of contributions that involve the notion of culture, Rousseau (1990) notes that disagreement among organizational researchers is not concerned with the nature of culture. Consensus can be discerned about the essential characteristics of culture. According to Adler (1991), culture is something that is shared by all or almost all members of some social group, something that the older members of the group try to pass on to the younger members, and something (as in the case of morals, laws, or customs) that shapes behaviour, or structures one's perception of the world.

The confusion that surrounds 'culture' appears to be concerned not with its nature, but rather with its theoretical conceptualization and, correspondingly, the manner in which it is investigated. 'In many respects, it is not the definitions of culture that vary so widely across organizational researchers, but the types of data researchers collect' (Rousseau, 1990). This section holds that a large part of the discussion coincides with two classic debates in the social sciences. One is concerned with ontology, the philosophical theory of what exists; the other is concerned with epistemology, the philosophical theory of knowledge. The ontological debate refers to the question whether the ultimate constituents of society are individuals and their interaction, or whether reality can also be assigned to social structures that transcend individual consciousness. This conflict is related to culture, because it determines the level of being at which culture should be analysed. Should culture be conceived as a structural phenomenon with properties irreducible to individuals, or is culture just the sum of properties of individuals that constitute the cultural group? The second debate, on epistemology, is between positivism and hermeneutics. The relevance for culture relates to the nature and scope of knowledge that can be acquired about culture. Can culture be characterized by universal dimensions or should culture be understood in terms of the unique characteristics of a particular cultural group? The two debates are combined in the fourfold categorization of Table 4.1. Each quadrant can be characterized by a particular conceptualization of culture. We examine in what follows how each concept of culture has been applied to the study of the employment relationship. However, before examining the four quadrants individually, it will be useful to reflect on the two debates that constitute the two dimensions of Table 4.1. First, the opposite views of individualists and holists are outlined, then attention is shifted to the contrast between positivist and hermeneutic approaches to social science. Finally,we mention the shortcomings of the four approaches towards culture and indicate a way to overcome the confusion that surrounds it.

Table 4.1 Four approaches to studying culture

	Individualism	Holism
Positivism	Culture as shared values	Culture as collective consciousness
Hermeneutics	Culture as subjective meanings	Culture as common meanings

Individualism versus Holism

At what level should culture be studied? Is culture the product of vast numbers of choices by individual members of the society or is culture something more? Should culture be explained by reference to the individual actor or is culture a collective property that emerges out of the interaction of individual actors and, as such, irreducible to the individual actor? This debate between individualists and holists, which has a long tradition in social science, is at the core of any conceptualization of culture (Archer, 1995). The two opposite positions are briefly examined in the following.[3]

Individualism

Philosophical individualism involves a specific ontological perspective on the essence of social life. Individualists view society as constituted merely by human actions and their effects. This perspective is based on the recognition that all actions are ultimately performed by individuals. Social structures are thought to have no existence and reality outside the actions of individuals. Elster (1989) denies even the existence of societies; there are 'only individuals who interact with one another'. All social activities are carried out by people, separately or in groups. When an act occurs on behalf of a collective group, such as a company, a ministry or a trade union, individual persons conduct the real acting. For example, a war consists of fighting soldiers, a slump refers to bosses sacking workers and inflation arises from sellers raising their prices. In sum, individualists deny any autonomous properties to social structures. Instead, they hold that 'Men, however, in a state of society, are still men; their actions and passions are obedient to the laws of individual human nature. Men are not, when brought together, converted into another kind of substance, with different properties' (Mill, 1875, cited in Hollis, 1994, p.10).

The individualist perspective on the essence of society is accompanied by a particular methodology to explain social phenomena: methodological individualism.[4] It is the doctrine that facts about societies, and social phenomena in general, are to be explained solely in terms of facts about individuals. Thus social events are only explained if their origins in the actions of individuals are uncovered. A classic interpretation of this imperative is given by Watkins: 'There may be unfinished or half-way explanations (say, inflation) in terms of other large-scale phenomena (say, full employment); but we shall not have arrived at rock-bottom explanations of such large-scale social phenomena until we have deduced an account of them from statements about the dispositions, beliefs, resources and inter-relations of individuals' (Watkins, 1968, p.271).

Central to an individualist explanation of social phenomena is human action. An essential premise for individualists is that such human action is purposeful and goal-directed.[5] 'Individual and purposeful action is regarded as the steam driving the socio-economic engine' (Hodgson, 1988, p.60). However, the account of the origins behind the purposes of the individual differentiates individualistic-oriented social scientists among themselves. Lukes (1973) distinguishes a 'continuum of individual predicates', but generally individualists may refer to either the 'homo economicus' or the 'homo sociologicus'. Economic man derives his or her purposes from an instrumental evaluation of his or her position. Economic man 'calculates' the most effective means to achieve a certain end. The 'ends' or the preferences are allowed to change across different cultures, but the process of preference formation is taken to be beyond the scope of analysis. Obviously, the concept of culture is not relevant to explaining the action of 'homo economicus'.[6]

Culture becomes of interest if individualist analysis is based on the 'homo sociologicus'. The purposes of this individual originate in the social and cultural environment in which he is embedded. For social man, the pursuit of socially and culturally formed preferences might drive out the weighing of instrumental costs. Individualist analysis can grasp culture by reducing it to properties of the social individual. Most commonly, it is proposed that culture should be explained in terms of 'values' or 'meaning', depending on the adoption of, respectively, a positivistic or a hermeneutic perspective on social reality. The distinctive aspect of culture is always the shared nature of such individual properties among a certain cultural group.

Holism

The holistic conception of society contrasts sharply with the individualist perspective. While an individualist views the essence of social life solely in terms of human actions, a holist focuses attention on how social 'forces' condition individual behaviour. This can be taken to the extreme perspective where such social forces appear to be autonomous entities with a distinct identity (Rutherford, 1994). Thus holists do not deny that society consists of individuals, but society includes properties that cannot be reduced to the individuals that constitute it. Society is 'no more decomposable into individuals than a geometrical surface is into lines, or a line into points' (Comte, 1851, cited in Lukes, 1973, p.111). Society is thought to have its own existence with specific properties that arise out of interaction between individuals, in the same way as molecules consist of atoms and organic bodies of cells: 'By virtue of this principle, society is not the mere sum of individuals, but the system formed by their association represents a specific reality which has its own characteristics. Undoubtedly no collective entity can be produced if there are no individual consciousnesses: this is a necessary but not sufficient condition. In addition, these consciousnesses must be associated and combined, but combined in a certain way. It is from this combination that social life arises' (Durkheim, 1895, p.129).

Durkheim captures the specific reality of society by the notion of 'societal fact'. Societal facts depend on individual human beings for their creation, but, thereafter, they are thought to have their own existence beyond psychological attributes of individuals. The essential characteristic of societal facts is their power to exert outside pressure on individual consciousness. The individual 'cannot cause them to cease to exist or be different from what they are. Willy-nilly he is therefore obliged to take them into account' (ibid., p.45). Thus social facts are not considered as mere regularities resulting from the behaviour of interacting individuals. Instead, the behaviour of individuals is governed by the social context. The holistic ontology pictures actors at the receiving end of the social system. Individuals are treated as 'indeterminate material' who are socialized into society's central values and into the norms appropriate to the roles they are to play. Individual action is the product and derivative of the social system. 'Men act as they do, they are what they are, because of the societies in which they live' (Ayres, 1952, cited in Jensen, 1987, p.1055).

The holistic ontological view results in an utterly opposite methodological principle to explain social phenomena to that proposed by individualists. Because society is more than an aggregation of human beings, social facts cannot be explained by reduction to individual properties. In contrast, it is held that 'every time a social phenomenon is directly explained by a psychological phenomenon, we may rest assured that the explanation is false' (Durkheim, 1895, p.129). Holists have proposed two other modes of explanation to account for social phenomena that are known as 'functionalism' and 'structuralism'. The former suggests explaining social structures merely by reference to the purpose they serve and the role they play in society. The latter argues that explanation of a social fact should refer to another social fact while the role of the human agent is limited to that of 'mediator'.

According to the holistic viewpoint, culture should be conceived as a collective phenomenon with needs and agency, irreducible to individual properties; rather, culture exists outside the individual and imposes external constraints on human behaviour. Durkheim captures this view of culture by the notion of 'collective consciousness'. Depending on whether one adopts a positivist or a hermeneutic perspective on social science, culture can be grasped in more accessible terms, such as tangible 'institutions' that can be analysed in an objective way, or more interpretative terms, such as common meanings.

Positivism versus Hermeneutics

How can knowledge be acquired about culture? Two issues are of concern to cultural researchers. First, throughout the history of the study of culture, there has been a dispute between those who stress the unique aspects and those who stress the universal aspects. An ideographic approach treats culture as a unique configuration, which can only be understood in its own terms. On the other hand, a nomothetic research style stresses the uniform aspects among different cultures and searches for general laws (Lammers and Hickson, 1979). A second debate is concerned with the distinction between culture as a variable and culture as a root-metaphor (Smircich, 1983). Some perceive culture as a distinct variable that a group possesses and which can be isolated. In the view of others, culture is not a discrete entity that can be examined in isolation from other social phenomena. Instead, culture penetrates all aspects of social life. Both questions are related to the contrasting epistemologies of positivism and hermeneutics. Below, both positions are briefly described.

Positivism

Positivism is a so-called 'naturalist' perspective on scientific methodology. It holds to the unity of scientific method across the natural and the human sciences. Positivism does not consider the human sciences to be essentially different from the natural sciences. The methods of natural science are thought to be equally applicable to the social realm. Boylan and O'Gorman (1995) identify nine characteristics of this positivist method. Three of them, empiricism, nomothetic laws and theory-neutral observation, are discussed below.

First, positivism is held to be a large subset of a wider empiricist approach which boils down to the view that sense data, or 'experience', are the ultimate sources of knowledge. Empirical data, based on sense experience, are the only sources of valid knowledge, with the exception of logic and mathematics. In this view, only atomistic events that can be observed or experienced are accepted for theory building. Measurement is the preferred mode of experience. This empiricist approach is closely related to the 'law-explanation orthodoxy', a second central element of the 'standard view' of positivism (Outhwaite, 1987). The basic theme is that all sciences should be devoted to the pursuit of explanations that take the form of constant conjunctions of events. That is, scientific generalizations should be stated as laws in the form of 'if x then y'. Such laws are generally known as 'Humean causal laws' or 'nomothetic laws'.[7] The validity of such laws is independent of time and place. Science develops when a new nomothetic law is added to the existing knowledge. In line with the 'law-explanation orthodoxy', prediction is held to be the objective of science. Friedman (1953) exemplifies this position, asserting that the 'ultimate goal of a positive science is the development of a "theory" or "hypothesis" that yields valid and meaningful predictions about phenomena not yet observed' (Friedman, 1953). Finally, the element that most crucially separates positivism from hermeneutic thought is the positivist assertion that empirical observation is theory-neutral; the investigator and the investigated 'object' are assumed to be independent entities. It is maintained that, if certain methodological procedures are rigorously followed, the investigator is capable of studying the object without influencing it or being influenced by it. The researcher can 'look from the outside' at the object and infer true and objective conclusions from that experience. No specific adaptations are thought to be necessary for the study of social phenomena: 'Social phenomena must (...) be considered in themselves, detached from the conscious beings who form their own mental representations of them. They must be studied from the outside, as external things, because it is in this guise that they present themselves to us' (Durkheim, 1895, p.70).

The consequences for cultural research can be derived from the three characteristics that were outlined above. A positivist student of culture regards culture as an atomistic event that can be experienced in an objective way by the researcher. Culture is treated as an independent variable that can be related to other social phenomena in the form of a constant conjunction of events.

Ultimately, theories of culture should be stated in the formulation of general predictive causal laws: 'if culture is x, then human action is y'. The derivation of such general laws requires a characterization of culture in nomothetic terms. Accordingly, culture is decomposed into dimensions that are thought to have universal validity. The cultural dimensions of one social group should be equally applicable to describing other groups.

Hermeneutics

The science that is concerned with the interpretation of meaning is called 'hermeneutics'.[8] Various schools in social theory can be brought under this heading. All of them are concerned 'with problems of language and meaning in relation to the interpretative understanding of human action' (Giddens, 1993, p.28). The various theoretical approaches are united by the centrality given to the notion of 'verstehen' in the study of human conduct. This notion is related to a radical separation between the problems of the natural sciences and those of the human sciences or the so-called 'Geisteswissenschaften'. Hermeneutic approaches emphasize a fundamental methodological difference arising from the particularity of the research object of the human sciences, to wit, 'human action' (Sayer, 1992).

Both natural and social researchers have to deal with the necessary 'concept dependence' of research activity. Researchers observe their object by means of existing practices, beliefs, meanings and concepts. Accordingly, the outcomes of research activity are equally concept-dependent. However, in the case of the human sciences this concept dependence extends to the objects of research, for the social phenomena under investigation cannot be disconnected from the beliefs, meanings and concepts of the people in society that produce those phenomena. Social issues, such as class distinctions and the role of work and gender, have different meanings across distinct time/space settings. Therefore these phenomena should be studied with reference to the meanings attached to them.[9] In other words, social science, unlike natural sciences, 'deals with a pre-interpreted world where the creation and reproduction of meaning-frames is a very condition of that which it seeks to analyse, namely human social conduct' (Giddens, 1993, p.166).

From this acknowledgment of the nature of the research object of human sciences, the hermeneutic tradition infers that the objectivity claim of positivism cannot be maintained. In the first place, it is emphasized that no observation can be independent of the conceptual framework, language and theoretical system of the observer. Moreover, social phenomena should be understood by reference to the meanings attached to them by the people in question. The researcher cannot grasp these 'meaning-frames' of other people from the outside. Instead, hermeneutic human science proposes that 'the social world must be understood from within, rather than be explained from without' (Hollis, 1994, p.16).[10] The distinctive task of human sciences is not causal explanation, but 'verstehen', that is, trying to 'understand' the meanings or motivations that underlie human actions.[11] Social reality should be interpreted rather than discovered. The analogy with a text is insightful: 'verstehen is rather like that used in and obtained from reading a book. We do not understand a book by observing and analysing the shape of words or their frequency of occurrence, but by interpreting their meaning' (Sayer, 1992, p.35). Hollis (1994) employs the analogy of a 'game'. The playing of a game requires understanding of the rules: moves in a game have meaning only within the rules. In the same way, meaningful social interaction requires understanding of the 'rules' that define social life.

The hermeneutic idea of social life as a 'fabric of meaning' has methodological consequences for the study of culture. For one thing, culture is not something that can be observed from the outside, but it should be understood from within. Geertz (1973) asserts that culture should be 'read' and 'interpreted' like a text. In other words, 'man is an animal suspended in webs of significance he himself has spun. I take culture to be those webs, and the analysis of it to be therefore not an experimental science in search of law but an interpretive one in search of meaning' (ibid., p.5). Consequently, the use of universal cultural dimensions is inconsistent with the hermeneutic approach to culture, for the set of meanings that characterizes one cultural group cannot be applied to another group that has its own distinct frame of reference. Attempts to describe unique cultures in nomothetic terms are rejected; the particularity of culture should be captured in its own terms.[12] With this aim, cultural research needs to reduce the distance between the researcher and the cultural group. Indeed, it is asserted that 'immersion in a form of life is the necessary and only means whereby an observer is able to generate such characterizations' (Giddens, 1993, p.169).

Four Concepts of Culture

The various positions one can hold in the debates between individualism–holism and positivism–hermeneutics have been depicted above, in Table 4.1. This section will discuss, for each of the four quadrants, how culture is characteristically conceptualized. The concepts will be clarified by reference to major empirical studies relating culture to the organization of the employment relationship.

Culture as shared values

The upper left quadrant of Table 4.1 combines a positivist perspective on science with an individualist ontology. This combination aims to describe culture in nomothetic terms that are grounded in properties of individual human beings. Researchers who accept both individualism and positivism have directed their attention to 'values' to capture culture. For, defined as a 'broad tendency to prefer certain states of affairs over others', a value is a measurable entity that can be attributed to individuals. Culture, then, is commonly defined as 'the whole of values that is shared by the members of a certain group'. The values are described in nomothetic terms with universal validity. For example, Triandis (1983) identifies 23 value dimensions that are thought to have universal relevance to describe cultural groups. The common research method to measure culture is the large-scale survey. Cultural studies that fit the characteristics of this quadrant are England (1975), Hofstede (1980), Shonen and Renkar (1985), Lincoln and Kalleberg (1990) and Trompenaars (1993).

A major exemplifying study that relates culture to the employment relationship is Hofstede (1980). This study focused on work-related values that have universal validity. By means of survey analysis of 160.000 employees of a multinational company across 40 countries, four value dimensions could be identified.[13] These four dimensions were labelled 'power distance', 'uncertainty avoidance', 'individualism–collectivism' and 'masculinity–femininity'.[14] Furthermore, the survey results allowed Hofstede to rank the various nations on the four value dimensions. Table 4.2 illustrates the outcomes of this approach for eight countries.

In proper positivistic fashion, the value scores are related to organizational phenomena in the form of universal Humean laws. For example, a value system characterized by high 'power distance' is argued to underlie higher wage differentials, a steeper form of organization pyramid and a higher proportion of supervisory personnel. High 'uncertainty avoidance' is related to the organizational desire to structure activities by means of formalization, specialization and standardization. 'Collectivist' societies call for greater emotional dependence and stronger moral involvement of members in their organizations, whereas more 'calculative' involvement prevails in individualist societies. Finally, highly masculine countries are characterized by steep career patterns and dominance of organizational interests over people's private lives. Hofstede proposes these relationships between the four dimensions and work organization as conceptual and speculative. Empirical verification of such universal laws has been left to later researchers (Sondergaard, 1994).

Table 4.2 Hofstede's value scores for eight nations

	Power distance	Uncertainty avoidance	Individualism	Masculinity
Canada	39	48	80	52
France	68	86	71	43
Germany	35	65	67	66
Great Britain	35	35	89	66
Japan	54	92	46	95
Italy	50	75	76	70
Netherlands	38	53	80	14
United States	40	46	91	62

Source: Hofstede (1980).

Culture as subjective meanings

The lower left quadrant of Table 4.1 combines a hermeneutic perspective on science with an individualist ontology. Accordingly, culture needs to be reduced to the individual. Moreover, the problem of meaning is central. In combination, cultural analysis should direct its attention to the sum of the subjective meanings that human agents attach to the world. The object of analysis is the self as it creates and derives meaning in the world of everyday life. The fundamental elements of culture are mental constructions that are shared among individuals. 'Culture consists of meaning: it represents the individual's interpretations of reality; and it supplies meaning to the individual in the sense of an integrative or affirming world view' (Wuthnow, 1987, p.11). In terms of games and rules; the players construct the rules of the game.

This cultural perspective has been applied to the analysis of organizational or corporate culture (Schein, 1985; Schultz, 1992; Linstead and Grafton-Small, 1992). To illustrate the results of such a cultural approach to the study of the employment relationship, attention is directed to Schein's analysis of different subcultures within manufacturing organizations (Schein, 1996). He distinguishes three occupational groups in the organization – executives, engineers and operators – who have different sets of basic beliefs about how the world is and ought to be. The approach of Schein intends to uncover the shared meaning-frames of these groups about the nature of business. A summary of his conclusions is given in Box 4.1.

Box 4.1 Three professional cultures

Assumptions of the operator culture

- Because the action of any organization is ultimately the action of people, the success of the enterprise depends on people's knowledge, skill, learning ability and commitment.
- No matter how carefully engineered the production process is or how carefully rules and routines are specified, operators must have the capacity to deal with surprises.

Assumptions of the engineering culture

- The ideal world is one of elegant machines and processes working in perfect precision and harmony without human intervention.
- Puzzles and problems are stimulating and can be solved by linear, simple cause and effect, quantitative thinking.

Assumptions of the executive culture

- Financial survival is equivalent to perpetual war with one's competitors.
- The economic environment is perpetually competitive and potentially hostile.
- The organization must be a team, but accountability has to be individual.

Source: Schein (1996).

Culture as collective consciousness

The upper right quadrant of Table 4.1 combines a positivist perspective on science with a holistic ontology. This combination focuses on observable social structures that have an existence outside the influence of individuals. In this way, culture can be conceptualized as Durkheim's 'collective consciousness'. Culture is an entity with its own autonomy independent of human agents and an imperative impact on their social behaviour. However, because of the problem of observing culture as a single structural entity itself, research in this tradition cannot directly analyse culture. To circumvent the problem of measuring culture in a direct manner, culture is considered as a residual variable. If a variance is observed between a certain structural relationship across different cultural groups, culture is added to such a nomothetic law to explain the variance. In other words, culture is taken as a 'black box' variable that can account for the different shape of structural relations across cultural groups.

This approach towards culture and its impact on the organization of the employment relationship is exemplified by the structural contingency model developed by the Aston group of researchers (Pugh, 1981). The Aston research programme aimed to derive the structural determinants of the formal organizational structure of the firm. It was hypothesized that there is no 'one best way' to organize the firm, but that an organization should respond and adapt to its environmental demands. There should be a 'match' or a 'fit' between the structural characteristics of the firm and the 'contingency variables' in the context of the firm.[15] Focusing on structural variables, these authors explain their choice in this way: 'The implicit assumption in this approach is that formal organizations, along with other social structures, manifest regularities which can be analysed in themselves, apart from any knowledge of the behaviour of their individual members' (Blau, 1971, p.viii). The Aston researchers developed scales to measure structure and context. The dependent variables were structural characteristics of the organization, such as specialization, formalization and centralization. These dimensions of the organizational structure were to be explained by the contextual variables: size of organization, size of parent group organization, a measure of technology and organizational dependence. The results on the relationship between context and structure are derived from the strength and consistency of the correlation. After initial studies in Britain, the findings have been replicated in numerous other countries to determine whether the relationships between the contextual factors and organizational structures are stable across different cultures. With the exception of technology, the findings showed that the contextual variables had a significant effect on the structure of organizations independent of their location in a particular society. Overall, the studies resulted in the conclusion shown in Table 4.3. This result brought Pugh and Hickson to the conclusion that organizations are 'culture-free': 'The uniformity of these processes happening in all the countries studied is quite striking. Size and dependence become the basis for an explanation of the broad features of organizations world wide. It appears to be more important to know how large an organization is, who set it up and what its dependence on the environment is, than the country in which it is located' (Pugh and Hickson, 1993, p.433).[16]

Table 4.3 Correlations between Aston variables

	Formalization	Specialization	Centralization
Size	+	+	–
Size of parent organization	+	+	0
Dependence	+	0	+

Source: Hickson and McMillan (1981).

Culture as common meanings

The lower right quadrant of Table 4.1 joins together a hermeneutic perspective on science and a holistic ontology. In this combination, culture is grasped by a focus on intersubjective or common meanings. Intersubjective or common meanings should be distinguished from shared subjective meanings, for intersubjective meanings 'are not just in the minds of the actors, but are out there in the practices themselves' (Taylor, 1989, p.48). Common meanings imply something more than shared subjective meanings. Common meanings have an autonomous existence in the social world: 'Common meanings as well as intersubjective ones (...) are not simply a converging set of subjective reactions, but part of the common world' (ibid., p.52). These common meanings are thought to be constitutive of the institutions and social practices of a society and, consequently, are imposed on individual human agents. Culture, in this approach, can be derived from the interpretation of institutions that embody the common meanings in society.

In the field of organization studies, the new institutionalist school in organizational analysis has adopted this perspective (Powell and DiMaggio, 1991).[17] 'The new institutionalism in organization theory and sociology comprises a rejection of rational-actor models, an interest in institutions as independent variables, a turn towards cognitive and cultural explanations and an interest in properties of supra individual units of analysis that cannot be reduced to aggregations or direct consequences of individuals' attributes or motives'

(DiMaggio and Powell, 1991, p.8). To understand the underlying meaning of social activity, it is claimed that attention should be directed to the 'extraordinarily power of exogenous institutionalized definitions of reality' and 'the extent to which (...) the cognitive and moral frames of activity at all levels are anchored in the broadest institutional (societal and world) levels' (Meyer et al., 1987, pp.23–4).

Problems with Individualism and Holism

The previous sections have distinguished four major approaches to the study of culture that are based on different philosophical starting-points. The objective of this chapter is to propose a concept of culture that can be used to understand the evolution of the employment relationship. This aim requires clarity on the methodological starting position. In order to achieve such clarity, the following discussion concentrates first on the ontological debate between individualism and holism, leaving the epistemological issues raised by positivism and hermeneutics to later discussion.[18]

The debate between individualism and holism has been of central concern to observers of cultural studies. Mayhew (1987) discusses how the issue of individualism and holism has divided various schools within economic anthropology:[19] 'The fundamental issue in the larger debate is whether or not the important task of anthropology should be to describe the ways in which people act because of their culture or to describe the ways in which their culture is determined by the ways in which people act' (p.589). In political science, a similar diagnosis of the problem of cultural studies is posed by Eckstein (1996): 'which is the deeper or ultimately real level: the society or the individual? Meanings no doubt reside in individuals. So social facts are of necessity individual facts. But from where do individuals get their meanings? As I have said from sources external to individuals, through learning. Thus they come from "collectivities" in some sense' (p.467). Finally, Jackson (1993) comments on the use of culture in economic theory: 'Culture thus broaches one of the key questions in social sciences, namely the interdependence of the individual and society. Some commentators on culture have attempted to give it individualistic foundations and reduce it to fixed individual behaviour or preferences (...) Conversely, culture can be depicted as structural, a form of social conditioning that dictates individual action' (p.454).

Both holistic and individualistic approaches towards the study of culture have received widespread criticism. On the one hand, holists propose a 'top-down' explanation in which individual action is reduced to social structures. In stressing the way in which actors are constrained by conditions not of their choosing, holists produce a 'dehumanized social science' that neglects the activity and the skills of individual actors (Sayer, 1992). It appears as if external cultural conditions do the acting and human subjects are nothing more than 'cultural dopes'. On the other hand, the 'bottom-up' explanation of culture proposed by individualists is problematic as well. Here culture is reduced to individual attributes, but the impact of the social context on the formation of these attributes is ignored. The problem of an individualistic viewpoint 'appears to be not so much that of how one could give an individualistic explanation of social behaviour, but that of how one could ever give a non-social (i.e. strictly individualistic) explanation of individual, at least characteristically human, behaviour' (Bhaskar, 1989a, p.28). Structural phenomena cannot really be eliminated; individualists can only 'sweep them under the carpet' (Lukes, 1972).

Individualistic and holistic positions contain fundamental drawbacks that cannot be resolved if one sticks to their principles.

> The point is sufficiently evident. In standard social scientific discussions of culture, the human world is divided in two, objective social structure on the one hand, subjective thoughts and perceptions on the other (...) Studies of culture have been inhibited by the assumption that culture can only be understood by relating it to social structure. This is reductionism. Instead of treating culture as an interesting phenomenon in its own right, social scientists have reduced it to some other level (...) Cultural analysis has also been limited by the assumption that only individuals have culture. This supposition is another form of reductionism (...) So defined, it is little wonder that culture has remained poorly understood, if not genuinely misunderstood (Wuthnow, 1984, pp. 5–7).

Therefore, in order to progress, Wuthnow (1984) emphasizes that the study of culture needs to transcend the terms of the debate between individualism and holism. To proceed with the study of culture, one has to strike a proper balance between the nature of human beings as individuals and as constituents of society. People are both individuals and members of society.

Various theorists in the social sciences have responded to the call to change the terms of the debate. The issue of connecting the individual and society or agency and structure has been explored by, among others, Elias, Habermas, Bourdieu, Bhaskar and Giddens.[20] A common element among the various approaches is to transcend the traditional dualism between agency and social structures that is maintained by both individualists and holists. A dualism means a separation of two entities, so that they have a well-defined boundary with no shared territory. Conceptualized as a dualism, society is always divided into two separable and opposed elements, individual agency and collective structures, with no middle ground between them (Jackson, 1996). The coming sections will explore two approaches that aim to overcome the simplified perspective of a dualism. First, we explore the approach of Roy Bhaskar (1989a, 1989b). His approach can be labelled 'analytical dualism', since he maintains the ontological division between the two poles, but introduces possibilities for the analysis of their interplay. A second approach replaces the concept of 'dualism' as a theoretical starting-point with 'duality'. As a duality, the two categories agency and structure are conceptually distinguished, but, ontologically, they are conceived as mutually constituting one another and no longer separate or opposed. This view has reached its furthest state of advancement in the work of Anthony Giddens.

NEW PERSPECTIVES ON AGENCY AND STRUCTURE (I): BHASKAR'S TMSA

Bhaskar (1989a) criticizes both individualistic and holistic theories on the relationship between people and society, but not on similar grounds. On the one hand, he argues that individualistic approaches are wrong to assume that characteristically human behaviour can be studied without taking the social into account. On the other hand, holistic theories, as exemplified by Durkheim, are not criticized for their holistic perspective, but rather for their commitment to positivism. Furthermore, Bhaskar is not satisfied with the alternative conception of connecting society and agency as two moments of the same process.[21] Instead, he suggests 'a radically different conception of social activity', which he has labelled the 'transformational model of social activity'(Bhaskar, 1989a, p.34). To grasp Bhaskar's perspective of society, this section is divided into two parts. In the first part, the 'transformational model of social activity' is examined. To gain a deeper understanding of this model, its foundation in the critical realist philosophy is then considered.

The Transformational Model of Social Activity

The transformational model of social activity (TMSA) is founded on the acknowledgment that both social structure and human praxis possess a dual character. The duality of structure refers to the conception that society is both 'condition' and 'outcome' of human agency. The duality of praxis refers to the view that conscious human activity, at the same time, unconsciously 'reproduces' society. These building blocks of the TMSA are explained below.

First, the duality of structure is considered. Bhaskar preserves the individualistic notion that society cannot exist without human activity. Human activity underlies all social structures. However, he does away with the myth of creation that is sustained by individualists. People do not create society. Instead, Bhaskar argues that social structures constitute a necessary 'condition' for any intentional human act: 'all activity presupposes the prior existence of social forms' (Bhaskar, 1989a, p.34). Social structure is always already there before individuals act upon it. For example, the member of a church finds the beliefs and practices of his or her religious life ready-made at birth. Likewise, speech requires language, making requires materials and activity requires rules. Following this line of reasoning, Bhaskar denies that agents create society. Society always pre-exists them. Agents reproduce society by acting according to the social structures. In the words of Bhaskar (1989b): 'society is both the ever-present "condition" and the continually reproduced "outcome" of human agency'.

The second building block of the TMSA is the duality of praxis. Bhaskar characterizes human agency by intentionality. People are able to initiate changes in a purposeful way and to monitor and control their performances. However, although human action is intentional, Bhaskar denies that each human action has intentional consequences. Most of the time, intentional human action unintendedly reproduces the structures of society. In other words, social structures are for the most part reproduced unconsciously by intentional human action.[22] For example, an individual's purpose in getting married is not to preserve marriage as a social institution. However, whether two people marry for love or for money, they contribute equally to the reproduction of the nuclear family (Collier, 1994). In the words of Bhaskar:

> The conception I am proposing is that people, in their conscious activity, for the most part unconsciously reproduce (and occasionally transform) the structures that govern

their substantive activities of production. Thus people do not work to reproduce the capitalist economy. But it is nevertheless the unintended consequence (and inexorable result) of, as it is also a necessary condition for, their activity. (Bhaskar, 1989a, p.35)

It follows from the above that people and society mutually presuppose each other in the TMSA. Society does not exist independently of conscious human activity. Society is conceived as an ensemble of structures, practices and conventions that individuals reproduce or transform, but which would not exist if they did not do so. Figure 4.1 depicts the TMSA schematically.

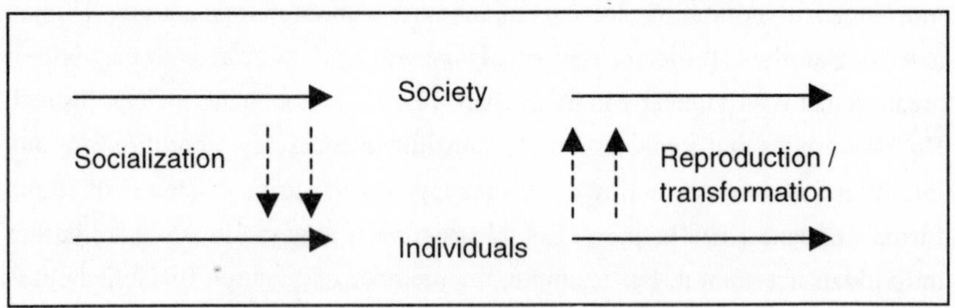

Source: Bhaskar (1989a).

Figure 4.1 The transformational model of social activity

To grasp the deeper nature of the TMSA, more needs to be said about the ontological status of the individual and social structure. As depicted in Figure 4.1, agency and social structure are considered as separate layers constituting social reality. Although agency and social structure presuppose each other, Bhaskar asserts that it is important to distinguish between human action and social structure, 'for the properties possessed by social forms may be very different from those possessed by the individuals upon whose activity they depend' (Bhaskar, 1989a, p.35). Human action is characterized by intentionality and purposefulness, while changes of social structures commonly occur unconsciously. Therefore Bhaskar explicitly states his intention to 'distinguish sharply between the genesis of human actions, lying in the reasons, intentions and plans of human beings, on the one hand; and the structures governing the reproduction and transformation of social activities, on the other' (Bhaskar, 1989b, p.79). Both the individual and social structures are allocated their own autonomy and causal powers. Bhaskar's assertion is based on a deeper philosophical perspective of social reality that is labelled 'critical realism'. To evaluate the TMSA as a social theory, we now examine its underlying realist assumptions.

Critical Realism

This section will describe Bhaskar's critical realist philosophy to grasp the origins of the autonomy of social structure and human agency. At the core of it is naturalism, that is, a common philosophical underpinning for both the natural and the human sciences.[23] In the first part, Bhaskar's perspective on the natural realm, named 'transcendental realism', is described (Bhaskar, 1978). The second part concentrates on the issue whether this transcendental realist perspective can be transferred to the social realm. Bhaskar is positive and gives his philosophy for the social realm the label 'critical realism' (Bhaskar, 1989a, 1989b).

Transcendental realism

Outhwaite (1987) identifies three ontological principles of transcendental realism: the stratification of reality into the domains of the real, the actual and the empirical; the distinction between transitive and intransitive objects of science; and the conception of causal relations as tendencies, grounded in the interaction of generative mechanisms. These principles guide the following outline of Bhaskar's views on transcendental realism (Bhaskar, 1978).

The domain of the real Realism in the philosophy of science commonly refers to an ontological thesis about the nature of being. Its central conviction is that 'the actual world exists independently of any and every knowing subject' (Boylan and O'Gorman, 1995, p.90). However, realists are divided among themselves on the issue of the 'constituent parts of the actual world' or 'the intransitive objects' of science.[24] Indeed, 'any position can be designated a realism, in the philosophical sense of the term, that asserts the existence of some disputed kind of entity' (Lawson, 1993, p.219). This broad definition leaves room for different kinds of realism that are distinguished by the type of entity that is asserted as 'real'.

What is thought to constitute the domain of the 'real' clarifies the difference between transcendental realism and the empirical realism that underlies positivism (Outhwaite, 1987; Lawson, 1995). In the world-view of empiricism, the 'real' is restricted to objects, events and phenomena that can be experienced.

Only events that can be perceived, observed or measured are admitted to the domain of scientific investigation.[25] However, Bhaskar (1978) arrives at the conclusion that such an empiricist perspective is inadequate, for scientific experiments can only be rationalized if the world consists of powers or mechanisms that are inaccessible at the empirical level.[26] The individual effects of these mechanisms are not manifest in the empirical world, because the various causal powers commonly operate in different directions. The whole purpose of scientific experiments is to isolate one mechanism from the effect of others, to see what that mechanism does on its own. This is reason for Bhaskar to picture a world that is characterized by a multitude of 'invisible' mechanisms with their own causal powers.

This conclusion is incorporated in the 'domain of the real' advanced by transcendental realism. The 'real' is not limited to events and our experience of them, but includes also '(irreducible) structures, mechanisms, powers and tendencies that, although perhaps not directly observable, nevertheless underlie actual events and govern or facilitate them' (Lawson, 1995, p.13).[27] Transcendental realism, then, distinguishes between three domains of reality: the empirical (experience, impression, perception), the actual (events, states of affairs) and the 'deep' or the 'real' (structures, mechanisms, powers and tendencies).[28] Table 4.4 sums up these elements of the real.

Table 4.4 Domains of reality in transcendental realism

	Domain of real	Domain of actual	Domain of empirical
Mechanisms	*	–	–
Events	*	*	–
Experiences	*	*	*

Source: Bhaskar (1978).

In conclusion, transcendental realism holds that there is an objective structure to the world, which is not immediately 'visible' in human experience, but which is scientifically discoverable. In this view, science should aim at 'the illumination and elaboration of the structures and mechanisms that govern the events of experience' (Lawson, 1995, p.13). The central objects of scientific activity are thus 'structures' and 'mechanisms'. To grasp the nature of these concepts, it is necessary to introduce the realist conception of a stratified world.

Stratification and emergence The mechanisms that govern the actual course of events are ordered across different layers of nature. In the world presented by Bhaskar, nature is stratified in various 'levels of being' that can be ranked from more to less basic. For example, matter is said to be more basic than organic life, which in turn is more basic than human society. Mechanisms that operate at the more basic layers have some explanatory primacy over those operating at higher layers. That is, laws of physics and chemistry may in some sense explain the laws of biology. 'There can be no biological mechanisms unless there are chemical ones, while the reverse does not hold' (Collier, 1994, p.108). Bhaskar perceives this primacy of the more basic layers not in reductionist terms, but by means of the principle of 'rootedness' or 'emergence'.[29]

Emergence theories maintain that the higher-level mechanisms are rooted in or emergent from more basic mechanisms. Adoption of the notion of 'emergence' recognizes that 'the more complex aspects of reality (e.g. life, mind) presuppose the less complex (e.g. matter)', but also insists that 'they have features which are irreducible, i.e. cannot be thought in concepts appropriate to the less complex levels (...) because of the inherent nature of the emergent strata' (ibid., p.110). Although mechanisms of more basic sciences explain something about the mechanisms of less basic ones, they cannot explain them away.[30] Many cases of emergence relations refer to relations of composition. For example, society is composed of people who are constituted by cells that consist of molecules that are constituted of atoms. Each level of composition is thought to be a proper object of scientific study if its objects are thought to have 'emergent powers', powers which cannot be reduced to those of their constituents.[31] Bhaskar's stratified world is thus made up of 'real, irreducible wholes which are both composed of parts that are themselves real irreducible wholes, and are in turn part of larger wholes, with each level of this hierarchy of composition having its own peculiar mechanisms and emergent powers' (ibid., p.117).

Possibility of naturalism

The second part of Bhaskar's philosophical project is to establish the possibility of naturalism (Bhaskar, 1989a, 1989b). Bhaskar holds that the world picture described for the natural realm extends to the social realm qualified by a number of limitations due to the specific character of the subject matter of the human sciences.[32] Below, we concentrate on the common ground between the natural and the social realm.

Like the natural realm, three domains of the real constitute the social realm: empirical experiences, actual events and 'deep' generative mechanisms.[33] The contention that hidden mechanisms figure in the social realm presumes a stratified view of the social world. Bhaskar's TMSA distinguishes between people and social structure as the two major strata to constitute the social realm, implying that both people and social structures possess distinct causal powers which emerge from, but are irreducible to, a lower stratum.

First, the causal power of people is ascribed to their ability to act on reasons, which include mental concepts such as beliefs, desires and intentions. Bhaskar argues that individual psychology should be an autonomous layer, because the 'reasons for action' cannot be reduced to mechanisms that belong to other strata. He refutes the position of material reductionists that mind can be reduced to the neurophysiological processes that take place in the brain. Moreover, he denies that reasons for individual action are determined by their embeddedness in particular social structures. Individuals are thought to have their own identity constituted by their own beliefs.

Second, society is regarded as the whole of social structures that are conceived as enduring relations between individuals or groups. Sayer (1992) notes that emergent powers are explained by reference to internal relations as opposed to external relations. Therefore the reality of social structures as autonomous strata should be established by reference to the internal relations among their constituents. People are internally related if they are what they are by virtue of their relationship to others.[34] For example, one can be an employee only in relation to an employer, a husband in relation to a wife, a buyer in relation to a seller, or a wage earner in relation to a capital owner. Internal relations determine the nature of the social objects. In this way, internal relations constitute emergent powers, because they modify individual powers in fundamental ways and are irreducible to the individual.

NEW PERSPECTIVES ON AGENCY AND STRUCTURE (II): GIDDENS' STRUCTURATION THEORY

Since the 1980s, Anthony Giddens has become a central figure in the social sciences, which is reflected by the numerous books that elaborate on his contributions (Cohen, 1989; Held and Thompson, 1989; Clark et al., 1990;

Bryant and Jary, 1990, 1997; Craib, 1992; Cassell, 1993). A central element in his work is the theory of structuration, most comprehensively outlined by Giddens (1984). Giddens motivates his development of structuration theory by his dissatisfaction with subjective, interpretative sociologies (symbolic interactionism, phenomenology, hermeneutics) and objective, functionalist and structuralist approaches. He characterizes the former as 'strong on action, but weak on structure', while the latter are thought to be 'strong on structure and weak on action' (Giddens, 1993, p.4). He holds that social scientists should focus neither on the experience of the individual actor nor on the existence of any form of social totality. Instead, the basic unit of analysis of social science, for Giddens, should be the 'recursive social practice', such as the daily trip to work on the train, the general election, the weekly seminar, and so on. According to him, the social sciences should focus their efforts on the processes of structuration or reproduction generating temporal and spatial order of social practices. Why are social activities 'stretched' across wide spans of time and space? Structuration theory offers a conceptual scheme that is designed to elucidate the 'chronic reproduction' of social conduct. At the core of Giddens' theory of structuration is the concept of 'duality of structure': 'The concept of structuration involves that of duality of structure, which relates to the fundamentally recursive character of social life, and expresses the mutual dependence of structure and agency. By the duality of structure, I mean that the structural properties of social systems are both the medium and outcome of the practices that constitute those systems' (Giddens, 1979, p.69). In this view, social structures are (re)produced by human agency while, at the same time, these structures mediate or enable human action. On the surface, the duality of structure resembles the TMSA of Bhaskar. However, a divergent ontological perspective separates the two theories. To grasp the differences between the theories, Giddens' conceptualization of 'human agency', 'structure' and 'social system' needs to be clarified.

Human Agency

Giddens draws heavily on the contribution of hermeneutic approaches in conceptualizing the human agent and its involvement in action. An essential feature of Giddens' actor is its knowledgeability or awareness of its actions: 'To be a human being is to be a purposive agent, who both has reasons for his or her activities and is able, if asked, to elaborate discursively upon those reasons' (Giddens, 1984, p.3). In Giddens' model of the human agent, the actor is continuously involved with the motivation, rationalization and monitoring of action. Although not all human action is 'purposeful' in the sense of being guided by clear purposes which the agent has in mind, action is always purposive in the sense that actors have a permanent understanding of the grounds of their own activity.[35] Discursive consciousness exemplifies the case where this understanding can be expressed verbally by the agent. However, more important to Giddens is practical consciousness, that is, the knowledge that actors possess about the social conditions of their own action, but that the actors are not able to express discursively.[36] In large part, routine activity appears to be of that kind. Practical consciousness guides the vast bulk of the day-to-day activities that have a habitual, taken-for-granted character.

However, action cannot only be analysed by focusing on the individual agent and its purposes. Although Giddens assumes reflexive actors, the continuous flow of human action has most of the time no intentional outcomes, for agents are bounded, both by 'unintended consequences'[37] and by 'unacknowledged conditions' of action.[38] In the words of Giddens, structuration theory

> presupposes the reflexive monitoring of agents in, and as constituting, the durée of daily social activity. But human knowledgeability is always bounded. The flow of action continually produces consequences which are unintended by actors and these unintended consequences also may form unacknowledged conditions of action in a feedback fashion. Human history is created by intentional activities but is not an intended project. It persistently eludes efforts to bring it under conscious direction (ibid., p.27).

Figure 4.2 summarises Giddens' conception of the actor and agency.

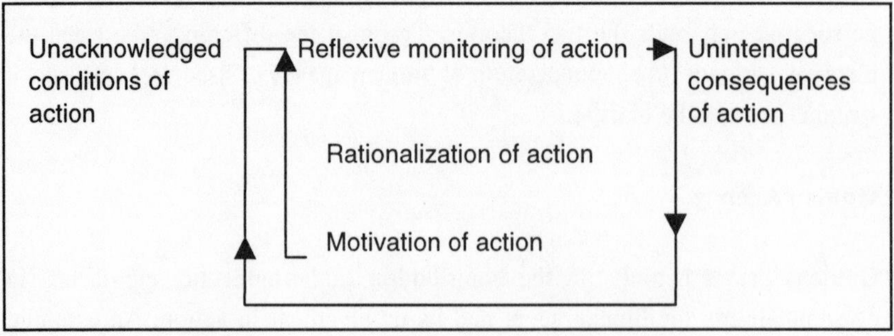

Source: Giddens (1984).

Figure 4.2 Stratification model of the agent

Structure

The prime conceptual innovation of Giddens concerns the concept of structure. Giddens does away with the traditional metaphors of social structure, like the girders of a building or the skeleton of society, for these conceptions picture structure as external to human beings. Instead, structure is intrinsically linked with human agency. Structure refers to virtual 'rules and resources' that come into existence when they are drawn upon by human agents. For example, the grammatical rules of language have no existence unless an individual who utters a correct sentence implicates them in social practice. Structure, as 'rules and resources', guides social interaction between individual agents. Individuals draw upon these rules to enact social practices. In this way, structure is both constraining and enabling. It is constraining because it limits the options available to individual action; it is enabling because it makes social interaction possible. To return to the example of language, the rules of language enable the transmission of messages, but those same rules constrain people by limiting the options of what can be said.

More needs to be said about the rules and resources that constitute structure. First, we consider the 'rules' of social life. They can be regarded as 'techniques' or 'formulae' that need to be understood and applied in social practice.[39] Rules are manifested in various forms. They can be classified as 'intensive' when they are constantly invoked in the course of day-to-day activities (such as the rules of language). They may be contrasted with rules that have only a superficial impact upon the texture of social life, such as certain forms of state regulation. Rules can be 'tacit', as opposed to 'discursive', if actors cannot codify them. Furthermore, rules can be formal, such as bureaucratic rules, but they can also be informal, like norms. Finally, rules can be classified on the basis of their sanction. Commonly, juridical laws are perceived as strongly sanctioned. Nonetheless, sanctions can also be applied with great strength if one departs from the informal rules that structure the variety of daily practices.

While rules refer primarily to the reproductive nature of human action, the incorporation of the notion of 'resources' in structure enables human agents to effectuate change. Resources are 'media through which power is exercised'. For Giddens, 'power' is the capacity to transform rules and effectuate change. Power is not confined to certain groups in society; each agent has the disposition of powers, for to be an agent means 'to be able to act otherwise'. An agent ceases to be if he or she loses the capability 'to make a difference', that is, to depart from the structural rules by exercising some sort of power.[40]

Duality of Structure

Now that its building blocks, human agency and structure, are clarified, the notion of duality of structure can be further elucidated. The duality of structure holds that, every time human agents draw upon the rules and resources to engage in social action, they reproduce, at that same moment, those rules and resources. In other words, 'the duality of structure holds that every act of production is at the same time an act of reproduction: the structures that render an action possible are, in the performance of that action, reproduced' (Thompson, 1989, p.58). Agents reproduce 'in' and 'through' their activities the conditions that make these activities possible. The example of language is once again illuminating. By uttering a syntactically correct sentence, individuals draw upon the rules of grammar to produce a social practice. However, at the very moment they speak, the rules of grammar are reproduced. Thus the communication of language in a correct way contributes to the reproduction of that language as a whole.

The importance of the conceptualization of the human agent should be clear. The 'knowledgeability' of the human agent is a necessary feature of the conception of the duality of structure: 'the reflexive monitoring action both draws upon and reconstitutes the institutional organization of society. The recognition that to be a (competent) member of society, every individual must know a great deal about the workings of that society, is precisely the main basis of the concept of the duality of structure' (Giddens, 1979, p.255). For the rules and resources that constitute structure are embodied in the knowledge of agents. Note that, in this scheme, structure has a virtual existence. It exists only as memory traces orienting the knowledgeable human agents: 'Structure has no existence independent of the knowledge that agents have about what they do in their day-to-day activity' (Giddens, 1984, p.26).[41]

Finally, structure should be distinguished from social systems. Structure refers to the 'structuring properties' of societies (rules and resources) that make it possible for similar social practices to exist across time and space. By drawing upon the structure of social life, social life is reproduced. As such, structure provides societies with a 'systemic' form. In other words, structure, as rules and resources, is better understood as a verb: rules and resources structure, or give shape to, social systems. 'Social systems, as reproduced social practices, do not have "structures" but rather exhibit structural properties' (ibid., p.17). 'Institutions' are regarded as those social practices whose sediment in time–space is deep, that is, social practices that are enduring and widespread among the members of society. The stretching in time and space of institutions is an implication of the circuit of reproduction.[42] Figure 4.3 sketches a reproduction circuit. Note that there are no arrows involved, for the relations between the boxes presuppose each other. Once again in the words of Giddens: 'The constitution of agents and structures are not two independently given sets of phenomena, a dualism, but represent a duality. According to the notion of the duality of structure, the structural properties of social systems are both medium and outcome of the practices they recursively organize' (ibid., p.25).

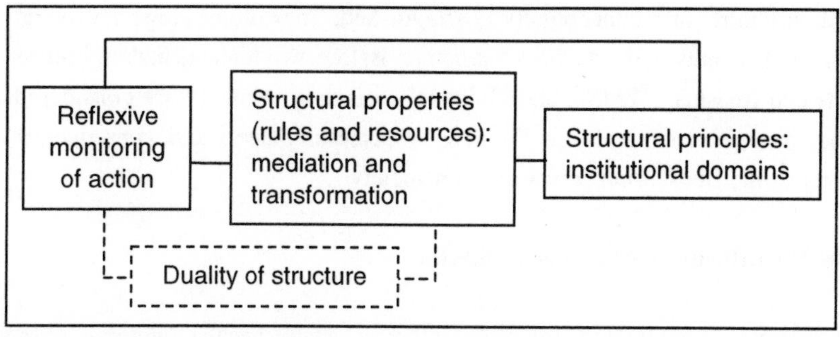

Source: based on Giddens (1984).

Figure 4.3 A reproduction circuit

ANALYTICAL DUALISM VERSUS DUALITY OF STRUCTURE

The purpose of this chapter is to ground the concept of culture in a sound theory of society. The first section rejected both individualist and holistic approaches and indicated the need to transcend the traditional dualism between agency and structure. Then two alternative conceptualizations were explored: Bhaskar's analytical dualism and Giddens' duality of structure. This section will put the two perspectives side by side.

From various points of view, structuration theory and the TMSA look very similar. The approaches share a common objective, to overcome the shortcomings of individualism and holism by emphasizing the mutual constitution of agency and structure. However, as rightly observed by Archer (1995), their common starting-point has concealed fundamental differences.

> Unfortunately, because realists and structurationists have both rejected the terms of the old debate between Individualism and Collectivism, there has been an over-hasty tendency to assume their mutual convergence and to lump them together as an alternative to the positions taken in the traditional debate. Instead the crucial point is that we are now confronted by two new and competing social ontologists. (Archer, 1995, p.14)

Indeed, the critical realist approach of Bhaskar's TMSA conceives the human agent and social structure as two separate layers of social reality with their own causal powers. In contrast, Giddens' structuration theory denies the existence of autonomous properties at the level of the actor and structure. Although action and structure are conceptually distinguished, they come together as an inseparable entity in the duality of structure. Below, two fundamental differences between Bhaskar's TMSA and Giddens' structuration theory are considered. They provide reason to favour Giddens' structuration theory and, consequently, to reject the Bhaskarian perspective on society.

The Stratification of the Social Realm

The TMSA, in contrast to structuration theory, establishes the autonomy of the individual and structure by reference to emergent causal powers of the autonomous strata of the social realm: individual psychology and social structure. In the words of Archer (1995, p.102): 'the fundamental argument between the Elisionists [like Giddens] and their opponents (at both the ontological and methodological levels) is about the stratified nature of social reality'. However, the assertion that the social realm is of a stratified nature is problematic. Although 'the evidence of stratification in the objects of the natural sciences is relatively good', it is 'rather patchy as regards society' (Sayer, 1992, p.120). In contrast with the natural realm, it is not possible to rank the strata of the social realm, the individual and society, as more or less basic to the other, for 'we are concerned here with two distinct strata, though mutually ontologically dependent ones' (Collier, 1994, p.147).

Bhaskar acknowledges this peculiar feature of the social realm. He describes the status of social structures as follows: 'unlike natural mechanisms, [social structures] exist only in virtue of the activities they govern and cannot be empirically identified independently of them. Because of this they must be social products themselves' (Bhaskar, 1989a, p.38). This observation is reason for Bhaskar to characterize social structures as only 'relatively autonomous' and 'relatively independent'. Nevertheless, in his view, individual human beings and social structure remain separate layers of social reality, for, in the words of Archer (1995), there is a distinction between 'those activities of agents which are exercises of their own intrinsic powers, and those activities which are really powers which reside in social structures, but operate through the activities of human agents' (Archer, 1995, p.17). Indeed, Bhaskar conceives society as an ensemble of tendencies and powers that are exercised in the last instance 'via' the intentional activity of human beings. In sum, Bhaskar concludes that, although social structure and human agency are 'existentially interdependent', they are 'essentially distinct' (Bhaskar, 1989b, p.92).

Giddens avoids the problem by dismissing the idea of a stratified social realm. To him, social reality is composed of just one layer, namely social practices that presuppose the mutual interdependence of human agency and structure. He rejects modelling the social realm by analogy with the natural realm. Although the hardness of bronze may not be attributed to the separate characteristics of copper and tin, but only to their mixing, Giddens emphasizes that human actors, as competent agents, do not exist separately from one another as copper, tin and lead do. Human agents do not come together out of nothing to form a new entity by their fusion or association. People and society are not like molecules in a gas: some are different from others and some have more effect on society than others. In Giddens' view, Bhaskar confuses a hypothetical conception of individuals, in a state of nature untainted by association with others, with real processes of social reproduction.

Structuralist Explanations

Bhaskar (1983) admits that he is 'inclined to give a stronger ontological grounding to structures' than suggested by structuration theory. Indeed, his picture of the social world provides for social structures which, although they operate through the activities of human agents, are external to people. This autonomy of social structures is based upon the assertion of the existence of emergent powers in the social realm. Consequently, it can be argued that

Bhaskar repeats the mistakes of structuralist sociologies, which look for the origins of human activities in phenomena (social structures) of which these human agents are ignorant. The causal influence of structures is supposed to operate outside the scope of the reasons that agents might have for what they do. The range of 'free human action' is restricted by structural constraints that are more or less equivalent to the impersonal causal forces of nature.

Giddens breaks with this naturalistic conception of social forces by emphasizing the knowledgeability of human agents. For Giddens, to be an actor means to be able to do otherwise. Action depends upon the capability of the individual to 'make a difference' to a pre-existing state of affairs. Giddens acknowledges that actors are commonly constrained in their action, but, nevertheless, he rejects the notion of a causal constraint operating independently of the reflexive monitoring of action by human agents. Structural constraints only 'place limits upon the range of options open to an actor in a given circumstance' (Giddens, 1984, p.177). It is true that structural constraints leave actors with the feeling of having 'no choice'. But, for Giddens, 'no choice' means that they are unable to do anything other than to conform to the constraint, given their motives or goals. For example, it has been said that workers 'must' sell themselves to employers, given the asymmetrical division of power in modern capitalist economies. However, if the knowledgeability of the human agents is accepted, this intuition should be understood as 'there is only one feasible option, given that the worker has the motivation to wish to survive'. Although social forces have an apparently 'inevitable' look to them, structural constraints do not operate independently of the motives and reasons that agents have for what they do. For Giddens, then, there is no room for structural explanation in the social sciences; all explanations need at least implicit reference to the purposive, reasoning behaviour of agents.

Conclusions

Although, in the first instance, Bhaskar's TMSA and Giddens' structuration theory look very much alike, this section has demonstrated their fundamental differences. The choice between these perspectives on society depends on whether one considers the human agent as knowledgeable rather than being forced into action by hidden social structures of which he or she is ignorant. Accepting that human agents are knowledgeable implies that Giddens' perspective is superior to that of Bhaskar, for as argued above, despite its attempt to incorporate human intentionality, the Bhaskarian perspective fails to avoid the traditional shortcomings of structuralism. It does so by ascribing reality to social structures external to human agents. The reality of such structures is justified by reference to the causal powers they possess over the agent's consciousness. However, Bhaskar fails to justify the existence of emergent powers on which the autonomy of social structures is based. It seems that Bhaskar's argument for their existence trusts more in intuitions and belief than in reality. The following quotation is illuminating in this respect:

> More particularly, I remain convinced by the notion that there are such things as underlying social structures, which are not easily visible, except in their effects, but have a different type of existence to the individuals who inhabit them and to the practice of those individuals. (...) As I write this, I am increasingly aware that it is a matter of assertion. My argument is that we cannot assert any knowledge of that order, but to engage in social analysis at all, we have to assume that perhaps such an order is there to be discovered. The possibility of there being some underlying social structure and historical process seems to share the status of Pascal's hidden god. (Craib, 1992, p.9)

However, intuitions and beliefs do not qualify for a sound ontological foundation for the notion of culture. The knowledgeability of the agent, although not an uncontroversial assertion, draws on stronger empirical evidence.[43] Accepting human beings as knowledgeable agents implies the rejection of the perspective of critical realism. For the conceptualization of culture, this implies that culture will not be conceptualized in Bhaskarian terms as an emergent power or a mechanism which, like the force of a magnetic field or the force of gravity, induces human agents to act in ways out of their control and consciousness. Instead, it is proposed to conceptualize culture on the basis of Giddens' structuration theory as a particular set of 'reproduced social practices'. The manner in which structuration theory can constitute a concept of culture is explored in the next section.

NATIONAL WORK-RELATED CULTURE

The first section of this chapter observed the confusion that surrounds the concept of culture. It was noted that alternative philosophical perspectives on social reality resulted in different concepts of culture. Therefore it was felt necessary, prior to adopting a certain concept of culture, to dwell upon deeper philosophical perspectives with regard to social reality. Now that Giddens' structuration theory is adopted as an adequate view of society, the chapter can conclude by developing a conceptualization of culture that serves the study of the evolution of the employment relationship. First, we provide a theoretical conceptualization of national work-related culture. Second, we mention some methodological recommendations for the study of culture. Finally, we elaborate the theoretical concept of national work-related culture into a concept that is workable for the purpose of empirical investigation.

A Theoretical Concept

In the perspective of structuration theory, one layer of reality, social practices that are ordered across space and time, constitutes the social realm. In the view of structuration theory, culture must be a theoretical concept to capture a certain part of the totality of such ordered social practices. Structuration theory has outlined that social practices are ordered, because human beings in their intentional social action draw upon 'rules and resources' which they, by so doing, unintendedly reproduce. In this way, underlying the ordered nature of those social practices that are captured by the notion of culture are certain 'rules and resources' that are reproduced by human beings. Accordingly, the starting-point of a definition of culture is the totality of rules and resources that structure human action. Culture is a theoretical concept employed by people to refer to a particular subset of the entire range of structural rules and resources. A definition of culture, then, should clarify the boundaries that circumscribe this particular subset. A review of the literature provides a number of widely shared intuitions about the nature of culture. Below, culture is specified according to three such common perceptions. Moreover, the concept of culture is qualified according to the particular objective of the study of the organization of the employment relationship.

A first specification concerns the endurability of culture over time. Culture is generally conceived as lasting over long spans of time. Therefore, among the totality of structural rules and resources, the concept of culture should refer to those rule–resource sets that are reproduced across long time periods. Following Giddens, those social practices with the greatest time extension are denoted as 'institutions'. Accordingly, a first element that is included in the definition of culture should be the institution.[44] A further specification relates to the sharedness of culture. Social scientists and laymen alike refer to culture when they observe certain social practices that are shared by a certain group of people as opposed to another group. Culture is considered to be something that is shared by all or almost all members of some social group. Therefore a definition of culture should specify the social group to which the concept of culture is applied. In this study, it is concentrated on national culture. Thus the social group is spatially confined to the territory of the nation state. Accordingly, national culture refers to the shared institutions that unite inhabitants of a nation state. A third element that needs to be incorporated into any definition of culture is coherency. The institutionalized features of a nation state cannot be overtly contradictory, because this will result in a process of social change at the 'fault lines' of the social system. Giddens understands such coherency by reference to 'structural principles' or 'principles of organization' that serve to produce a specific overall 'clustering of institutions' across time and space. Accordingly, the definition of culture needs to include the clustered nature of national institutions. A final element to confine the set of rules and resources relates to the object of analysis that is the organization of the employment relationship. In view of this objective, the definition of culture is specified one step further as 'clusters of work-related national institutions'.

Thus a theoretical concept of culture that serves the purposes of an international comparison of employment relations can be finalized as 'clusters of work-related national institutions'.[45] It should be recalled that in this conceptualization, culture, like its most elementary building blocks, 'rules and resources', has only a virtual existence. It exists solely when human agents draw upon the nationally institutionalized rules and resources to (re)produce a social action (or it exists as traces in the memory of human agents). Culture must be continuously produced and reproduced by man. This 'virtual existence' raises the question of how culture can become known. How can national culture be 'captured' by empirical research? The next section addresses some methodological recommendations.

Some Methodological Comments

As noted by Giddens (1990a, 1990b), structuration theory does not furnish a distinctive research programme. Structuration theory cannot be 'applied' in empirical research. It only provides an ontological perspective on society that can help us to understand the complexity of human social activity. The concepts of structuration theory should be regarded as 'sensitizing devices' useful for thinking about research questions and interpreting findings. They are not supposed to be translated into operational constructs to guide empirical studies.

How can the complexity of social reality be analysed according to structuration theory? To recapitulate, the structuration theory does not give primacy to either the human agent or the social structure. They are mutually dependent as they are intrinsically interlinked by the duality of structure. In and through their activities, agents reproduce the social conditions that make these activities possible. These circuits of reproduction structure social reality. However, although human agents and social structures are ontologically interdependent, for the purpose of empirical research they can be split apart by a methodological 'trick'. Giddens distinguishes two kinds of 'methodological bracketing' to disentangle the intricacies of the circuits of reproduction. First, empirical research can give primacy to the discursive and practical consciousness of the human agent. Such research can be denoted as the analysis of 'intentional conduct'.[46] This type of research concentrates upon the contextually situated activities of a certain group of actors and inquires why the human actors in question act as they do. In this way, such research avoids the enduring features of social life as incorporated by institutions. Instead, it focuses on the modes by which actors draw upon the rule and resource sets in the constitution of social relations.

The second type of methodological bracketing by which the complexity of the social realm can be reduced is called 'institutional analysis'. This kind of analysis directs attention to the chronically reproduced features of social systems. It suspends the skills and awareness of human agents and concentrates upon institutionalized practices across time. Although structuration theory allows for both methodological practices, it should be emphasized that neither type of analysis has primacy over the other. Both the structural relations indicated by institutional analysis and the intentional strategies of human agents should be understood as conditions of system reproduction. Indeed, the aim of social analysis is to demonstrate how the activities of knowledgeable human agents reproduce institutionalized practices and vice versa.

The objective of this study is to analyse national work-related culture. Because of its conceptualization as 'clusters of work-related national institutions', the analysis of national culture relies heavily on institutional analysis to derive the nation-specific institutional patterns.[47] However, the analysis of culture should not be limited to the identification of the clusters of enduring structural properties that 'compose' culture; insight is also required into the reproduction of culture by knowledgeable human action. Indeed, to show how the institutions that encompass the notion of culture are reproduced, one needs to direct attention to the individual human agents and their reasons and motivations behind their actions. Consequently, the analysis of culture, like all social research, should always incorporate a hermeneutic element to capture the reasons and motivations of action that underlie the reproduction of institutions.

Towards a Workable Concept for Empirical Study

In this final section the theoretical concept of work-related culture is specified somewhat further to make it a 'workable' concept for the purpose of empirical research on employment relations. Above, national culture as it relates to the organization of the employment relationship is conceptualized as the cluster of national work-related institutions. Thus national work-related culture refers to a particular subset of the totality of structural rules and resources, namely to those structural rules and resources that are enduring over time, that are shared by the inhabitants of a nation state, that are related to the employment relationship and that manifest themselves in clusters based on certain structural principles. Accordingly, the analysis of national culture should concentrate on those rule–resource sets that conform to these 'cultural conditions' and disregard those rule–resource sets that do not. Following this line of reasoning, a picture of culture can be construed by adopting the method of 'ideal type construction'.

Ideal types are abstract models that reduce a social phenomenon to its core elements (Parkin, 1982).[48] They are conceptual abstractions that isolate the significant aspects of complex social phenomena.[49] Ideal types provide insight into a social phenomenon by singling out or accentuating its basic features and by suppressing or downgrading those features that are marginal to it. The construction of an ideal type is a somewhat arbitrary affair. What is picked out or accentuated and what is left out or played down are to some extent influenced by the subjective predisposition of the researcher. Nevertheless, ideal types can accurately represent social reality. Although ideal types are unrealistic in the sense that they do not comprehend the totality of the social phenomenon in question, they can be true if they correctly represent the isolated essence of the social phenomenon; otherwise, they are false (Mäki, 1992).[50]

To construe ideal types of national work-related cultures of particular countries, some universal categories of work-related institutions can be selected beforehand. Institutions can be categorized on different grounds. For example, institutions are either shallow or intensive, either tacit or discursive, either weakly sanctioned or strongly sanctioned (Giddens, 1984). In the following, certain categories of work-related institutions that can be included in an ideal type of a national work-related culture are identified. This categorization of work-related institutions should not be understood as exhaustive and compulsory, but primarily as a starting-point and a frame of reference. First, a distinction is made between institutionalized patterns at the corporate level and institutionalized patterns at the societal level. Moreover, within the latter category, societal work-related institutions, a distinction is made between formalized and informal institutions. In sum, three main categories are distinguished: employment practices at the firm level, formalized societal work-related institutions and informal societal work-related institutions.[51] As a

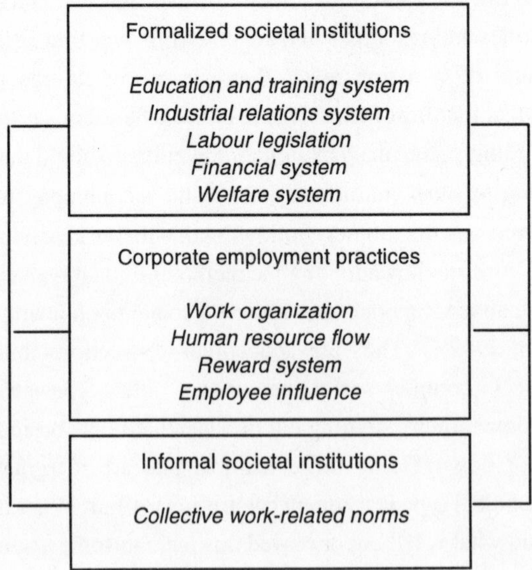

Figure 4.4 National work-related culture

heuristic device, an ideal type of work-related culture can be visualized as in Figure 4.4. Here the three categories are depicted as a coherent cluster. The three layers are discussed in more detail below.

Formal work-related institutions at societal level

Two distinct branches of literature provide insight into what formalized institutional domains at the societal level are relevant to the construction of an ideal type of work-related culture. The first type of literature concentrates on the design of employment practices at firm level and considers societal institutions as 'environmental variables'. For example, the 'outer context' of the human resource management model put forward by Hendry and Pettigrew (1990) comprises technological, economic, sociocultural and political institutions. Likewise, Sparrow and Hiltrop (1994) include the following factors under the institutional heading: national business system (which refers to the role of government, financial system, system of education and training, trade associations, and system of industrial relations), social, legislative and welfare context, and labour legislation. The second branch of literature starts from the institutional context and draws implications for the pattern of employment practices. For example, Whitley (1997) focuses on the institutional embeddedness of the employment relationship by means of the concept of

---

Box 4.2 Categories of formalized societal work-related institutions

Educational system
    How is formal education organized for both workers and managers? What is the degree of stratification? What is the importance of vocational versus general education?

System of industrial relations
    What is the role of each of the three players in the industrial relations system, that is, employers, collective labour and the state? How are conflicts solved?

Labour legislation
    What is the extent of government interference by means of labour legislation? What are the main objects of regulation? What principles underlie the jurisprudence?

Capital system and market for corporate control
    What is the relative importance of credit versus equity-based capital? Who are the main providers of capital? What are the checks on the performance of managers?

Social security and welfare system
    To what extent is the economic situation of people assured? How is responsibility for economic security divided among individuals, interest groups and the state?

'national work system'. To understand employment practices at firm level, he draws attention to two dimensions of the societal context. First, he refers to the position of the actors in the system of industrial relations: collective labour, employers and the state. Moreover, he is concerned with the institutions that account for the socialization of the actors. Major importance is ascribed to the institutions that govern the development of skills (education system), the availability of capital (financial system) and the sustenance of trust (welfare system). Box 4.2 lists five categories of formal work-related institutions. The questions illustrate some dimensions of these institutional domains that are relevant to constructing the ideal types.

Dominant corporate employment practices

The second category of the ideal-typical description of national work-related culture concerns the set of employment practices at firm level that are dominant in a particular society. What dimensions are involved in this category? For the purpose of cross-national comparison, the analytical framework provided by Beer et al. (1984) is recommended.[52] It classifies the domain of employment practices into the four areas that are listed in Box 4.3.

Box 4.3 Categories of corporate employment practices

Work organization: the manner in which labour and responsibility are divided among individual jobs.

Human resource flow: the flow of personnel into, through and out of the organization.

Reward system: the basis on which employees are rewarded for their commitment to the organization.

Employee influence: the modes of participation of employees with respect to managerial decisions.

Informal work-related institutions at societal level

The informal work-related institutions at societal level that make up the ideal-typical description of national work-related culture refer to work-related norms and values that are shared by the majority of the society's population. Classifications of work-related norms are provided by so-called 'international value studies' that have identified value dimensions with validity across nations. For example, based on a literature review, Triandis (1983) identifies about 30 value dimensions that are related to managerial practice.[53] A further example is

Hofstede (1980), who identifies four work-related issues that are relevant for every society.[54] A third relevant study is Hampden-Turner and Trompenaars (1993). They have distinguished seven value orientations to characterize various modern capitalist countries.[55] A final reference is Whitley (1992), who identifies a number of informal rules to characterize distinct national business systems. The rules refer to the degree and basis of trust between non-kin social groups, the commitment and loyalty to collectivities beyond the family, the importance of individual identities, rights and commitments, and the way authority is perceived.

CONCLUSIONS

This book aims to explain the course of development of the employment relationship across different cultural contexts in a period of powerful global trends. In the conceptual framework of Chapter 2, the employment relationship was depicted as intermingled between two 'forces'.[56] The development of the employment relationship hinges, on the one hand, on the dynamic 'force of globalization' and, on the other hand, on the 'conserving force' of national culture. Chapter 3 has explored the worldwide trends that impose pressures on firms to adjust the existing employment relationship to a common global standard. The present chapter has focused on the conceptualization of national work-related culture as the primary mechanism that preserves the existing cultural diversity.

In this chapter, it has been argued that a sound concept of culture needs explicit attention to the underlying philosophical perspective on the relation between individuals and society. The rejection of both individualism and holism led the analysis to explore the theories of Roy Bhaskar and Anthony Giddens. Both theories aim to overcome the dualism that separates the human actor from society. Both theories emphasize the mutual constitution of society and human agents. However, we have argued in favour of Giddens' structuration theory, because it takes the knowledgeability of the human agent as a starting-point. This theoretical perspective has, consequently, formed the basis of the conceptualization of culture. The impact of national culture on the employment relationship is conceptualized by a cluster of national work-related institutions. Further elaboration of this concept has resulted in a three-layer scheme that distinguishes between formal work-related societal institutions, informal work-related societal institutions and dominant employment practices at firm level. The remainder of this book will illustrate the conceptual framework by means of an empirical application. The study of the development of the employment relationship in, respectively, the Netherlands and the United States will illuminate the manner in which cultural rules shape the evolution of the way firms manage the employment relations in a context of powerful global trends.

NOTES

1. Kroeber and Kluckhohn (1952) propose the following definition to integrate the numerous definitions of culture: 'Culture consists of patterns, explicit and implicit, of and for behavior acquired and transmitted by symbols, constituting the distinctive achievement of human groups, including their embodiment in artifacts; the essential core of culture consists of traditional (i.e., historically derived and selected) ideas and especially their attached values; culture systems may, on the one hand, be considered as products of action, on the other, as conditioning elements of future action' (Kroeber and Kluckhohn, 1952, p.181).
2. The original and central domain of culture is anthropology. This discipline considers culture not as a theoretical concept to be incorporated in its theories, but as the central object of its research efforts. Developments in anthropology have exerted considerable influence on the study of culture in other disciplines. Overviews of the various schools of thought in anthropology are provided by Smircich (1983), Allaire and Firsirotu (1984), Eckstein (1988) and Sackmann (1991). It appears that the conceptual confusion with regard to culture in the social sciences is a reflection of the state of the anthropological discipline.
3. In this discussion of individualism and holism, the differences between the two positions are magnified by contrasting the more extreme views. The boundaries become blurred if more moderate standpoints enter the discussion (see Rutherford, 1994).
4. Note that philosophical individualism is necessary but not sufficient for methodological individualism. Methodological individualism can be rejected without rejecting philosophical individualism. However, without the latter ontology, methodological individualism is not coherent.
5. A second principle for methodological individualism to work is that individual purpose is a sufficient cause of all social action (Hodgson, 1988).
6. The major school in social science that starts from the instrumental individual is mainstream neoclassical economics. This school takes the preference functions as fixed and exogenous. The consequence is that variables in the domain of culture are ignored. Recent attempts of Casson (1991) and Becker (1996) to introduce social and cultural elements within this rational choice framework did not open the black box of preference formation.
7. Lawson (1995) argues that the positivist mode of explanation in terms of such Humean causal laws is intrinsically linked with its empiricist starting-point. For, if only atomistic events of experience can be considered for theoretical purposes, the

only sort of generalization left to scientific analysis is the search for constant conjunctions between such atomistic events.

8. A distinction can be made between an epistemological and an ontological hermeneutic thesis (Schwandt, 1994). In this section, the concern is exclusively with the methodological consequences of the epistemological thesis for the study of social phenomena.
9. Social science becomes even more complex when the existence of a double hermeneutic is recognized. Giddens (1993) emphasizes that there is a 'continual slippage' of the concepts that are constructed by the human sciences to the knowledge of the human actors that are, subsequently, the object of analysis. In other words, previous 'scientific' outcomes have an impact on the social action of people.
10. The hermeneutic perspective may result in scientific relativism if the 'closed' character of frames of meaning is overemphasized and, consequently, the translation of meaning from one frame to another is argued to be logically impossible.
11. The classic reference on the method of 'verstehen' for social science is Max Weber (1905/1949).
12. In extremis, this argument deems every comparative analysis among different cultures impossible.
13. In a later study, a fifth dimension was added: 'Confucian dynamism' (Hofstede and Bond, 1988). This dimension incorporates the time orientation of a cultural group (for example, long-term versus short-term time orientation).
14. 'Power distance' indicates the extent to which it is accepted that power in organizations is distributed unequally. 'Uncertainty avoidance' indicates the degree of tolerance for uncertainty and ambiguity. 'Individualism-collectivism' refers to the strength and the breadth of the social network in which people are engaged. Finally, 'masculinity' versus 'femininity' highlights the importance that people attach to material versus immaterial aspects of life.
15. Contextual contingencies that are commonly studied are technology, size, environmental uncertainty, industry, strategy and dependence (see Tayeb, 1988).
16. The importance of the 'culture-free thesis' is criticized by, among others, Maurice et al. (1986). They criticize the conclusion of the Aston researchers because their conclusions are irrefutable, given the generality of the concepts that they have employed: 'Since the structural and contextual variables used have been thoroughly de-socialized, it should come as no surprise that the research leads to the conclusion that the predictions of structural contingency theory are quite generally valid' (ibid., p.226). In their view, formalization, centralization and functional specialization within an organization vary in meaning according to the cultural context.
17. The new institutionalist school in organizational analysis has its roots in sociology and should be distinguished from the new institutionalism in economics. The theoretical background of this school has already been described in the second section of chapter 2.
18. Bhaskar and Giddens support the primacy of ontology above epistemology. Bhaskar writes: 'we must first know what kind of things societies (and people) are before we can consider whether it is possible to study them scientifically' (Bhaskar, 1989a, p.13). Likewise, Giddens notes: 'Concentration upon epistemological issues draws attention away from the more "ontological" concerns of social theory (...) Rather than becoming preoccupied with epistemological disputes, (...) those working in social theory, I suggest, should be concerned first and foremost with reworking conceptions of human being and human doing' (Giddens, 1984, p.xx).
19. Mayhew (1987) distinguishes between a 'formalist' and a 'substantivist' approach

in anthropology. The formalists assume that description of the processes of self-interested choosing is the most revealing task that economic anthropologists can undertake, while the substantivists assume that the description of the cultural context within which such choosing takes place is the most important thing to be done.

20. For a review, see Bryant (1995).
21. Bhaskar refers to Berger and Luckmann (1966) when he criticizes approaches that relate people and society as two moments of the same process. Archer (1995) notes that the same critique applies to Giddens' structuration theory.
22. Although change of social structures is normally not explained by the desires of agents to change them that way, Bhaskar holds that 'as a very important theoretical and political limit, it may do so' (Bhaskar, 1989a, p.35).
23. Note that Bhaskar does not start from naturalism, but that he is guided by the question whether naturalism is possible. However, conditioned by some peculiarities of the social realm, in the end his answer is in the affirmative.
24. The objective structures, or the real constituents of the world, are referred to as the 'intransitive objects' of scientific inquiry. The product of science, that is the theoretical knowledge advanced by scientists about these structures, is 'transitive', which means that such knowledge is always open to transformation.
25. This view of knowable reality has resulted in the perseverance of Humean causal laws as the primary form of explanation of science: 'once the empirical realist ontology is accepted, then for successful science to be possible, the "whenever event x then event y" formulation necessarily follows' (Lawson 1995, p.12). This perspective on scientific laws is heavily criticized, because its relevance is restricted to closed systems.
26. Most of Bhaskar's leading ideas on transcendental realism are rooted in the single 'transcendental' question, 'how are experiments possible?'
27. Reality can be ascribed to underlying mechanisms on the basis of a causal criterion, by which the real existence of an object is ascertained by demonstration of its capacity to bring about changes in material things. 'On this criterion, to be is not to be perceived, but rather (in last instance) just be able to do' (Bhaskar, 1989a, p.12).
28. The three distinct domains are not synchronized. Experience does not necessarily correspond to actual events. That is, observations of the same event can conflict among different individuals. Moreover, underlying mechanisms are typically not manifest in actual events as a result of the existence of numerous countervailing causal powers.
29. According to 'reductive materialism', a fully developed science of matter could explain everything so that the laws of 'higher-level' sciences (biology, psychology) are redundant (for example, human behaviour entirely explained by the material constitution of the genes).
30. For example, the emergence of organic life can be explained in terms of the physical and chemical elements out of which organic things were formed. However, the proliferation of brightly coloured objects at a certain stage of natural history must relate to biological laws of natural selection.
31. For example, the power of water to extinguish fire cannot be derived from the power of its constituents, for both oxygen and hydrogen are highly inflammable.
32. Bhaskar (1989a) mentions three ontological limitations for a possible naturalism: (1) social structures, unlike natural structures, do not exist independently of the activities they govern; (2) social structures, unlike natural structures, do not exist independently of the agents' conceptions of what they are doing in their activity; (3) social structures, unlike natural structures, may be only relatively enduring (so that

the tendencies they ground may not be universal in the sense of space–time variants).

33. Like natural phenomena, actual social events ultimately result from the interaction of a multiplicity of different mechanisms. However, the solution of natural science, to bring about artificial closure of the open system by means of experimental activity, is not available to social scientists. Because of the specific nature of human action to produce novelty and qualitative change, social sciences are sciences without closure. The working of a single mechanism can never be isolated from other mechanisms: 'The chief epistemological limit on naturalism is not raised by the necessarily unperceivable character of the objects of social scientific inquiry, but rather by the fact that they only ever manifest themselves in open systems' (Bhaskar, 1989a, p.45).
34. On the other hand, external relations between individuals do not have an impact on the nature of their social being (for example, two passing strangers or taxonomic collectivities).
35. Giddens recognizes the importance of unconscious motivation, but concentrates on practical and discursive consciousness as he emphasizes the intentional nature of action.
36. There is no clear dividing line between discursive and practical consciousness. It is often the case that agents, if asked, can give a rational account of what they are doing, although they do not bear that account in mind all time.
37. Giddens distinguishes between three types of unintended consequences. First is the cumulation of unintended consequences that follows a single event in particular circumstances, like for example the firing of the bullet that killed Archduke Ferdinand at Sarajevo. The second type is the unintended consequence that results from a complex of individual activities. An example is the development of ethnic segregation as an unintended consequence of numerous individual decisions to move. The third type of unintended consequence is the reproduction of institutionalized practices. For example, the regular consequences of speaking or writing English in a correct way is to contribute to the reproduction of the English language as a whole. It is the last sort of unintended consequences that are emphasized by Giddens.
38. In the view of Giddens, it is especially this characteristic of the social realm, the instability of the knowledge that actors have about the circumstances of their own action, that inhibits the social sciences from producing universal laws.
39. Giddens holds knowledgeability about the social rules as a core characteristic of human agents: 'Awareness of social rules, expressed first and foremost in practical consciousness, is the very core of that "knowledgeability" which specifically characterizes human agents' (Giddens, 1984, p.22).
40. Giddens distinguishes between two types of resources: allocative and authoritative. Allocative resources refer to capabilities that generate control over aspects of the material world, while authoritative resources refer to capabilities that generate command over human agents.
41. In the words of various commentators on structuration theory: 'Structurationists deliberately turn their backs upon any autonomous features which could pertain independently to either "structure" or "agency"' (Archer, 1995, p.97). On the one hand, human agency is not autonomous: 'a human agent worthy of his name must be a competent agent. As a competent agent, his action draws upon a rich reservoir of mutual knowledge, conventions, and resources, which makes his action possible' (Mendoza, 1997, p.247). On the other hand, social structure is not autonomous: 'structure has no reality except in so far as it is "internal" to agents in the form of

memory traces; it is agents who bring "structure" into being, and it is "structure" which produces the possibility of agency' (Cassell, 1993, p.12). In sum, 'though structure and action are not the same thing, they are not different things either; rather they are two aspects of the same thing: social practices' (Craib, 1992, p.34).

42. Giddens provides two more definitions. 'Structural principles' are the most deeply embedded structural properties, implicated in the organization of societal totalities. He draws on such structural principles to distinguish capitalist societies from feudal and tribal societies. Furthermore, in the vocabulary of Giddens, 'structures' (the plural of structure) are sets or distinct clusters of rules and resources implicated in social reproduction.
43. Giddens refers to major ethnomethodological and phenomenological studies of authors, like Goffman and Erikson, which illuminate the importance of practical consciousness.
44. Giddens classifies institutions into three groups: signification, legitimization and domination. That is, there are institutions that constitute meaning (signification), there are institutions to sanction certain modes of social conduct (legitimization) and, finally, there are institutions that express forms of power (domination).
45. This definition of culture resembles other notions for capturing the national specificity of the organization of the employment relationship, like Whitley's (1997) 'national work system', Hollingsworth and Boyer's (1997) 'social system of production' and Edwards' (1994) 'national regime of labour regulation'.
46. The notion of 'intentional conduct' is preferred to the term 'strategic conduct' that is employed by Giddens himself, for in the realm of management and organization studies and economics, the notion 'strategic' refers to highly conscious interpretations of alternative courses of action. In line with the insights of structuration theory, intentional conduct does not have to be deliberate, but can be guided by practical consciousness. Most of the time, it refers to routine activity, for which the actor is able to specify his reasons and motivations only if he is asked to do so.
47. A study that illustrates the broad conception of the mutual constituency of the individual and society, but restricts itself to institutional analysis for demonstrating the societal effect (or cultural effect) on the employment relationship, is Maurice et al. (1986). In this study, attention is focused on three interrelated institutional domains in which human agents are socialized: the education system, the work organization and the industrial relations system.
48. The introduction of the method of ideal type construction in social science dates back to Max Weber (1902).
49. The term 'ideal type' is somewhat misleading, since it does not refer to a normatively preferred type. Ideal types are ideal only in the sense that they capture the 'heart of the story' and abstract from secondary factors; they are not ideal in the sense of being desirable or good.
50. Likewise, we disagree with Weber (1902, pp.43 and 92), who suggests that ideal types only have a function in empirical investigation as some sort of yardstick against which empirical cases can be evaluated to acquire a better comprehension of the social phenomenon in question. Here, a realist perspective is favoured above such an instrumentalist notion of the use of ideal types. That is, the construction of ideal types can recommend itself as an end of scientific activity. For, when they are rightly constructed, they can provide insight into the essence of a certain social phenomenon (Mäki, 1992).
51. Note that the distinction between formalized and informal institutions is commonly blurred. For example, labour law as a formalized institution inhibits many informal

institutions, such as the value judgments that are involved in actual jurisprudence. Similarly, the industrial relations systems incorporate formal regulations that provide unions with a legal basis. However, equally important are the informal institutions like common norms, mutual expectations and trust relations.

52. Poole (1990) recommends the Harvard model of Beer et al. (1984) as a 'basic framework for defining human resource issues which are relevant for international or comparative analysis'. Other authors who have adopted the Harvard framework for cross-cultural comparative purposes are Begin (1992) and Gronhaug and Nordhaug (1992).
53. Triandis (1983) refers, among others, to the cultural dimensions of Parsons and Shils (affectivity, specificity, universalism, quality versus performance), Kluckhohn and Strodtbeck (human nature, man's relationship to nature, time orientation, activity orientation, man's relationship to other human beings), McClelland (need for achievement, need for power), Glenn (universalism–particularism, associative–abstractive, Apollonian–Dionysian).
54. The four dimensions are labelled 'power distance', 'uncertainty avoidance', 'individualism–collectivism' and 'masculinity–femininity'. Some years later, Hofstede and Bond (1988) added a fifth dimension called 'Confucian dynamism' (see the first section of this chapter).
55. The seven dimensions of Hampden-Turner and Trompenaars are: universalistic versus particularistic; analytical versus integrative; individualistic versus communitarianistic; inner-directedness versus outer-directedness; time as sequence versus time as synchronization, achieved status versus ascribed status; equality versus hierarchy.
56. From the discussion in this chapter, it should be clear that the notion of force is used as a metaphor. The notion of force originates from the natural sciences, where it refers to a real mechanism with actual causal power. In the social realm, there are no such outside forces that compel human agents to act in a certain way. The notion of 'force' in social science is nothing but a metaphor to denote that the conditions in which human agents find themselves limit the number of feasible alternatives, given their reasons and motives to act.

5. An empirical illustration: the United States versus the Netherlands

INTRODUCTION

In what direction will the employment relationship evolve under pressure of the altered circumstances in the global economy? Does the exposure of firms across the world to similar global trends leave them no other choice than to organize the employment relationship in the same way, or can a substantial influence of national culture be observed, resulting in a continuous divergence of employment practices across nations? To take a position in the convergence/divergence debate, the impact of national culture on the organization of the employment relationship needs to be identified. The identification of the impact of culture should not be limited to the mere observation of organizational differences across cultural boundaries, because such findings treat culture as a black box. Mere reference to cross-cultural differences leaves the question of how the organization of the employment relationship is affected by national culture unanswered. Instead, the claim for cultural persistence in the organization of the employment relationship should be accompanied by a specification of the mechanism(s) by which national culture affects the course of developments in the realm of employment relations.

The above questions inform the empirical study that is illustrated in this chapter. This chapter presents evidence on the development of the employment relationship in, respectively, the United States and the Netherlands. The data are collected in such a way that the impact of national culture can be derived from the findings. The first section describes the research design. It provides the rationale for the cross-cultural comparison between the United States and the Netherlands. The second section substantiates the work-related cultures of the United States and the Netherlands. The third section reports on concrete developments in the realm of employment management in four multinational companies that operate both in the United States and in the Netherlands.

RESEARCH DESIGN

A research design is an action plan for getting from the initial research questions to some set of answers for these questions. It must ensure a logical link between the theoretical research question, the empirical data and the conclusions. With this aim, this section outlines a research design that aims to identify the impact of national culture on the evolution of the employment relationship. How can the impact of national culture on organizational changes of the employment relationship be demonstrated? In the previous chapter, culture was defined as the nation-specific 'rules and resources' that are drawn upon by actors when they engage in social action. Accordingly, the influence of national culture on the development of firms' employment practices is elucidated when one can show that the actors who shape the employment relationship draw upon a different set of rules and resources in a certain national cultural context than in another one. With the objective to demonstrate this, the research design in the following study consists of two elements: cross-cultural comparison and matched samples. Both elements are considered in more detail below.

Cross-Cultural Comparison

National culture is understood as a particular part of the totality of structural rules and resources that underlie human action, namely that part which is enduring, nation-specific and clustered. Human agents are hardly aware of those rules and resources, because social activity involves a great amount of commonsense knowledge or practical consciousness. This commonsense nature of cultural rules and resources imposes problems for identifying their national specificity, for human agents cannot themselves distinguish which part of their action is particular to their national context if they have no knowledge about the common practices in other national settings. Therefore a cross-national study is indispensable. By means of a cross-national study, one can question the commonsense nature of certain rules and resources by contrasting them with the rules that are instantiated by human actors who are socialized in other national environments. It is the task of the researcher to identify which parts of the rule-resource sets are national–specific and belong accordingly to the realm of national culture, and which parts are not.

Which nations should be incorporated in a cross-national comparison? As a general condition, research should focus on nation states that are different in their cultural orientation but similar in terms of their economic development.[1] With this condition in mind, the comparative analysis in this chapter focuses on the Netherlands and the United States. These countries can be considered as exemplars of, respectively, the so-called Rhineland and the Anglo-Saxon models of capitalism: two distinct variants of capitalistic economic organization that have achieved similar levels of economic development (Albert, 1990).[2]

Matched Samples

It is generally acknowledged that social events are the outcome of a 'plurality of causes'. The objective of the empirical study, to infer a causal relationship between national culture and developments in the employment relationship, is hampered by the recognition that a multitude of explanatory variables can be identified that can account for the shape of the employment relationship. Variables such as 'applied production technology', 'labour market conditions', 'size of the company', 'corporate identity', 'state regulation' and 'personal features of executive management' can, in principle, be important to explain and understand changes of employment practices at a particular firm. Accordingly, to infer the impact of a single causal variable, such as national culture, a requisite of the research design is that it brings about some sort of closure to the observed social phenomena. As a natural scientist uses the experiment to control for the effects of other variables, the social scientist needs to 'isolate' the relationship of interest from other impinging factors.

The case study appears to be most suited as a research method to illuminate the causal processes that relate culture to developments in firms' employment practices.[3] Following Giddens, the influence of culture should be revealed by the analysis of practical consciousness of the actors. Case studies can fulfil this condition, for they leave the real-life context of the phenomenon in question unimpaired so that the practical consciousness underlying the human activity can be explored (Yin, 1994). Moreover, case studies can fulfil the condition of closure through the careful selection of the case. The 'method of matched samples' is especially suited to isolating the impact of national culture on firms' employment practices (Sorge and Warner, 1986). The strength of the method of matched samples is twofold. On the one hand, the method maximizes the variance of the variable of most interest. In this study this variable is 'national work-related culture'. Comparing developments in employment practices across firms that are located in different national cultures, respectively, the Dutch and the American culture, creates variance in this variable. On the other hand, the method of matched samples minimizes the influence of other impinging variables. Variables other than national culture can be ruled out by holding the context of the Dutch and American firms constant. Factors that impinge on firms' employment practices but which lie outside the domain of national culture should be kept constant among the firms where the data collection took place. In this study, based on the method of matched samples, firms are selected that operate in the same industry, that have a similar organizational culture, that follow a similar strategy, that use the same technology, that have a similar size and that occupy a similar position vis-à-vis the parent organization.[4] If the paired comparison fails to satisfy any of these conditions, it can always be suggested that observed results are due to the fact that the samples are imperfectly matched. Table 5.1 outlines the manner in which this study fulfils the matching requirements.

Table 5.1 Operationalization of matching criteria

Criterion	Operationalization
1. Presence in both USA and NL	Focus on Dutch and American multinational companies
2. Similar corporate identity	Focus on establishments of the same multinational company
3. Active in the same industry Exposed to international competition	Focus on multinationals that operate in the chemical industry
4. Similar position of dependence vis-à-vis the parent organization	Focus on production plants based in the USA and the NL
5. Similar strategy Similar technology	Focus on production plants that produce the same product
6. Similar size	Focus on production plants that employ the same number of shift workers

It is argued that the comparison of production plants of the same multinational company satisfies the matching procedure for the factors 'corporate culture' and 'dependence on parent organization'. Furthermore, the production plants are selected on the basis of corresponding size and similar product. It is assumed that, by comparing production plants that produce the same product, matching for the factors 'strategy' and 'technology' is achieved. The choice of the chemical industry emanates from the global nature of the industry and the high degree of international competition (Grant and Paterson, 1994). In this way, it can fairly be assumed that the production plants have been exposed to the global trends that influence the organization of the employment relationship. Furthermore, a stronger base from which to generalize the outcomes is achieved by a fourfold replication of the method of paired comparison.[5] Four firms that operate in the chemical industry are selected. Two firms are of American origin, namely Dow Chemical and General Electric; the other two, Akzo Nobel and DSM, are of Dutch origin. For each company, the employment relations in an American production plant are compared with those in a similar Dutch production plant. Table 5.2 specifies the contextual conditions of the selected production facilities. The selection of case study sites in this way ensures that the findings can be meaningfully interpreted in terms of national work-related culture.

Table 5.2 Specification of selected production plants

Company	Product	Location	Size
General Electric (US)	Noryl plastic	Selkirk (New York, US) Bergen op Zoom (NL)	100 shift workers 80 shift workers
Dow Chemical (US)	Light hydrocarbons	Oyster Creek (Texas, US) Terneuzen (NL)	40 shift workers 80 shift workers
Akzo Nobel (NL)	Hydroprocessing catalysts	Pasadena (Texas, US) Amsterdam-Noord (NL)	30 shift workers 45 shift workers
DSM (NL)	EPDM-rubbers	Addis (Louisiana, US) Geleen (NL)	60 shift workers 50 shift workers

Logic of the Research Design

The study aims to demonstrate the importance of national culture for the explanation of the evolution of the employment relationship. By showing that the actors who shape the employment practices in the United States draw upon a different set of rules and resources than their counterparts in the Netherlands, the influence of national culture is elucidated. With this objective a research design is developed that is composed of two branches. Figure 5.1 provides a schematic overview of the entire research design.

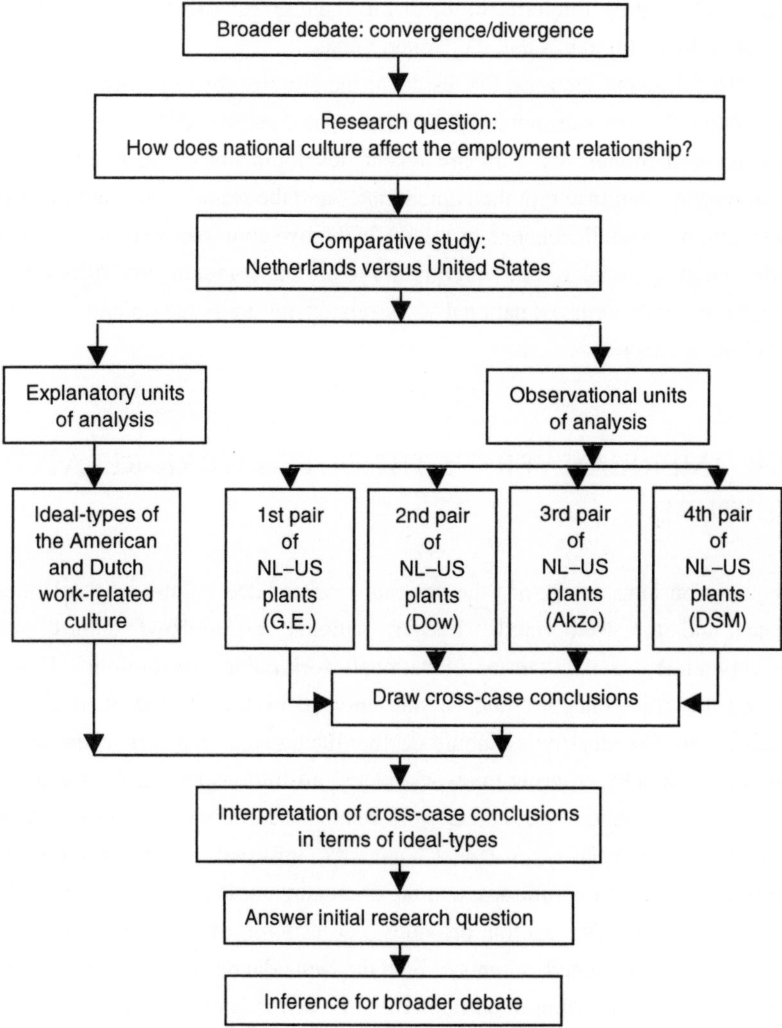

Figure 5.1 Research design

First, the explanatory units of analysis, that is the work-related cultures of the Netherlands and the United States, are specified. Second, data on the observational unit of analysis, that is change processes in the realm of employment relations, are collected among Dutch and American production plants. In the third step, the two branches are combined. Any significant differences between the change processes of the selected Dutch and American plants are interpreted in terms of the distinct cultural rules that guide individual action in the Netherlands and the United States.

In the following sections, the results of the aforementioned research design are presented. After substantiating the work-related cultures of the United States and the Netherlands, we compare recent developments in the realm of the employment relationship in the United States and the Netherlands, and identify the extent to which the change processes in the two countries exhibit similar or differentiating aspects. The interpretation of the common and differential developments in terms of national work-related culture is the objective of the concluding chapter.

THE AMERICAN VERSUS THE DUTCH WORK-RELATED CULTURE

This section aims to specify the national work-related culture of the United States and the Netherlands. Earlier, national work-related culture was conceptualized as the 'cluster of national work-related institutions'. It was argued that this concept could be substantiated by the method of ideal-type description. The ideal-types should capture the essential features of the work-related cultures by ordering the work-related institutions into distinct national clusters. Three kinds of concrete work-related institutions were proposed to constitute such ideal-types (see Chapter 4): informal societal institutions, formalized societal institutions, and the dominant employment practices at the level of the firm. This section provides a description of the three constituent parts of the work-related cultures of both the Netherlands and the United States. To illuminate the cultural particularity of each country, we focus on the differences between the two nations rather than their common characteristics.[6]

American and Dutch Informal Institutions

This section contrasts the dominant norm and value patterns that prevail in the United States and the Netherlands. For this purpose, both idiographic and nomothetic studies are referred to.[7] The first part of this section examines various idiographic studies of the United States and the Netherlands. The picture of the American value pattern relies primarily on the works of Lipset (1990, 1996), who emphasizes the exceptional nature of the American value structure. The description of the dominant value system of the Dutch is primarily based on the work of the German sociologist Zahn (1989).[8] The second part of this section analyses the American and Dutch value patterns by referring to two major nomothetic studies. Attention will successively be given to the cultural studies of Hofstede (1980, 1991) and Hampden-Turner and Trompenaars (1993). Both studies have developed certain universal value dimensions that enable a direct comparison of the American and Dutch value patterns.

Idiographic value studies

The American creed Lipset (1990, 1996) emphasizes the unique nature of the historical origins of the United States. While the origin of other Western nation states resides in a common history, the foundation of the United States is based on a common ideology, that is, a set of dogmas about the nature of a good society. Classic statements of illustrious personalities in the history of the United States illustrate this point. It was Emerson who proclaimed that 'becoming an American is a religious – that is, an ideological – act' (Lipset, 1990, p.19). Likewise, Churchill declared that 'Being an American (...) is an ideological commitment. It is not a matter of birth. Those who reject American values are un-American' (ibid.). Such statements presuppose the existence of a distinct well-circumscribed American ideology. Lipset (1990) describes this ideology in four terms: anti-statism, individualism, egalitarianism and populism. Below, each of these elements of the American creed is examined.

The first value, anti-statism, refers to classical liberalism and 'laissez-faire' politics.[9] This notion of 'anti-statism' is reflected in the peculiar constitution of the United States (Glendon, 1992).[10] The repudiation of the authority of government is in alignment with the dominance of the market mechanism to sustain economic order in society. Both left- and right-wing politicians in the United States profess mistrust of government and stress the virtues of free market competition.

The second dominant American value, 'individualism', is expressed in various ways (Bellah et al., 1985). Aram (1993) distinguishes three forms of American individualism, all consistent with the anti-state ideology. 'Political individualism' refers to freedom from arbitrary and oppressive state action. Private property establishes a sphere of personal action beyond the reach of the state. An American citizen has the right to challenge government in the courts, through organization and by electoral activity. 'Economic individualism' refers to the unhampered opportunity to pursue profits for the purpose of self-interest. Economic freedom is assumed to result in superior national prosperity. Economic freedom encourages people to utilize their abilities fully and to reward them in proportion to their contributions. This type of individualism is related to the characterization of American society as meritocratic, achievement-oriented and materialistic. 'Social individualism' relates to the concern for the social circumstances of individuals. Voluntary involvement rather than state involvement should be an expression of such social commitment. The spread of voluntary organizations in the United States reflects this kind of individualism.

The third value, 'egalitarianism', refers to equality of opportunity and respect for individual human beings. The egalitarian spirit underlies the historic role of the United States in the development of the public school system to provide a common educational background for all people irrespective of descent. Moreover, equal opportunity underlies the non-discrimination regulation that was implemented in the 1960s. American egalitarianism corresponds to the notion of 'economic individualism', for the egalitarian nature of American society entails only equality of opportunities and does not involve the equality of result or outcome. Personal destiny is supposed to be determined by the free interplay of competitive forces.[11]

Finally, the value 'populism' relates to the political system of the United States. This value holds that the will of the people should dominate elites. Public choice is viewed as superior to professionalism. This value is reflected in the practice that almost all figures in law enforcement at the national and state level are directly elected by citizens or appointed by elected officials.

The Dutch: regents, rebels and reformists The dominant American value pattern originates from a common ideology. The identity of other Western nations, such as the Netherlands, originates from a common history. Therefore, to understand the value orientation of the Dutch, the historical development of the Netherlands needs to be examined. Zahn (1989) identified certain continuities in the history of the Netherlands: 'The political and social history of the Netherlands is through and through a history of religion: the history of relations between denominational parts of the population, churches, sects and non-church related philosophical traditions like humanism, liberalism and socialism' (p.43). The unique concourse of different religious and non-religious groups of people in the Netherlands is reflected in the value pattern of its inhabitants. Zahn summarises the Dutch value orientation by reference to three roles: the 'rebel', the 'reformist' and the 'regent'.[12]

The 'rebel' refers to the 'protest potential' and the 'resistance to authority' of the Dutch. Rebellion against the Spanish Court of the Habsburgs stood at the origins of the Dutch Republic founded in 1579 by the Union of Utrecht. A major reason for the revolt against the Spanish and the Roman Church was concerned with the freedom of religion. In accordance with the principles of Erasmian humanism, the right to express differences of opinion was in need of defence. The recognition of freedom of religion was emphasized by the Union of Utrecht. Dutch society is therefore formed by resistance to authority and tolerance of different opinions rather than by its identification with a dominant power.[13] From the early beginnings of the Republic, Dutch society has been dominated by the interplay of two other distinct roles, the 'regent' and the 'reformist' (or 'merchants' and 'clergymen').

The 'reformist' plays a major role in Dutch history. This role refers to the population of farmers, fishermen and 'insignificant citizens' who practised orthodox Calvinism. Various outside observers have noted a Calvinist legacy in the value system of the Dutch. For example, Lawrence (1991) traces a 'dislike of vanity, eccentricity, needless risk-taking and material self-indulgence' as characteristic traits of the Dutch back to this Calvinist background.

The other role, the 'regent', refers to the tolerant urban population. The regent, who adhered to a moderate, accommodating, liberal, Erasmian type of Protestantism, played an important role in the administration of the country and the cities. Its leading position was based on the profitable business of trade. The administration that was led by the Dutch regents was never one of a strong, powerful authority, but entailed a myriad of oligarchic bodies that were controlled by civil society. Executive power of the state was shared with various private organizations, committees, councils and chambers. This involvement of civil society in public authority has been a continuous feature of Dutch society (Waarden, 1992). Zahn emphasizes the impact of this typical form of governance on the value pattern of the Dutch: 'In the Netherlands the collegiate relationships among the regents have put their stamp on administrative structures and civilian patterns of behaviour and they have influenced lower echelons. (...) Collegiate relationships are related to decentralization, oligarchic governing bodies and a non-authoritarian style of governance' (Zahn, 1989, p.58).

The liberal 'regents' controlled the oligarchic governing bodies that dominated Dutch societal organization until the late nineteenth century. Since then, the dominance of the regents has come to an end as a result of the emancipation of orthodox Calvinists, Catholics and socialists. Each of these social groups aspired to a role in public government. However, the coexistence of a diverse set of beliefs was not accompanied by dogmatic struggle. Instead, the different subcultures coexisted and pursued a common objective: each group supported a strong state as a means of realizing the emancipation of their subculture. Zahn comments that it is not so much the strong state that interferes with the life of the citizens; rather, the Dutch citizens are involved with the many details of state policy through numerous groups, parties and associations. Lijphart (1969) notes that the involvement of different cultural groups in state and civil organization reinforced the Dutch societal model of search for consensus, accommodation and tolerance: 'The fundamental convictions of other blocs must be tolerated, if not respected (...) Most issues do require some kind of substantive decision. An attempt is then made to involve all blocs in finding a fair compromise (...) Decisions are not made by a majority simply outvoting a minority' (p.124).

Nomothetic value studies

Hofstede maps different nations on the basis of five universal value dimensions (see Chapter 4, first section). His study (1980) can be used to identify the differences in value orientation between the Dutch and the Americans. It appears that the most significant difference in value orientations between the Dutch and the American populations is found in the dimension 'masculinity'. While the American value system is characterized as masculine, Dutch society reflects highly feminine values. Table 5.3 relates this value difference to general norms, workplace attitudes and the perspective on the role of the state.

Table 5.3 Key differences between feminine and masculine societies

	Feminine (Netherlands)	Masculine (United States)
General norms	Care for others and preservation People and relationships are important Everybody should be modest Sympathy for the weak	Strive for material progress Money and tangible things are important Men should be assertive Sympathy for the strong
Work-place attitude	Work in order to live Stress on solidarity and quality of work life Managers strive for consensus Resolution of conflicts by compromise Team job enrichment	Live in order to work Stress on competition among colleagues Managers are expected to be decisive Resolution of conflicts by power Individual job enrichment
Role of the state	Welfare society ideal The needy should be helped Preservation of environment has priority	Performance society ideal The strong should be supported Maintenance of economic growth has priority

Source: Hofstede (1980).

Except for the masculinity dimension, the value orientations of the United States and the Netherlands appear to be fairly similar. According to Hofstede's results, the Dutch are more threatened by uncertain or unknown situations and the Americans have a shorter time horizon for decision making. However, the differences are seemingly unimportant. The position of both countries on the dimension 'individualism' is striking. Both the United States and the Netherlands are characterized as highly individualistic. However, this finding presents some interpretative difficulties, for individualism is not a homogeneous concept and can assume different meanings. It can be argued that the notion of individualism in the United States is related to dislike of state intervention. In this meaning, a big state is assumed to be in opposition to the freedom of individual citizens. In contrast, in the Netherlands, individualism can be interpreted in a manner that enhances the role of the state, for the state is expected to ensure the 'freedom to act as one pleases' by the emancipation of the various subcultures in the country.

Here individualism is closely related to the emancipation of groups and can be labelled as cultural individualism rather than economic individualism. This interpretation of individualism in the Netherlands appears to be more in line with the comments of various foreign observers of Dutch culture. For example, Phillips (1985) expresses his doubts about Dutch individualism by demonstrating the importance of group conformism in the Netherlands. He notes that the Dutch demonstrate a high degree of tolerance between groups, but within groups non-conformism is hardly accepted: 'Much more than in the United States, the Dutch are organized in closed groups. They largely associate with other people of the same age, social background and professional status. Much more than in the United States academics associate with other academics (of the same age, sex and status), students with other students, workers with workers (...) Of course, the various groups tolerate each other. But within a particular group there is little room for non-conformism' (Phillips, 1985, p.25).

Hampden-Turner and Trompenaars (1993) provide a second source for comparing the American and Dutch value structures across universal dimensions. They describe national value systems by means of seven dilemmas that need to be solved by each country. The inclusion of both the Netherlands and the United States in their study provides an opportunity to compare the Dutch and American value orientations in a direct manner. Table 5.4 lists the seven dilemmas and the approach preferred by, respectively, the Americans and the Dutch. Most notably, it appears that the Dutch and the American value pattern diverges on the dilemmas 'inner-directedness' and 'ascription of status'. The outcome of the latter dilemma is that Americans ascribe status to individuals on the basis of their achievements and performance, while status and authority in the Netherlands originate mainly from knowledge and education. The former dilemma refers to whether people regard personal fate to be determined by external conditions (outer-directed) or individual decisions (inner-directed). The inner-directed orientation of the Americans corresponds to the view that each person is responsible for his or her own destiny. The Dutch appear to attribute more importance to environmental circumstances that are beyond the control of the individual. In sum, Hampden-Turner and Trompenaars conclude that 'American managers are also more inner-directed, i.e. they locate the source of the organization's purpose and direction in the inner convictions of its employees. (…) Americans believe you should "make up your own mind" and "do your own thing" rather than allow yourself to be influenced too much by other people and the external flow of events' (Hampden-Turner and Trompenaars, 1993, p.48).

Table 5.4 Culturally based preferences to solve seven universal dilemmas

Dilemma	United States	Netherlands
1. Universalism versus particularism	Strongly universalistic	Moderately universalistic
2. Analysing versus integrating	Strongly analytical	Moderately analytical
3. Individualism versus communitarianism	Strongly individualistic	Moderately individualistic
4. Inner-directed versus outer-directed	Inner-directed	Outer-directed
5. Time as sequence versus synchronization	Sequential	Sequential
6. Achieved versus ascribed status	Status based on achievement	Status based on knowledge
7. Equality versus hierarchy	Equality	Equality

Source: Hampden-Turner and Trompenaars (1993).

American and Dutch Formalized Institutions

This section examines the dominant characteristics of, respectively, the American and Dutch formal institutions that structure society. The manner in which individuals relate to the state is the main axis across which American and Dutch societal organizations are contrasted. Following Waarden (1992), the relationship between individuals and the state can be characterized on the basis of two dimensions. The first dimension refers to the strength of the state; the second dimension concerns the extent to which civil society is organized in different interest groups. On the basis of these two dimensions, a fourfold categorization can be constructed (see Table 5.5).

In this scheme, the organization of society in the United States is labelled 'liberalism'. In the absence of a strong state and organization of civil interests,

Table 5.5 Typology of societal organization

		Strength of the state	
		Strong	Weak
Strength of societal interests	Strong	Social corporatism (e.g. the Netherlands)	Clientelism (e.g. Switzerland)
	Weak	Etatism (e.g. France)	Liberalism (e.g. United States)

Source: Waarden (1992).

the dominant mode of societal organization is the 'market'. In contrast, the manner in which society is organized in the Netherlands is characterized as 'social corporatism'. In this case, the state has a tendency to intervene in societal organization. However, the state is not autonomous, but tightly connected with civil society. Societal organization consists of numerous relations between the state and civil society in the form of bi-, tri- or multipartite intermediary agencies. In the Netherlands, a myriad of semi-state agencies and committees that participate in policy making in areas such as health, social welfare, industrial relations, quality control and vocational education can be identified (Waarden, 1987).

Below, the description of American and Dutch work-related culture is divided into five institutional categories. Successively, attention is given to the following spheres of societal organization: education, industrial relations, labour legislation, corporate governance and welfare provision.

Educational system

The United States The main institutions of the American system of education are depicted in Figure 5.2. The high school is the central institution after primary education. At high school, the student is offered a choice between a college preparatory, a vocational and a general programme. After graduation from high school, the student faces four options. However, the major divide occurs between those high school graduates who choose to learn a trade on the job and those who choose to follow a four-year college or university course to attain a 'bachelor degree'. Trade vocational and business schools ('certification') and two-year community colleges ('associate degrees') attract mainly older, working people (NEDO, 1984). The following characteristics of the education system are relevant to grasping the American work-related culture.

- The education system incorporates a strong form of stratification between college-educated and non-college-educated students.
- Free choice is a basic tenet of the education system. There is no effort to track students along certain educational paths at an early point in their lives. General education is emphasized to enable students to switch careers at any point.
- Vocational education is not much developed (Osterman, 1988). The educational background of non-managerial workers is restricted to high school. The trade is primarily learned 'on the job' (Carnevale et al., 1990).
- There are no uniform national standards of education. This fact reflects resistance to a strong state and a preference for decentralization. Moreover, the low level of collective organization of employers inhibits the development of business-oriented curricula (Waarden, 1992).
- Colleges and universities are ranked according to status. Admission to high-status universities is dependent on performance at high school. Student grades reflect the performance relative to other students at the same high school. This feature induces students of the same high school to compete with each other.

The Netherlands The organization of the Dutch education system diverges from the American system of education on various accounts. As implied by Figure 5.2, the Dutch system of education embodies a rich variety of educational programmes (CEDEFOP, 1991). After primary school, the Dutch student faces a variety of secondary schools. Four educational levels are distinguished: lower, middle, higher and academic education. Second, general and vocational education are distinguished. Below, various features of the Dutch education system that are relevant to grasping the Dutch work-related culture are listed.[14]

- The Dutch education system is highly stratified according to educational levels. This has resulted in small differences between graduates of different levels. Status is assigned on the basis of the attained level of graduation.
- A broadly developed system of vocational education with three different levels (VBO, MBO, and HBO) exists. The degree of practical orientation is relatively low in these programmes. With the exception of the

'Leerlingwezen', the practice of mixing normal work experience with further education is not widespread. However, periods of practical work experience are obligatory in both MBO and HBO.

- Employers are involved in the development of educational programmes and vocational qualifications at industry level (Gordon et al., 1994).
- The government holds responsibility for the standardization of diplomas. This has resulted in solid and reliable standards on a national scale.
- University education is characterized by the absence of a ranking system. Centres of excellence are non-existent. The level of education is supposed to be uniform across the various universities. Performance in terms of grades plays a marginal role in the selection of graduates by universities.

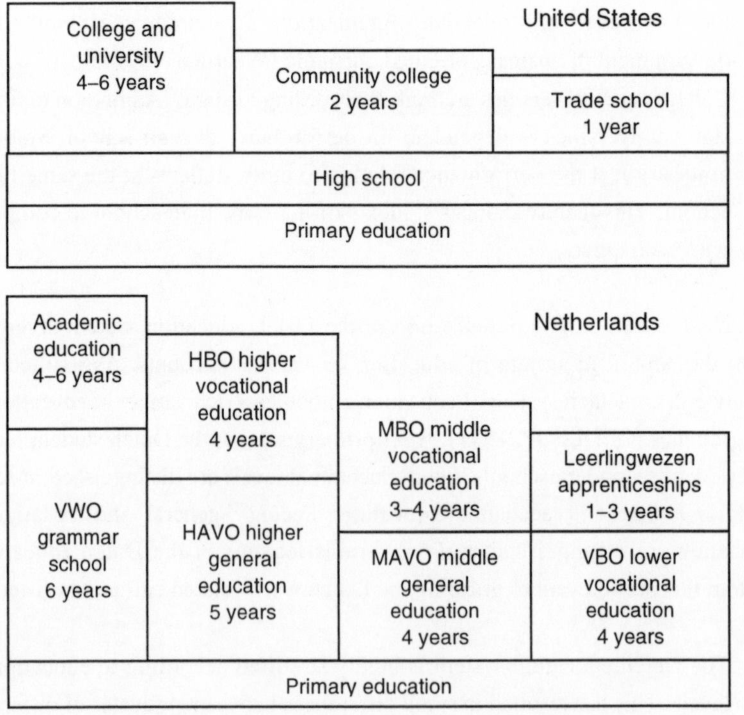

Figure 5.2 The American versus the Dutch educational system

Industrial relations

The United States The American system of industrial relations is characterized by a weak role of the state, a decentralized system of collective bargaining and an adverse relationship between employers and unions (see Table 5.6).

Table 5.6 The American versus the Dutch system of industrial relations

	United States	Netherlands
Role of the state	Weak (focus on process)	Dominant (focus on outcomes)
Reliance on jurisprudence	Strong	Weak
Locus of power	Decentralized	Centralized
Union influence	Local	National/sectoral
Interaction	Power bargaining	Consultative
Nature of relationship	Adversarial	Consensual

Source: Nijs (1996).

Historically, both employers and employees have resisted state intervention (Wheeler, 1993). The proper functioning of the market mechanism is supposed to reconcile the opposite interests of the employers and employees. The only role left to the state is to ensure that the market process is not obstructed by the presence of dominant market power on the side of either the employers or the employees. Accordingly, government regulation in the United States is directed towards the accomplishment of an appropriate balance of power between employers and employees. The state does not interfere with the terms and conditions of employment. Rather, the state ensures a 'fair' bargaining process through which the contract between the market actors is shaped.[15]

A further principle that is reflected by the American industrial relations system is the idea of populism. Unions acquire the right to act as representative of employees in a collective bargaining process only after a so-called 'representation ballot' has demonstrated the support of the majority of the workers.[16] Such ballots take place at the level of the 'establishment', such as the production plant, which gives the American system of industrial relations its decentralized nature. Moreover, the system of representation elections has divided American industry into a unionized and a non-unionized sector (Kochan et al., 1986).[17] Since managers in a non-unionized environment have more discretion and control, as they are not hindered by union interference, American management tends to use power to keep its workforce union-free. This feature contributes to the adversarial relationship between employers and unions (Jacoby, 1991).[18]

Owing to the limited role of government regulation, the American system of industrial relations is highly influenced by the attitudes and judgments of the jurisdiction. A number of rights and obligations of employees and employers are not written down as laws, but are legitimized by the jurisprudence of the American courts. The right of employers to replace strikers and the duty of fair representation and no-strike clauses are examples. Court decisions are also the basis of the distinction between mandatory and permissive bargaining subjects. The distinction holds that unions can only play a role in setting wages and working conditions. Management is given the right to manage and will retain the initiative with respect to strategic and entrepreneurial decisions ('management prerogatives'). The workers' right to negotiate is restricted to the impact of managerial decisions on employment conditions.

The Netherlands The traditional system of industrial relations in the Netherlands is largely a product of the reconstruction of the economy after the Second World War (Visser, 1992; Albeda and Dercksen, 1994). The system reflects the basic values of Dutch society, such as a preference for state intervention and decision making based on consultation and consensus (Burgess, 1991). Above, Table 5.6 lists some main features.

The role of the state in the organization of the industrial relations system was particularly dominant in the Dutch situation after the Second World War. During the period of 'centralized wage policy' (1945–63), market principles played no role in determining the wage level. The conditions of social–economic life were constructed by a cooperative effort of government, employer associations and unions. Furthermore, the state issued laws that regulated the employment relationship (for example, dismissal protection, collective bargaining, codetermination and working conditions). The objective of these legal provisions was to ensure just outcomes and to eliminate conflicts between employers and employees. Most of these institutions are still in existence.

The traditional Dutch system of industrial relations is further characterized by its centralized nature. At national level, the relation between employers and employees is institutionalized by organizations such as the 'Stichting van de Arbeid' (Foundation of Labour) and the 'SER' (Social Economic Council). At industry level, the interaction between employers and employees is formalized by the negotiation of the collective labour agreement. The influence of individual employers and local union officials in this system of industrial relations is limited. The interaction of employers and employees at the workplace level is realized by the instalment of the works council. Finally, it should be noted that the attitude of the industrial players is characterized by an emphasis on 'consultation' and 'striving for consensus'. This attitude is in contrast with the principle of bargaining that underpins the interaction in the American industrial relations system (see Table 5.7).

Table 5.7 Distinction between consultation and bargaining

	Consultation (NL)	Bargaining (US)
Starting-point	A problem	A conflict of interest
Objective	Consensus	Contract
Attitude	Cooperative	Competitive
Means	Discussion	Pressure/power

Source: Nijs (1996).

Labour legislation

The United States It was pointed out earlier that the position of the national government in the United States is relatively weak.[19] The American constitution requires public government to share its power with the various jurisdictional bodies. This peculiar division of power stresses the importance of law and renders the jurisprudence of courts influential: 'The exceptional focus on law here as compared to Europe, derived from the Constitution and the Bill of Rights, has stressed rights against the state and other powers. America began and continues as the most anti-statist, legalistic and rights-oriented nation' (Lipset, 1996, p.20).

In view of the above, a sufficient account of American labour legislation needs to refer to formal labour laws, as well as to their interpretation by the courts. Atleson (1983) analyses the judgments of the American courts in order to uncover their underlying values with respect to the employment relationship. He concludes that the American courts are driven by five hidden assumptions. First, 'continuity of production must be ensured'. This assumption is reflected by the right, bestowed upon employers by the courts, to replace strikers. Second, 'employees act irresponsibly unless they are controlled'. It is assumed that employees are 'strike-prone' and that greater employee freedom would result in 'anarchy'. Third, 'employees owe a certain degree of respect and deference to their employers'. Fourth, 'the enterprise should be under control of management'. The workplace is perceived as the property of the employer. Although the notion of a 'common enterprise' is present in labour law, judicial decisions assume that employees constitute a relatively minor part of this entity. The emphasis on property rights denies the employee the right to regulate their work effort and to solicit for union organization on company property. Fifth, 'employees are not considered full partners in the enterprise'. It is believed that such a consideration would interfere with the inherent and exclusive managerial rights of employers.

According to Atleson (1983), one needs to trace the roots of these underlying assumptions back to the merger between contract and master–servant law. Master–servant law stresses certain assumptions of obedience and obligation. Contract law reflects a free market system of voluntary cooperation. Employees are employees at will. Employees voluntarily choose to accept the employer's authority in exchange for a wage. Accordingly, in the absence of an employment contract stating otherwise, every contract of employment can be terminated at will.[20]

The Netherlands Unlike the government in the United States, the Dutch government has significant control over the legal system. It has developed a system of labour legislation that contrasts with the American labour law. This contrast reflects the different assumptions about the employment relationship. Dutch law recognizes the role of employees as stakeholders in the private enterprise. The regulation of codetermination, the peculiar position of the supervisory board and the regulation of the employment contract are institutions that reflect this recognition. Moreover, Dutch labour law is primarily concerned with the legal rights of the employees as a collective and pays only limited attention to employees as individuals (Peijpe, 1990).[21] Below, three main areas of state regulation that are in contrast with the American work-related culture are considered.

The first main element of regulation of the employment relationship is the regulation of the individual employment contract. The employment contract delimits the rights and duties of the employer. Commonly, the employment contract does not specify the period of the employment relationship. Rather, the duration of the contract is assumed to be unlimited. Dutch labour law makes firing procedures lengthy and costly for employers.[22]

A second group of regulations concerns working conditions. The Work Environment Act is the main regulation in this area. The Act is characterized by a broad perspective on working conditions. An essential element, besides aspects such as 'safety' and 'health', is the quality of working life. Moreover, the Act prescribes that proper working conditions should be achieved by codetermination of employer and employees.

The third group of regulations concerns codetermination. The Works Council Act of 1950 (amended in 1971 and 1979) addresses this issue. This Act aims to democratize the corporation by giving employees certain rights on managerial issues. Works councils consist of directly elected employees from the enterprise who are independent of management. The works councils are granted a number of statutory rights. These are grouped into 'information rights', 'consultative rights', 'rights of agreement' and 'rights of appointment'.

Corporate governance

The United States Corporate governance refers to the relationship between capital–owners and the management of the private enterprise. Different models of corporate governance can be distinguished across different nation states (Charkham, 1994). The American model of corporate governance is characterized as a 'shareholder democracy'. This term indicates that corporate management is primarily subject to the appraisal of shareholders (Blair, 1995). The various characteristics of the American system of corporate governance that justify this label are listed in Table 5.8.

The power of shareholders in the American system originates from several features of the system. A first source of the shareholders' power is the right to elect the Board of Directors to which executive management is accountable (Charkham, 1994).[23] The other main source of the power in the hands of shareholders to discipline management is the exit option, which shareholders use if they disagree with management's strategies or if they are disappointed by the performance of the company. Falling share prices signal the necessity for managers to improve performance. The exit option is effective in disciplining management, because a substantial part of management's earnings is related to the value of the stocks. Moreover, threats of hostile takeover bids are realistic since protective measures to prevent hostile bids are difficult to implement.

Table 5.8 Corporate governance models of the United States and the Netherlands

	United States	Netherlands
Main source of finance	Equity	Balance between equity and credit
Monitoring board		
- System	- one-tier board (board of directors)	- two-tier system: independent monitoring board
- Appointed by	- shareholders	- 'cooption' + approval of shareholders and works council
- Objective	- shareholder value	- continuity of the company
Shareholder control		
- position of shareholder	- strong	- weak
- managerial shareholding	- significant	- small
Creditor control		
- position of creditor	- weak	- strong
- representation on monitoring board	- none	- substantial
General assessment	Market orientation, focus on short-term objectives, profit-oriented, shareholder value	Inside orientation, focus on long-term objectives, market share, stability and continuity

Source: Gelauff and Broeder (1996).

The Netherlands The Dutch system of corporate governance deviates in a number of respects from the American system (Gerlauff and Broeder, 1996). Management in the Netherlands is fairly shielded from the whims of the shareholders. Appraisal of management is conducted by an independent supervisory board whose members are appointed through cooption. Both shareholders and works council have the right of approval. The supervisory board is legally obliged to transcend a narrow focus on the company's stocks and to assume a role in ensuring the continuity of the company. The efficacy of protective mechanisms against hostile takeovers and the absence of widespread managerial shareholdings further weaken the power of the shareholder. The weakness of the shareholder's position is balanced by a relatively strong position of creditors. Commonly, representatives of the main creditors occupy a seat on a company's supervisory board. They monitor the company from a creditor perspective. Such a perspective emphasizes continuity and stability rather than the magnitude of the profits in the short term.

Welfare system

The United States The welfare system of the United States corresponds to the liberal value system (Esping-Andersen, 1990).[24] The market mechanism is sovereign in a liberal welfare system (see Table 5.9). Social problems are to be solved primarily through the market. Illness, disability, unemployment and ageing should be dealt with by means of private insurance companies. Poverty is the main problem that cannot be solved by the market. Hence the provision of welfare to the poor is the major component of the liberal welfare system. However, such state intervention should not disturb the working of the market. Accordingly, benefits are low, their duration is short and the criteria for eligibility are strict. Furthermore, benefits are 'means-tested'. One is eligible only in the case of objective needs and in the absence of other resources. The central characteristics of the American welfare state are in line with this liberal model: limited social security programmes, emphasis on economic opportunity and concern for individual and local responsibility (Maremor, 1990).

The Netherlands The difference between the American and Dutch welfare system can be traced to the difference between the economic individualism in the United States and the cultural individualism in the Netherlands. While the American welfare state reflects the liberal ideology, the Dutch model of welfare is characterized as 'a typical product of consociational concertation and compromise' (Engbersen et al., 1993). The Dutch welfare system reflects the division of power in Dutch society across the different ideological and social groups (liberals, social democrats, Calvinists and Catholics). It contains elements of all three models (see Table 5.9). Compulsory workmen's insurance that has been the guiding principle of the corporatist model is reflected by the general disability plan, sickness insurance and unemployment provisions. The social democratic model is reflected by the universal state pensions, widows' insurance and children's allowance plans and exceptional health costs. The National Assistance Act reflects the liberal strand in Dutch society. Furthermore, liberalism is partly expressed by the national system of health insurance and pensions. For, if one's personal income exceeds a certain level, one needs to acquire insurance from private firms.

Table 5.9 Characteristics of different welfare systems

	Liberal		Corporatist	Social-democratic
Type of social security	means- and needs-tested	voluntary insurance	state-compulsory social insurance	flat-rate state pension
Institution protected	market	market	family, church, private associations	government agencies
Population coverage	small	small	medium/large	large
Target group	the poor	middle class	Employees	all citizens who satisfy criteria
Level of benefits	low	variable	high	low
State involvement	high	low	medium	high
Predominant in	USA, Australia	USA, Australia	Germany, Austria	Sweden, Norway

Source: Engbersen et al. (1993).

American and Dutch Corporate Employment Practices

The previous sections illuminate the formal and informal societal institutions that constitute the American and Dutch work-related culture. They show that the American cultural system emphasizes, among other things, economic individualism, power bargaining, reliance on market principles and masculinity. The Dutch cultural system emphasizes, among other things, group thinking, consensual decision making, state interference and femininity. This section will analyse the interdependence of these broader cultural traits with the employment practices that dominate among private firms. Four areas of employment practices are distinguished: work organization, human resource flow, reward system and employee participation. Each element is considered below.

Work organization

Work organization refers to the division of work into separate jobs. The work organization defines the job content for the individual worker in terms of responsibilities and required skills. It is argued below that the contrast between work organization in the United States and in the Netherlands corresponds to the contrast between a 'Taylorist' and a 'sociotechnical' approach towards work organization (see Table 5.10).

Table 5.10 Work organization (US versus NL)

	United States	Netherlands
Job content	Jobs are narrow, work is fragmented;	Broad job design to emphasize whole task;
	Sharp delineation of individual responsibilities;	Responsibilities are defined for the group;
	Coordination and control rely on rigid formal rules and procedures;	Coordination and control based on shared goals and values
	Separation of doing and thinking	Combination of doing & thinking
	Individual job restructuring	Group job restructuring
Required skills	Skills are specific to the job;	Broad and in-depth work skills;
	Skills are acquired by 'on-the-job' training;	Reliance on public vocational education;
	Emphasis on behavioural features	Emphasis on professional skills

The United States Taylorism is the dominant principle of work organization in the United States. The scientific management principles put forward by Taylor can be summarised by three elements (Littler, 1982). First, work is decomposed into its simplest constituent elements. Individual jobs should be limited to a single task. Second, planning and doing are separated. The 'planning department' coordinates the entire manufacturing process. It prescribes the sequence of tasks and the standard operating procedures to accomplish the tasks. Third, the Taylorist work system is characterized by the division of individual responsibility: everybody works for a direct supervisor who coordinates and allocates the responsibilities. Subordinates are held individually accountable and report to their direct supervisor. In this system, there is always an individual who is responsible for taking a decision; that is, 'someone who runs the show' (Iribarne, 1989).

The enduring influence of Taylor's principles on work organization in the United States is recognized by a wide variety of management pundits (Littler, 1982; Beer et al., 1984; Walton, 1985; Skinner, 1985; Dertouzos et al., 1989; Appelbaum and Batt, 1994).[25] The reliance of American management on scientific management principles is not turned off by the introduction of new flexible manufacturing systems in the United States (Jaikumar, 1986). Further evidence of the enduring influence of Taylorist work methods is delivered by a study on skill requirements of American industry (NCEE, 1991). The results of the study present 'a picture of an economy that has designed most of its non-college graduate jobs for unskilled workers with little educational attainment' (ibid., p.2). They show that hiring decisions are completely disconnected from the education system, for American employers do not perceive lack of education as a major deficiency. Employers are more concerned with the attitudinal characteristics of the workforce.[26]

The Netherlands The Taylorist model in its pure form has not been introduced in the Netherlands owing to the critical stance of the Dutch labour movement towards the developments taking place in the United States. Yet, in the 1920s, it accepted scientific management under certain provisions that aimed to mitigate the negative consequences of rationalization (Laurier and Pot, 1983; Bloemen, 1988). Employee participation, social control and reduced working times were among these conditions. Sorge (1992) notes the conflict in the Netherlands between the Tayloristic hierarchical and professional specialist control and the strong traditional forms of peer control based on group thinking. He argues that this conflict has been overcome by the implementation of so-called 'sociotechnical approaches' to work organization. In these approaches, peer control has been retained in work organization by means of job enrichment, autonomous work groups, shortening of hierarchical distances and participation in decision making.

In the course of the 1980s, work organization in the Netherlands was further influenced by the sociotechnical approach through the academic work of De Sitter, the consultancy firm 'Koers' and experiments within the Dutch Postal Services and the electronics company, Philips (Haak, 1994). According to the sociotechnical model, groupwork and integration of control and operations should replace the division of labour and the creation of individual tasks (Sitter et al., 1997). It prescribes the instalment of 'whole task groups' at the shopfloor level. Such a group is responsible not only for work directly related to production, but also for supportive and control tasks, such as planning, material handling, small repair jobs, maintenance and problem solving. Moreover, individuals are able to switch tasks with other group members. This ensures more variability in the job content of the individual group member.

Human resource flow

Human resource flow refers to the flow of people in, through and out of the corporation. Management of the human resource flow is thus concerned with recruitment, training, promotion and termination. The differences between the American and the Dutch mode of managing the human resource flow coincide with reliance on, respectively, external or internal labour market mechanisms (see Table 5.11).

Table 5.11 Human resource flow management (US versus NL)

	United States	Netherlands
Recruitment	Focus on quantity and 'on-the-job' performance	Focus on quality and educational background
Performance appraisal	Individual is accountable Objectives are clearly spelled out Criteria are quantitative and objective Performance appraisal is linked with pay Emphasis on low and high performers	Teams are accountable Role in the team is emphasized Criteria are open to outside influences Appraisal is linked with needs of the employee Emphasis on large middle group
Promotion	Rapid promotion tracks for good performers	Promotion track is steady and structured
Training	Priority for market to 'buy' trained people	Priority for training to preserve productivity of incumbent employees
Termination	Dismissal is easy and frequent	Commitment to life-time-employment

The United States American firms are unaffected for the most part by government regulation of staffing policies. Hence American firms were able to develop employment policies that gave them maximal freedom to move employees into and out of the organization (Begin, 1997). American companies regard the external labour market as a cost-effective mechanism to fill job positions. In accordance with the principles of scientific management, individual jobs are designed in such a way that the dependence of the organization on individual availability, ability or motivation is minimized. In a Tayloristic work organization, workers are interchangeable resources for the organization. Accordingly, firms invest only a limited amount of financial resources in the formal training of their employees (Osterman, 1995). The main form of training is 'on the job'. The preference for the external market is reflected in the practice of attracting trained people from outside the corporation. Accordingly, job mobility is high. 'Job hopping' is regarded as a way to ensure promotion and to increase salary (Begin, 1997). However, well-performing employees are considered as assets that should be retained. Accordingly, management of personnel is characterized as 'management of the tail'. Attention is focused on those employees who perform with above-average efficiency and those employees whose performance is below average. The upper performers are to be retained and to be shielded from the external labour market by means of pay rises, job opportunities and training. The low performers are to be returned to the external labour market. Dismissal based on poor performance is legitimate.

The Netherlands Sorge (1992) notes the prevalence of paternalistic concepts of the enterprise in the Netherlands. This paternalism has resulted in a sensitivity towards employees' work, career and social needs 'from the cradle to the grave'. An extensive system of fringe benefits, pension funds, employment guarantees and reliance on internal labour market mechanisms is a reflection of this sensitivity.

The reliance on the internal labour market entails various mechanisms to foster the mutual dependence between the company and the employees. Social group pressure, promotion opportunities and the provision of benefits increase the dependence of the employee on the firm. Social group pressure emphasizes company loyalty and rejects so-called 'job hopping' (Lawrence, 1991). Promotion trajectories are slow and steady and based on skills and seniority. Moreover, benefits are partly tied to the company.

The dependence of the company on its employees follows from the work organization and is reinforced by social pressure and labour law. The sociotechnical approach to work organization requires a broadly skilled and trained workforce. The provision of cross-training increases the value of the employee to the organization. Furthermore, Dutch companies tend to be reluctant to sanction poor performance in terms of dismissal. One reason for this is the protection offered to the employee by labour legislation. However, Lawrence (1991) regards morality as the decisive factor. He emphasizes that the Dutch are reluctant to judge individual behaviour without taking external factors into account.

Since dismissal is rare and job mobility is slight, managerial attention is not confined to the 'tail'. Instead, the large middle group of average performers is the main object of performance appraisal. Appraisal is concerned with the individual's contribution to group objectives. Moreover, ample attention is given to the manner in which the productivity of the employee can be sustained during his or her employment by the company.

Reward system

The reward system can be categorized on the basis of two dimensions. First, rewards can be extrinsic to the job performed, such as material rewards, or the reward can be intrinsic to the job. Second, rewards are provided on either an individual or a collective basis. The different reward preferences of American and Dutch employees reflect the difference between the value patterns in the United States and the Netherlands (see Table 5.12). The dominant reward system in the Netherlands emphasizes 'collective benefits' and 'job satisfaction'. The American employee favours pecuniary rewards on an individual basis.

The United States American reward practices reflect the dominance of masculine and individual values. Masculinity underlies the preference for extrinsic rewards and the low emphasis on job satisfaction.[27] Employee commitment is bought by money. The influence of individualism is apparent in a number of practices. Merit pay systems emphasize individual performance (Begin, 1997). Wide pay differentials are accepted. Supervisors have more possibilities to reward subordinates on an individual basis.[28] Likewise, an employee can bargain on an individual basis to arrive at a salary level that reflects his personal worth to the company. Furthermore, individualism is reflected by the limited importance that is accorded to benefits. The individual is held responsible for guaranteeing future life security.

Table 5.12 Reward systems (US versus NL)

	United States	Netherlands
Intrinsic versus extrinsic	Preference for material incentives, such as pay	Preference for intrinsic rewards, such as job satisfaction, congenial colleagues and work environment
Collective versus individual	Focus on individual performance (merit rises)	Focus on employees as group (profit sharing)
	Ample room for individual recognition	Rigid collective pay structures
	Pay is geared to individual job evaluation	Pay is linked to seniority and skills
	Wide pay differentials are accepted	Pay differentials are muted
	Benefits are individualized	Collective benefits are emphasized

The Netherlands The Dutch reward system reflects the dominance of group thinking and the feminine value pattern in the Netherlands. Hofstede (1975) demonstrates how femininity underlies the relative importance that Dutch employees attach to various work goals. Relative to other European workers, Dutch workers attach more importance to work goals, such as 'to live in an area desirable to you and your family', 'to have good fringe benefits' and 'to work with people who cooperate well with each other'. Moreover, the Dutch attach the lowest importance to monetary earnings. Accordingly, Hofstede (1975) concludes that the Dutch are a people 'who care more about benefits than earnings, who value the family more than the company, who find cooperation with colleagues more important than advancement and excelling in the eyes of others; for whom job freedom counts more than success (...) and who finally are not preoccupied with employment security' (p.26).

A historical analysis of Dutch union policy confirms this preference. Generally, Dutch unions have accepted wage moderation, but they have stressed extension of benefits and reduction of working hours (Visser, 1992). Emphasis on benefits and the rigid structure of pay levels reflect the Dutch values of group thinking, solidarity and uncertainty avoidance. Individual rewards are uncommon. Moreover, the collective payment of bonuses that reflect corporate performance is a widespread practice.

Employee participation

Employee participation refers to the relation between management and employees at two levels: first, the relation between supervisor and subordinate at the workplace level; second, the relation between management and employees at the plant level. Below, it will be argued that at both levels the distance between managerial and non-managerial employees is greater in the United States than in the Netherlands (see Table 5.13).

Table 5.13 Employee participation (US versus NL)

	United States	Netherlands
Workplace relationships	Sharp status distinctions Room for discretionary power of supervisor Use of authoritarian pressure and sanctions	Status differences are muted Little discretionary power of supervisor Use of consultation to reach consensus
Participation at plant level	Voluntary management method to increase productivity Focus on the needs of the company Management prerogatives	Societal obligation to promote industrial democracy Focus on the needs of employees and company Participation concerns wide range of issues

The United States American workplace relations are characterized by a large power distance between the supervisor and his immediate subordinates. The Taylorist way to organize work (individual accountability) in combination with ample discretionary powers of the supervisor (performance appraisal, determination of pay level, disciplining) seems to be responsible for the existence of fear at the workplace (Starkey and McKinlay, 1993). The following description of unwritten rules is typical of American shopfloor relations: 'Don't disagree with the boss; Don't rock the boat; Look busy even if you're not; Don't smile, let alone laugh too much; Be obsessive about getting your numbers right, estimates won't help; CYA (cover your ass); If a colleague gets into trouble with the boss – don't help, be grateful it's not you; Observe the dress code' (Starkey and McKinlay, 1993, p.43).

At the plant level, the relationship between workers and management is characterized by the existence of so-called 'management prerogatives'. Since there is no public policy mandating worker participation, employees can only get involved in governance activities by management on a voluntary basis. The needs of the company are central rather than the quality of work life. Moreover, programmes designed to enhance the participation of workers do not affect the so-called management prerogatives (Jaggi, 1992). Instead, programmes to enhance cooperation between management and employees concentrate on the survival of the company. The initiative for employee participation programmes is with management, who support their introduction as a method to improve effective communication. Programmes such as work committees, employee suggestion schemes and quality circles are accepted within the framework of productivity, profitability and management prerogatives.

The Netherlands Iribarne (1989) characterizes human relations on the typical Dutch workplace by the absence of authoritarian power. To coordinate work organization, a Dutch supervisor cannot make use of his hierarchical position by giving orders and using sanctions. The only means at his disposal is persuasion on the basis of convincing arguments and discussion. In the process, it is necessary to accept the recommendations of his subordinates and to reach consensus. The following observation captures the position of the Dutch supervisor: 'Speaking, discussing, explaining and convincing pay off. The Dutch appear to be as open to good reason as they are allergic to pressure (...) It is necessary to speak a lot. Motivating is easy if one takes the effort to explain. When I give an order, I always have to explain and speak. If I don't, I run the risk that the order will not be carried out. Explaining should be considered as the most efficient way to manage in the Netherlands, in the same way as one speaks about sanctioning in the United States' (Iribarne, 1989, p.213).

Employee participation at the plant level is a formal arrangement based on a wider concern to democratize labour relations. The conflict of interest between employees and management is acknowledged, but codetermination is seen as a means to resolve this conflict. The primary mechanism is regular consultation with the works councils and the union representatives. McFarlin et al. (1992) reveal the different attitudes towards employee participation as between

American and Dutch managers. First, they observe that American management prefers to implement employee participation by means of formal programmes, such as self-directed work teams. Furthermore, employee participation is considered by American management as a tool to enhance performance ('improving the bottom line'), rather than as a means to improve relationships and quality of working life. Also, American managers are less convinced that their subordinates desire participation. In contrast, Dutch managers appear to be sceptical about certain American initiatives. They view participation as a societal obligation to workers. Dutch managers do not understand the need for a separate programme to improve participation, because the works council already provides ample opportunity. Furthermore, Dutch managers reject the American 'obsession' with formal, programmatic efforts to improve productivity via employee participation programmes. They feel that the programmatic, formalized nature of American efforts to improve participation is inconsistent with their own style for dealing with the needs of their subordinates. The societal expectations in the Netherlands force managers to operate on an informal basis. To get anything done, one needs to ask for subordinate input on a regular basis and to rely on persuasion rather than hierarchical power.

Clustering the Work-related Institutions

The previous sections examined the various societal institutions that make up the ideal-type of the American and Dutch work-related culture. To complete the ideal-type construction, the final task is to relate the various institutions in a coherent cluster. Below, the cluster of work-related institutions of, respectively, the United States and the Netherlands are outlined. Figure 5.3 depicts them in a schematic way.

American work-related culture

The previous sections outlined the dominant work-related institutions of the United States. The distinct value pattern of the American population is characterized by anti-statism, individualism, equality of opportunity, populism, masculinity and inner-directedness. The organization of society is based on the rejection of state interference and the prevalence of the market mechanism. The dominant employment practices are a Taylorist work organization, reliance on external labour market principles, a reward system that is based on individual

Figure 5.3 The American versus the Dutch work-related culture

and material rewards, and limited employee participation. Below, some of the major links between the three parts of the work-related culture are explicated.[29]

- The sharp delineation of individual responsibilities that characterizes a Taylorist work organization is consistent with the dominance of the individualist value pattern. Furthermore, a Taylorist work organization is consistent with the reliance on the market mechanism as workers are replaceable on the external labour market.
- A work organization based on Taylorist principles is more likely to develop in a society where 'management prerogative' prevails. The absence of state interference and the limited degree of employee participation leave management with the freedom to organize the workplace. Generally, management values efficiency and control at the cost of the quality of

working life.

- The American education system has developed in accordance with the Taylorist principles on which business is organized. The division into college-educated and non-college-educated that results from the education system corresponds neatly to the distinction between managerial and non-managerial employees. Moreover, the lack of a vocational education and, consequently, sophisticated technical skills at the workplace level does not harm a Taylorist work organization in which jobs are defined in a narrow manner and responsibilities are sharply delineated.
- The adverse relationship between managerial and non-managerial workers at both the plant and the workplace level can be related to the system of industrial relations (ballot system) and the education system (college- versus non-college-educated students). Moreover, the dominant position of the managerial population is reinforced by the limited welfare system and the lack of government regulation to protect employees from dismissal.
- The reward system (individualist, materialist) is consistent with the American masculine and individualist value pattern.

Dutch work-related culture

The cluster of Dutch work-related institutions has its origins in the interplay between the various groups that have dominated Dutch history: liberals, Protestants, Catholics and socialists. Underlying the organization of Dutch society is the pursuit of consensus and accommodation between these groups. The responsibility of the relatively strong state is to bring about such a consensus. Accordingly, one can trace elements of each subgroup in the organization of Dutch society. In brief, societal organization is based on consultation and accommodation. The dominant value pattern in the Netherlands includes group conformism, a pursuit of equality of outcome and femininity. The dominant employment practices are a work organization that is based on principles of sociotechnical work design, reliance on internal labour market mechanisms, a reward system that is based on intrinsic incentives and that ignores individual differences among employees and, finally, ample room for employee participation. The major links between the three institutional categories include the following:

- The reliance of the work organization on sociotechnical principles is related to the educational system (workers tend to have high skills), reliance on internal labour market principles and the role that is assigned to collective representations of labour.

- The view on employee participation is based on the orientation towards consensus and the preference for accommodating differences of interest.
- The lack of authoritarian power of Dutch managers cannot be understood without reference to the educational system (there are only gradual differences in skill levels), the Dutch labour law (inhibits dismissal), the welfare system (minimizes risks of dismissal) and the role of collective representations of labour.
- The reward system (collective, intangible) is consistent with the Dutch value pattern that includes values such as femininity, group conformism and the Dutch preference for equal outcomes.

CHANGE OF THE EMPLOYMENT RELATIONSHIP

The comparative study of the United States and the Netherlands comprises two branches (see Figure 5.1). The aim of the first branch is to describe, respectively, the American and Dutch work-related culture. This task has been completed in the previous section. The present section focuses on the second branch of the research design. It describes recent developments in the realm of the employment relationship in both countries. The aim is to identify the extent to which the employment relationship has developed in a similar or a distinct manner in the two countries.

Data on the development of the employment relationship are collected by analysis of recent change processes that are realized by private firms. This section is based on data that are collected by means of case studies of four multinational enterprises operating in the global chemical industry: General Electric, Dow Chemical, Akzo Nobel and DSM. Pot (1998) contains a detailed report on the employment developments across these companies during the period 1985–97. This section presents a summary of the main findings of this study. The inquiry focused on three aspects of employment-related change processes, namely the strategic content, the procedure and the actual outcomes.[30] Furthermore, the inquiry incorporated change processes that are initiated at various hierarchical levels of the corporations, such as the corporate, business unit, geographical and production plant level. The data were collected primarily by means of company documents and interviews with key actors. The investigation at the higher hierarchical levels of the companies, such as the corporate, business unit and geographical level, relied relatively more on document analysis. Interviewing was the dominant research method at the level of the production establishments.[31]

The specific selection of the case study sites allows for three types of comparative analysis. The three modes of comparison are represented by Figure 5.4. The first comparison (I) concentrates on the common developments in employment relations. In other words, it identifies the trends that are similar across the four companies in both the Netherlands and the United States. The findings that have resulted from this analysis are described next. There follows a comparative analysis based on the distinct nationality of the parent company (II). The analysis separates the two Dutch from the two American multinational firms. This mode of comparison focuses on the new employment practices that are initiated at the higher hierarchical levels, such as the corporate, business unit and geographical level. Finally, we concentrate on the level of the production plant (III). For each company, the developments in the American plant are contrasted to the developments in the plant that is located in the Netherlands. In this way differences between the change processes at the level of the production plant are identified.

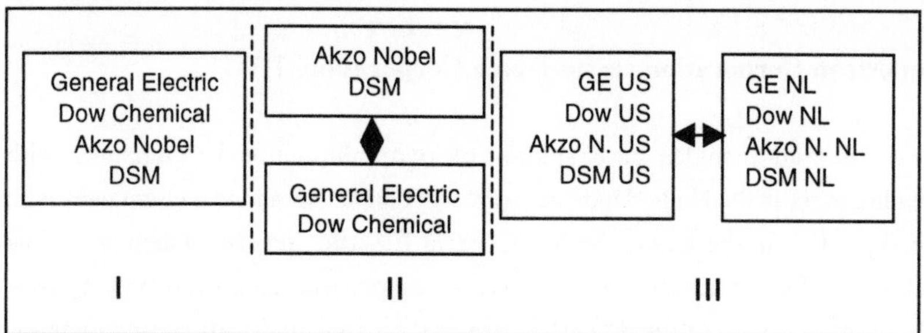

Figure 5.4 Three modes of comparative analysis

Similar Trends across the Four Cases (I)

A number of similar trends can be observed across the four companies that are independent of cultural background. Most notably, all companies have engaged in substantial delayering efforts and rationalization of the organizational structure. This development has been accompanied by a substantial reduction of employment in all companies. The new, leaner organizations are characterized by a dual management structure that consists of management layers at the corporate and the business unit level. In line with this reorganization of responsibilities, the autonomy of business unit management has increased, while the role of other management levels, such as the geographical and functional organizational layers, has been reduced. These organizational layers are increasingly considered as service units for corporate and business unit management.

A further common development is the adoption of similar management methods. Customer focus, business process re-engineering, total quality management, empowerment and teamwork have become common terminology within each company. These abstract management principles have been applied concretely at the plant level. The production facilities are increasingly operated by fewer operators. This is a trend that has been accompanied by the introduction of more advanced production technologies, the functional integration of operational activities, the introduction of team-based forms of work organization and the involvement of operators in improvement trajectories. In line with these changes, the firms expect greater functional and temporal flexibility from the operators.

American Corporation versus Dutch Corporation (II)

The research includes case studies of two multinational companies with headquarters in the Netherlands, Akzo Nobel and DSM, and two companies with headquarters in the United States, General Electric and Dow Chemical. This selection of the research objects allows for the pairwise comparative analysis of Dutch-based multinationals versus American-based multinational companies. The hierarchical layers that are the objects of this comparative analysis are the corporate, business unit and geographical level. At these levels, the terms of employment are shaped that condition the employment relationship at the level of the production plant. In this section, we point out some crucial differences in the change processes of employment relations that are realized by, respectively, the two American and the two Dutch companies. The following analysis is split up into a comparison of the strategic direction, the procedure and the actual outcomes of the change process.

Strategic direction

First, the developments in employment relations that are initiated by the corporate layers of the American companies, General Electric and Dow Chemical, are considered. The major development in the corporate employment strategy of General Electric entails a shift from bureaucratic control mechanisms, such as scientific management and a military-style hierarchy, towards a value-based organization that relies on shared values and common goals among management and workers.

To foster this objective, GE-corporate introduced a number of instruments. First, General Electric defined its corporate values. The 'GE-values' stated the desired mental attributes of the workforce, such as 'to have vision', 'to be accountable', 'to have a passion for excellence', 'to believe in teamwork', 'to stimulate change' and 'to be able to energize others'. Further, General Electric announced that so-called 'type IV managers' would be removed, for such managers, although they do deliver on their performance, do not believe in and promote the GE-values. General Electric continued its 'cultural transformation' with the initiative called 'Work-Out'. The emphasis that has been placed on this method is reason for Tichy and Sherman (1993, p.197) to characterize the Work-Out programme as 'one of the biggest planned efforts to alter people's behaviour since Mao's cultural revolution'. The programme aimed to redefine the relationship between the boss and the subordinate. It obliged salaried and hourly personnel to engage jointly in problem-solving exercises. Jack Welch, the chief executive officer of General Electric, comments as follows on the philosophy underlying Work-Out: 'My view of the 1990s is based on liberation of the workplace. If you want to get the benefit of everything employees have, you've got to free them, make everybody a participant. Everybody has to know everything, so they can make the right decisions by themselves' (ibid., p.204). Finally, at the geographical level, programmes to instal empowered teams on the shop floor were developed. Such empowered teams are defined as 'groups of people working together in a coordinated effort towards a common goal'. They are expected to result in productivity gains to the company as workers are provided with more responsibility.

The Dow Chemical Company initiated similar developments. Ever since the mid-1980s, Dow Chemical has followed, in its own terms, a 'Quality Performance Journey'. This journey involved, among other things, the introduction of quality circles and a continuous improvement philosophy. In 1993, a further step on the journey was taken with the launch of the programme 'Strategic Blueprint'. Among other things, the Blueprint entailed an effort to reduce the distance between management and workers by the instilling of a common mindset among Dow employees and the introduction of empowered teams on the production floor. The declaration of nine Dow corporate values, such as 'customer focus', 'value-driven', 'innovative' and 'accountable', was supposed to create the common mindset. The empowered teams were defined as 'teams that, within set boundaries, are authorized, capable and willing to manage their own activities to produce an agreed upon set of target outcomes'.

Next, consider the employment initiatives of the Dutch multinationals, Akzo Nobel and DSM. The strategic direction that underlies the many initiatives is the increase in flexibility among the various aspects of the employment relationship. At Akzo Nobel Netherlands, the primary strategic guideline since 1988 is captured by the concise phrase: 'the stronghold employee in the manoeuvrable firm'. In other words, the firm must be flexible to respond to changing requirements of the business world, while employees should become able to take care of themselves rather than to rely on the care of the corporation. This guideline is reflected by successive collective labour agreements that were negotiated with the national trade unions. The employment relationship has become more flexible on the aspect of human resource flow through measures such as the differentiation of working hours and the ability provided to employees to trade days of leave for monetary pay. Moreover, flexibility has been introduced in the reward system by means of performance-based pay and the development of flexible early retirement schemes. Finally, flexibility of the work organization is enhanced by the stress on the employability and continuous training of the employee. Akzo Nobel's chairman of the Board of Directors mentions employability as the core theme of the coming decade: 'The time is over that training was just one of the "charities" to facilitate a moderate wage development. The training provisions in the collective labour agreement will gain meaning and significance as broad employability of the employees has become a central objective' (internal communications magazine, Akzo Nobel Netherlands, September 1996).

At DSM Netherlands, a similar development has occurred. The common thread that runs through the various initiatives that apply to the Dutch employee population of DSM is the increase of flexibility. Flexibility is enhanced by a multitude of measures. Examples are the strategy to hold a minimum of fixed capacity that is assisted by a maximum of temporary assignments, a proactive outflow policy in management development programmes, an employment philosophy that is 'conscious of age', aiming to keep ageing employees valuable to the company through continuous training, more flexible reward systems, the use of labour pools and the enhancement of the employability of the employees.

Procedure

Consider first the procedure by which the change processes were realized at the two American companies, General Electric and Dow Chemical. It appears that the dominant actors that shaped the employment conditions were staff members who operate at the corporate management level. Both at General Electric and at Dow Chemical, management at the corporate level designed the employment strategy and associated tools that were supposed to apply to each local establishment, irrespective of national boundaries. At General Electric, the 'Work-Out' programme and the formulation of the 'GE-values' reflect this procedural aspect. At Dow Chemical, the various global programmes that resulted from the overarching framework of the 'Strategic Blueprint' are illustrative. In accordance with the dominant position of the corporate level, the role of other organizational layers in shaping the employment initiatives is limited. The role of business unit management and geographical management is restricted to the proper implementation of the global programmes. Moreover, other stakeholders, such as trade unions, play no part in the formulation of the employment strategy. Corporate management in consultation with staff and external management consultants shape the employment conditions that apply to the company's establishments irrespective of national borders.

Within the two Dutch multinational corporations, Akzo Nobel and DSM, the role of corporate management with regard to the development of the employment strategy is limited. The corporate layers of Akzo Nobel and DSM have issued a few guidelines with global width. However, since these guidelines are few and of a very general nature, the lower management layers are left with ample autonomy. Accordingly, both the business unit layer and the geographical layer play a more important role in creating the employment strategy. At the business unit level, employment programmes are designed that have worldwide applicability to the establishments of the business unit. The actors that are involved in the design of such programmes are cross-national teams supported by external consultants. The programmes that are designed in this way are in close alignment with the global management literature, such as Akzo Nobel's 'Managing Total Quality' programme and the global change programme 'Olympus' initiated by DSM business unit Elastomers.

A further distinct characteristic of the procedure by which the employment conditions are created among the Dutch companies is the presence of a separate national layer for employment issues in the Netherlands. While no distinct American division separates the corporate level from the local sites with regard to employment issues in the United States, the Dutch companies have installed a specialized Dutch personnel department. At this level, a set of employment strategies is designed that applies solely to the Dutch employees. It is important to note that the relevant actors at this level are not confined to the management representatives. Instead, the employment strategy is a result of a close collaborative effort that includes management, the national trade unions and the national works council. Through regular consultation and joint study groups, management and unions develop new employment strategies that are acceptable to both. It should be noted that the interaction between management and representatives of the trade unions are no 'one-time' negotiations. The case studies of Akzo Nobel and DSM demonstrate that potential problem areas are identified at an early stage, after which management and unions engage in joint study groups to design solutions. The products of this continuous interaction are formalized after several years by the collective bargaining agreement.

Figure 5.5 contrasts the distinct roles of the various management layers in the design of the employment strategy for the American and Dutch companies.

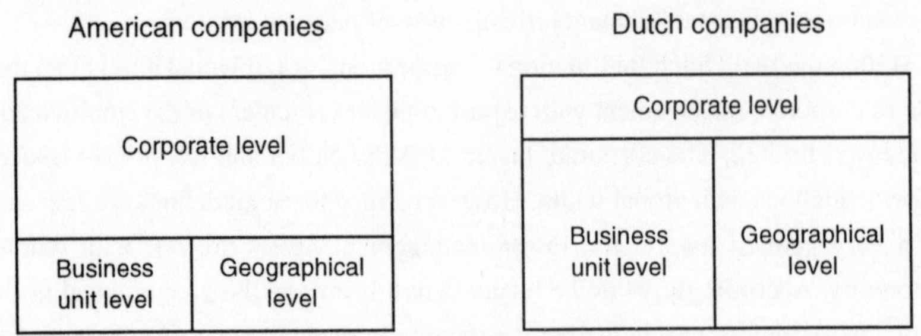

Figure 5.5 Actors involved in the formulation of the employment strategy

Actual outcomes

The prime objective of the employment strategy of the American firms was to redefine the relationship between the supervisor and the subordinates. Whether the strategic objectives have been realized should be asked at the level of the production plant. The next section, which focuses on the developments at plant level, will discuss the actual operation of the American attempts to create empowered teams on the shopfloor.

With regard to the objective of the Dutch companies to make the employment relationship more flexible, some remarks should be made on the actual outcomes. Most significantly, one can observe that flexibility is not pursued solely at the expense of employees. The trade-off between working time reduction and flexible working hours that came out of the negotiations between Akzo Nobel Netherlands and the national trade unions is illustrative. The agreement entailed that employees can be told by management to adapt their working hours to the needs of the business. At the same time, Akzo Nobel management agreed to reduce working hours from 38 to 36 hours on average a week. A similar illustration of a trade-off is the introduction of the new system of performance evaluation at DSM. The new system allows management to rank employees on the basis of performance. The agreement of the unions to link ranking with remuneration was obtained through the condition that the level of the basic salary was left unaffected. Furthermore, the issue of the rising number of temporary workers has been subjected to discussion by unions and employers' associations at a national level. In 1996, a compromise that contained, on the one hand, the facilitation of the hiring of temporary workers by firms and, on the other hand, the guarantee of sufficient rights for temporary workers was obtained (Ministerie van Sociale Zaken en Werkgelegenheid, 1995; Stichting van de Arbeid, 1996). Finally, the employers' desire to ensure the employability of the employee to enhance the flexibility of the employment relationship is given substance in consultations with the trade unions and works councils.[32] In the agreements of Akzo Nobel and DSM with trade unions, the notion of employability refers primarily to the need to preserve the skill level of the employee on both the internal and the external labour market. This is substantiated by the mutual responsibility of both employer and employee to engage in continuous training.[33]

American Plant versus Dutch Plant (III)

This section concentrates on the employment developments that are initiated at the level of the production plant. Each of the four case studies includes a matched pair of a production plant in the United States and a production plant in the Netherlands. This selection of research objects allows for the comparative analysis of change processes at the plant level between the United States and the Netherlands. The employment developments at, respectively, the American and the Dutch plants are contrasted below. Again a distinction is made between the analysis of the strategic direction, the procedure and the actual outcomes.

Strategic direction

The broad strategic direction in which the production organization develops appears to be similar across the American and the Dutch context. At each plant there are initiatives to reduce the number of operators at the shopfloor level by the introduction of more advanced production technologies and the functional integration of operational activities. Furthermore, at each plant, this trend is accompanied by the development of 'on-the-job' training systems, the introduction of various forms of teamwork and a reconsideration of the role of the first-line supervisor.

Procedure

Three interrelated elements contrast the procedural manner by which the employment-related changes have been realized at, respectively, the American and the Dutch plants: the formulation of the change objectives, the time span of the change process and the extent of interaction between management and non-managerial employees.

First, among the American plants, the change process was scheduled as a clearly defined project. Beforehand, the objectives and the time planning were strictly defined. In contrast, among the Dutch plants, the change processes were defined in process terms. The problem was identified, but the final objectives were not clearly formulated. The answers to the problems were expected to develop in a gradual manner. A prime example is the contrast between the plants of General Electric in Selkirk (USA) and Bergen op Zoom (NL). Both plants intended to organize production workers by means of 'empowered teams'. Since a corporate blueprint did not guide the transformation, management of both sites could shape the transformation according to their own insights. In the Netherlands, the transition can be characterized as a gradual change process. In the words of a Dutch manager: 'One needs to change the mind-set before one can change the structure. So we've spent a lot of time training the managers and operators in order to make the need for change clear. Then we slowly changed the structure, like a flower growing, a very natural change' (quoted in Pot, 1998, p.148). Moreover, the change process was not confined to a given time period: 'it is a continuous process in which, in the end, everybody is doing other things than they did before' (ibid., p.153). And no clear objectives were prescribed beforehand: 'if we eventually get to self direction, that's fine, but that's not the objective, the objective is to deliver on business targets' (ibid., p.147). The change process in the American plant of General Electric followed a different procedure. The shift towards empowered teams was implemented according to a planned schedule. The management manual described five stages according to which the teams should be implemented. Each stage was described in terms of the realized objectives. The complete change process was planned to take a period of 18 months. By then, teams were expected to have gained autonomy in various areas, such as disciplinary action, budgeting, performance appraisal, purchase, vacation scheduling and so on. In the words of an operator: 'They gave us a date, then it's gonna happen, then you'll be self-directed whether or not you're ready for it' (ibid., p.155).

A second respect in which the change procedure differs in the Dutch and the American context is time orientation. Across the Dutch plants, the time span of the change process was consistently longer than that observed across the American plants. The contrast between the change processes at the plants of Dow Chemical in Oyster Creek (USA) and Terneuzen (NL) illustrates this difference. The plants faced a similar 'change management model' that was diffused on a global scale by corporate management. The model entailed the shift towards empowered teams at the production establishments. Management of the American plant effectuated the whole change process within six months. At the Dutch plant, the implementation of the change process according to the change management model failed because there was no support from the operators. Thereafter, a new change process was initiated that aimed to achieve its objective, the functional integration of two separate plants, in six years. Akzo Nobel provides another illustration of the differences in time orientation. Plant management in the Netherlands initiated a change process that was expected to lead to self-direction within a period of ten years. In the words of the plant manager: 'We will gradually introduce the new work organization to the operators. First, we need to create acceptance (...) It is a long-term process. It is important to think before you jump. Everybody should be on the same line' (ibid., p.180). In contrast, the management of the site in Pasadena completed an organizational change in a couple of months.

A final procedural difference that separates the typical Dutch change process from the one that is observed among the American plants concerns the quality of interaction between management and operators. Across the Dutch plants, changes are effectuated through the interaction between operators and management; in contrast, in the United States, the control over the change processes resides with management. The developments at DSM illustrate this point. Site management at the American plant directed the organizational change to such an extent that even key operators were not involved. According to the newly appointed production manager: 'they announced the new organizational structure and, thereafter, I was asked to become polymerization manager' (ibid., p.192). At the Dutch plant of DSM, the organizational change involved more interaction between management and operators. After management had convinced the shift leaders of the need for change, the shift leaders themselves designed a new organizational structure. They proposed a model that was ultimately accepted by all higher managerial layers. The other case studies confirm this observation on the extent of management–worker interaction during the change processes. At the Dutch plant of General Electric, higher management convinced the shift supervisors of the need for change. However, the intention to remove the shift supervisor out of the organizational structure originated with the shift supervisors themselves (at least in their perception): 'Management made it clear to us that change was necessary. We came up with the idea that we, as shift coaches, should make ourselves superfluous' (ibid., p.151). In contrast, at the American plant no input of the workers in the change process towards empowered teams was observed. In the words of an operator: 'This change has been thrown at us. If the teams would have decided themselves, they would have kept the e-tech and appoint one of the e-techs as coordinator' (ibid., p.157). The case of Dow Chemical is also illustrative. The lack of employee participation was the primary reason for the failure of the global change management model at the Dutch plant. Workers who felt ignored during the design of the change were not committed to the objectives of the change. The acknowledgment of workers' involvement during the restart of the change process resulted in a change programme that received broad support. In contrast, although the workers were included in the design teams at the American Dow plant, workers perceived the change process as directed by management. Some major decisions were made by management while other decisions were perceived as being decided in advance or being manipulated by management. An operator commented, 'we tried to make decisions, but it was almost as if we were coached to go in a certain direction' (ibid., p.167).

Actual outcomes

The strategic aim to reduce the number of operators that has been found across the American and the Dutch plants has led to a reconsideration of the role of the shift supervisor. The idea is that supervisory tasks add little value to the production process. Accordingly, personnel costs can be reduced if operators can be supervised in other ways than direct supervision, for example by means of technological control or by dividing the supervisory tasks among the shift workers. Although the strategic motives are similar, the outcome that resulted from this reconsideration separates the Dutch from the American plants. A different pattern emerges across, respectively, the Dutch and the American plants. Across the Dutch plants, the hierarchical position of the shift supervisor is preserved. The shift supervisor retains his or her position in the organizational hierarchy, but he or she is given new responsibilities. The shift supervisor is expected to participate in problem-solving projects, rather than to direct the operators in their day-to-day activities. However, across the American plants, the policy has been to remove the position of the shift supervisor as a hierarchical layer above the operators. The implementation of empowered teams was supposed to make the role of the supervisor redundant. Operators are expected to work in teams without the authority of a shift supervisor. Supervisory responsibilities are given to these teams of shift workers. Earlier, the introduction of such empowered teams was observed as the prime strategic shift in the realm of employment relations that was initiated by the American corporations. The success of its implementation is considered below.

Consider first the attempt to introduce empowered work teams at the American plant of General Electric. The new organizational model aimed to increase the multi-skilling of the employees and the decision-making authority of the operators. However, both objectives were frustrated by the manner in which the organizational change was introduced. The lack of employee involvement and the tight time schedule by which management aimed to realize the organizational change inhibited the transition from the traditional work organization to a self-directed workforce. Instead, the workforce clung to the old rules. The antagonistic relationship between supervisors and operators remained in place. Originally, it was intended by management to remove the production supervisors from the hierarchy. However, efficiency broke down and the supervisors were reinstalled. A production supervisor comments: 'We had to move back. It was communicated that the teams couldn't run their lines efficiently' (Pot, 1998, p.155). Although the supervisors were supposed to coach the teams and to refrain from command–control behaviour, the authority to make decisions still belonged to the production supervisors. Consider the following comment of an operator: 'There are still supervisors. The production lead runs the show. They don't leave their men alone. We still don't have control over the line. On meetings they say we should decide ourselves to shut a line, but the production lead still tells us that the line should be running to get the tons right. Although management tells us that they want us to be self-directed, they have left us with that guy who tells us what to do. Management overlooks it. They just let go. You can't teach an old dog new tricks' (ibid., p.155). Furthermore, the degree of multi-skilling of the operators has not increased. In contrast, a return to more specialization was observed. Former team responsibilities, such as pigment weighing and colour operations, were reassigned to individual operators. Moreover, the frequency of job rotation by operators was set at 18 months. Given this low frequency, the operators cannot be considered to form a multi-skilled workforce. Management prefers specialization, because it ensures individual accountability and a higher production quality. Consider the following comment of a production supervisor: 'I like specialists in my shift. I only need a few operators for rotation. Let's face it, experts get the product out. They can fix something, they are good for the yield and they have less red tags. As a rule, you can say that shifts with experts run the lines better' (ibid., p.155). Accordingly, the empowered work teams that operate at the General Electric plant in Selkirk are best characterized as baseball teams. According to a personnel manager: 'We will still have teams in the future, but it depends on how you see a team. Look at baseball. They never change a winning team. If the pitcher knows how to throw and the catcher catches the balls, you should not remove them from their posts' (ibid., p.155).

Next, consider the attempt at the American plant of Dow Chemicals to implement empowered teams at the workplace. Guided by the Dow's global change management model, 'Strategic Blueprint', the introduction of empowered teams promised to endow operators with broader skill levels and more decision-making authority. However, the theoretical merits of team-based forms of work organization appear not to be realized. First, the managerial prerogatives have been preserved. Although Dow's global change management model prescribed employee participation by means of so-called 'design teams', operators doubt whether a true 'bottom-up' procedure was followed, for management decided on important matters, such as the move from a five-shift to a four-shift schedule. Moreover, the feeling among operators was that management manipulated them to go in a certain direction. An operator recalled: 'I think we were guided on how to design. Our ISB-leader came back from Canada with a bunch of paper that we were supposed to use as a starting point' (ibid., p.167). Furthermore, the instalment of a so-called 'Operate Plant Team' did not affect managerial prerogatives. The Operate Plant Team in which operators were represented was supposed to be the decision-making body for the plant. However, its potency was disputed. In the first place, the democratic intentions were frustrated by the majority rule: 'Decisions in the OPT are already pre-decided by the day technicians and leave little influence to the schedules. It doesn't matter what we say. They will do what they want. If you don't nod your head, you'll get banned' (ibid., p.169). In the second place, the aim of consensual decision making was not understood by the operators: 'The OPT doesn't make clear decisions, but tries to please everybody. They ask everybody whether they can live with it, or support it. I don't think it's important whether I can live with it. The key is whether a decision is good for Dow because that's where the money comes from' (ibid., p.169). Furthermore, although in the new organizational scheme all supervisory positions were removed from the hierarchy, new antagonistic relationships have emerged. The common unwritten rules that were discovered are 'never voice your opinion without fear of reprisal' and 'always tell management what they want to hear'. The primary result of the removal of supervisory positions appears to be confusion. The senior operators, the day technicians and the production engineers became involved in a new struggle for decision-making authority instead of cooperating. According to the operators, the new organization is characterized by disorganization: 'Now there are too many chiefs and too few Indians. Everybody is on the same layer and everybody wants to be the boss. It is disorganized, which causes confusion and frustration, because one person says this and the other tells us something else. There is no chain of command. Sometimes there must be a leader who shows the direction' (ibid., pp.168–9). Finally, the development of a multi-skilled workforce was not realized. Although some operators were cross-trained, their actual job content was not broadened. Accordingly, the operators perceived cross-training as a waste of effort and time.

CONCLUSIONS

This chapter has reported on an empirical study that was designed to identify the impact of national culture on the development of the employment relationship. A central feature of the research design is the cross-national comparison between the Netherlands and the United States. The chapter has described the national work-related culture of each country. Moreover, the developments in the employment relationship of each country have been outlined by means of case studies of four multinational companies. The chapter has been solely descriptive. So far, we have refrained from interpretation. It is the purpose of the concluding chapter to interpret the developments in the employment relationship in terms of the work-related cultures. Is reference to the American work-related culture necessary to understand the course of developments in the realm of the employment relationship in the United States? Likewise, to explain the employment developments in the Netherlands, does one need recourse to variables that describe the Dutch cultural context? The following chapter will shed light on these questions.

NOTES

1. The rationale of incorporating countries that are equally developed in economic terms is derived from the well-known 'logic of industrialization' put forward by Kerr et al. (1960). In that study, it is asserted that cross-national differences in the organization of production are related to differences in their stage of industrialization. Cross-national differences are expected to vanish if nation states achieve similar levels of economic development.

2. A major practical consideration in incorporating the United States and the Netherlands is the collaboration of the researcher with the Roosevelt Study Centre. This research institute maintains a wide relational network of Dutch and American multinational companies and was helpful in providing entry to the empirical field.
3. There are two other methods to infer a causal relationship between separate variables (Sayer, 1992). First, at an abstract level, one might simply assume the social system to be confined to the variables of interest. In other words, the social world is assumed to be 'closed'. Under certain conditions, this approach can be a sufficient approximation of reality. However, the assumption of closure is inconsistent with the study of developments in the realm of the employment relationship in a period of shifting conditions in the global economy. A second way to instal closure is by means of statistical techniques. Through the analysis of a large number of quantifiable observations, one can identify statistically significant regularities between different variables. The main disadvantage of this method is its inability to include the rich detail of the practical consciousness of human agents and their reasons and motivations for action. It detracts from any meanings that human actors ascribe to their social conditions. Consequently, statistical techniques are helpful to answer the question whether there is a regularity between national culture and firms' employment practices, but they are incapable of demonstrating a causal sequence. The process of 'how' culture affects firms' employment practices remains unilluminated.
4. Analysis of human resource management literature suggests three categories of explanatory factors. First, the design of human resource management practices is affected by nation-specific environmental factors which in this study are included in the definition of national work-related culture, such as labour legislation, the system of industrial relations and the education system. Second, the contingency approach relates the content of human resource management practices to various universal factors in the context of the organization. The common contingency variables are industry, size, technology and dependence on parent organization (Tayeb, 1988). The third group of variables influencing the shape of human resource management is specific to the organization. Of most importance are the variables corporate strategy (Fombrun et al., 1984) and corporate culture (Schein, 1985).
5. In this study, the cases are selected according to the principle of 'literal replication' (Yin, 1994). According to this principle, a conclusion is replicated if multiple cases demonstrate the same results. Table 5.2 specifies the contextual conditions of the involved production facilities. To ensure the comparability of the American plants, an additional criterion has guided the selection of the American production facilities. All four American plants are non-unionized. We have chosen to focus on the non-unionized sector of American industry since, historically, it is the dominant segment of American industry (Dunlop, 1993).
6. The ideal types are primarily constructed on the basis of secondary resources. The ideal-types are confirmed by interviews that were held with field experts. Pot (1998) reports on the outcomes of a large number of interviews that were conducted with employees who had ample work experience in both the Netherlands and the United States.

7. Nomothetic studies distinguish different cultures in terms of similar value dimensions. Idiographic approaches, in contrast, deny the existence of such universal value dimensions and emphasize the unique value configuration of each culture.
8. Dijk and Punch (1993) and Iterson (1997) give other idiographic interpretations of Dutch informal work-related institutions.
9. Semantic confusion might arise about the labels 'liberalism' and 'conservatism' in the United States, as 'what Europeans have called "liberalism", Americans refer to as "conservatism": a deeply anti-statist doctrine emphasizing the virtues of laissez-faire' (Lipset, 1996, p.36).
10. The suspicion of government is commonly explained by reference to the domination of the English monarchy before the War of Independence: 'The liberalism of the eighteenth century was essentially the rebellion (...) against the monarchical and aristocratic state – against hereditary privilege, against restrictions on bargains. Its spirit was essentially anarchistic – the antithesis of socialism. It was anti-State' (Wells, 1906, cited in Lipset, 1996, p.32).
11. Critical observers of American society comment that the combination of equality of opportunity and economic individualism has resulted in a concern with the achievement of ends rather than the use of appropriate means. 'In a country that stresses success above all, people are led to feel that the most important thing is to win the game, regardless of the methods employed in doing so. American culture applies the norms of a completely competitive society to everyone. Winners take all' (Lipset, 1996, p.47). In other words, 'the moral mandate to achieve success thus exerts pressure to succeed, by fair means if possible and by foul means if necessary' (Robert Merton, 1957, cited in Lipset, 1996, p.47).
12. The 'reformist' refers to the member of the strict branch of the Dutch Reformed Church.
13. Zahn (1989) emphasizes the persistence of the 'rebellious' nature of the Dutch. He speaks about the 'institutionalization of unconventional behaviour'. Non-conformity is respected and agreement with other people's opinions without any form of criticism is rare.
14. A further characteristic of the Dutch education system is the variety of educational organizations based on distinct religious world-views. Although this feature of the education system is interesting in view of the broader Dutch cultural inclinations, it is not linked to the work-related culture of the Netherlands.
15. The first major government regulation in the area of industrial relations aimed to strengthen the 'market position' of employees to offset the traditionally more powerful employers. The National Labour Relations Act, or Wagner Act, of 1935 gave employees a federally protected right to organize themselves and to strike (Rothman and Briscoe, 1993). The second major intervention of the government (Taft-Hartley Act, 1947) limited the power of unions by the prohibition of certain organizing and bargaining practices.
16. Representation by the union coincides with the separation between non-exempts and exempts. Only non-exempts participate in the election procedure. The union contract extends only to this group of employees, who are usually hourly, non-managerial workers.

17. The 1940s and 1950s were characterized by the growth of the unions and the development of the collective bargaining system. Union influence stagnated in the 1960s and continued to decline in the next decades. Private sector union membership density had fallen from 35 per cent in 1954 to 11 per cent in 1994 (Strauss, 1995).
18. Relatedly, Peter Lawrence, an observer of cross-cultural management, mocks the academic term 'industrial relations' as it applies to the United States. For the phrase 'system of industrial relations' with its connotations of rules, procedures, institutions and reciprocal expectations is 'a far cry from the American scene of interest-driven pugnacity. In the USA there is no system, it is all the more basic. If the company is non-union it will fight to keep it that way; anyone who wants to unionize it must be prepared to fight. If the company is unionized it is an article of faith that union power must be contained, that the management prerogative will be preserved at all costs, and that the company will be on the defensive at all times, ready to fight organized labour if it has to' (Lawrence, 1996, p.95).
19. Badie and Birnbaum (1983) relate the relatively weak position of the state in the United States to the adoption of the British common law system. While the Roman legal system justifies the existence of an autonomous state, British common law pays less attention to the definition of a separate public sphere. The legal system of the Netherlands is based on the Roman civil code, which partly explains why a strong central state exists in the Netherlands (see also Waarden, 1992).
20. Note that the doctrine of 'employment at will' is constrained by shared norms and the fear of lawsuits. First, to keep the commitment of their workforce, employers need to make sure that the dismissal of an employee corresponds to the expectations of the employees, that is, the dismissal needs to be 'fair' (Iribarne, 1989). Second, dismissal is liable to result in wrongful termination lawsuits if the dismissal concerns an employee who belongs to one of the groups that is protected by the various non-discrimination laws, such as ethnic minorities, the elderly and women (Mendelsohn, 1990; Olson, 1991). Lipset (1996, p.40) notes that 'the weakness of the state, the emphasis on individual rights and a constitutionally mandated division of powers gives lawyers an uniquely powerful role in America and makes its people exceptionally litigious'.
21. For example, grievance law, which is emphasized in the United States, is relatively undeveloped in the Netherlands.
22. For example, to dismiss an employee, the employer is obliged to get approval of the regional employment office (see Burgess, 1991).
23. However, this source of shareholder power has weakened, since the composition of the board has become dominated by executive management of the corporation (Charkham, 1994).
24. The adjective 'liberal' is understood here in its continental European meaning; that is, reluctance of the state to interfere and a preference for the market mechanism.
25. Peter Drucker, the well-known expert on American management, emphasizes the influence of scientific management principles on American work organization: 'Personal Administration and Human Relations are the things talked about and written about whenever the management of worker and work is being discussed. They are the things the personnel department concerns itself with. But they are not the concepts that underlie the actual management of worker and work in American

industry. This concept is Scientific Management (...) Indeed, Scientific Management is all but a systematic philosophy of worker and work. Altogether it may well be the most powerful as well as the most lasting contribution America has made to Western thought since the Federalist Papers' (Drucker, 1954, cited in Braverman, 1974). More than 30 years later, management scientists rediscovered the dominance of the Taylorist principles. See, for example, the following quotation from Walton (1985, p.242): 'The common theme of the many elements of the traditional model is to establish order, exercise control and achieve efficiency in the application of the work-force. The model's antecedents include the bureaucratic organizations of the military and church. But it is Frederick W. Taylor who deserves the credit for developing and promoting the industrial model. Because it was consistent with the prevailing ideologies of U.S. management and because it worked satisfactorily for many decades, the model was internalized by successive waves of managers. It has been reinforced by the policies of the U.S. labour movement.'

26. During his visits to American companies, Lawrence (1996, p.129) observed that 'blue collar workers and their supervisors could not do simple maths, could not work out percentages, did not understand the difference between the mean and the average, could not keep the score on scrap rates, did not have the educational resources to implement quality improvement programmes and were sometimes handicapped by simple illiteracy'.
27. Samuel Gompers, the illustrious labour leader of US history, expressed this attitude to work as follows: 'A job is a job; if it doesn't pay enough, it's a lousy job' (quoted in Cascio,1992, p.106).
28. Lawrence (1996) notes the consistency of praise in management with the American commitment to individualism: 'When individuals are praised it is for qualities that differentiate them, not integrate them.' In contrast, Lawrence (1991) notes the restricted individuality in the Dutch business environment where eccentricity, boastful pride and self-glorification are condemned. 'This emphasis on not being different, not setting yourself apart, not playing the tunes of glory (...) colours attitudes to such subjects as promotion, ambition, rewards and leadership' (Lawrence, 1991, p.15).
29. The main principles that underlie the presentation of the American work-related culture coincide with characterizations of other authors. Walton (1985) describes the dominant way to organize work in the United States as the 'traditional control model'. Appelbaum and Batt (1994) have labelled their model the 'traditional American HR model'. In a similar way, Hollingsworth (1991) has called his model of traditional American manufacturing the 'Fordist system'. Beer et al. (1984) describe Tayloristic human resource management as the 'traditional work system'.
30. The 'strategic content' denotes the desired outcome of the change and the tools to achieve that objective. The 'procedure' refers to the quality of the interaction between the various actors that are involved in the realization of the change. The 'outcome' refers to the actual operation of the strategic change and should be distinguished from the desired outcome.
31. Research methods such as direct observation and participant-observation are unsuited to revive the change processes that were implemented in the past. The use of surveys by means of standardized questionnaires is problematic as they provide only a superficial insight into the experience of the individual actors.

32. In 1995, the central works council of Akzo Nobel issued a response to the managerial perspective on the notion of employability. The works council approved the role of the employer to enhance the responsibility, flexibility and independence of the employee through personal development and training. However, the view of the employee as a 'business partner' who maintains his or her skills and 'sells' them to the company is rejected. In the view of the works council, employees should be managed by means of collective provisions to maintain cooperation and solidarity among employees.
33. For example, a paragraph in the 1997 collective labour agreement of Akzo Nobel states: 'The employee has the right of reimbursement of the costs related to educational programs that have the objective to maintain or strengthen his labour market position inside or outside the company.'

6. Discussion

INTRODUCTION

Global convergence or continuing divergence of the organization of the employment relationship? Owing to the homogenizing influence of the ongoing process of globalization, this question is on the agenda of many organizational researchers. Inspired by this problem, this book concentrates on the impact of national culture on the dynamics of the employment relationship. The convergence/divergence debate cannot be settled without proper insight into the manner in which national culture has an impact on the way that the employment relation is organized, for national work-related culture constitutes the major barrier to global uniformity. Accordingly, central to this book are the following questions. How does national work-related culture affect the way the employment relationship is organized and changed? By what mechanisms does national culture inhibit the global standardization of the organization of the employment relationship?

This final chapter addresses these research questions. The earlier chapters have provided the requisite building blocks. Chapter 4 has proposed a theoretical conceptualization of national work-related culture on the basis of the structuration theory of Anthony Giddens. On the basis of this conceptualization, a comparative study was designed that included the Netherlands and the United States. Chapter 5 reported on this study, presenting, on the one hand, ideal types of the work-related cultures of the Netherlands and the United States and, on the other hand, data on change processes in the realm of the employment relationship that are realized by private firms in the Netherlands and the United States. By the inclusion of the Netherlands and the United States in the research design the research question can be specified as follows. Does the organization of the employment relationship evolve to a standard that is similar in both the Netherlands and the United States? If this question should be answered in the negative, is reference to the American cultural background required to explain the course of the employment relationship in the United States? Likewise, to explain the developments of the employment practices in the Netherlands, does one need reference to variables in the cultural context of the Netherlands?

The first section of this chapter presents evidence that points to the emergence of a global standard to which the organization of the employment relationship should conform irrespective of cultural borders. Nonetheless, the evidence is not robust. Only if the analysis is limited to the strategic objectives of upper management can the conclusion of global convergence be inferred. If the analysis is conducted in more detail and includes the actual outcomes, the case for divergence becomes more plausible. The second section presents evidence in favour of the divergence thesis. The differences between the outcomes that have resulted from the change processes in the Netherlands and the United States are demonstrated. In the third section it is argued that the continuing influence of national culture has caused these divergent outcomes, for national culture shaped the procedure by which the strategic objectives were converted to actual outcomes. The procedure of change appears to be designed in fundamentally different ways across, respectively, the Dutch and the American context. The final section shows that the change procedures are firmly rooted in the national work-related cultures of the United States and the Netherlands.

EVIDENCE FOR GLOBAL CONVERGENCE

Convergence of the organization of the employment relationship may arise in two ways. First, actors, irrespective of national borders, adopt similar newly developed management methods. In this way the employment relationship develops in an imaginary new direction. A second case for convergence is based on cross-cultural learning. Actors in countries that organize the employment relationship in a relatively inefficient manner imitate the employment practices that are applied by actors in better-performing nation states. In this way the employment relationship converges to a model that combines employment practices that are universally considered as 'best practice'. Below, evidence for both pathways to global convergence is presented.

Towards a New Model

The comparative analysis of the four case studies showed that a number of similar trends are going on that are independent of cultural background. It was observed that all companies have engaged in an effort to rationalize the organizational structure. The new organizational structures provide ample autonomy for the business units that coordinate the business of the product group on a global scale. In line with this reorganization of responsibilities, the responsibility of other management levels, such as the geographical and functional layers, has been reduced.

Furthermore, the analysis of the four case studies showed that firms, irrespective of national borders, have adopted similar management methods. Customer focus, business processes re-engineering, total quality management, empowerment and teamwork have become common terminology within each company. At the plant level, the application of these management principles has led to a substantial reduction of employment. As a consequence of more advanced production technologies and the functional integration of operational activities, the production facilities are operated by fewer operators. Accordingly, the firms expect greater functional and temporal flexibility on the part of the operators. Moreover, operators are expected to engage in improvement trajectories. Across all companies, attempts are made to unlock the knowledge of operators for the goal of continuous quality improvement.

The common developments that were observed among the four firms can be considered as evidence for convergence. The organization of the employment relationship appears to have developed in a similar direction, independent of cultural context. Seemingly, the actors that are involved in shaping the employment relationship are constrained by various global social processes. Owing to the increasingly global business environment, the actors seem to have no choice but to adopt a new model of employment relations that is characterized by decentralized structures that are coupled with team-based cultures to foster innovation. How can these observations be accounted for? Chapter 2 distinguishes various theories of the employment relationship. Each theory suggests a different mechanism to explain the adoption of similar employment practices across diverse cultural contexts. First, an efficiency argument can be put forward. In a context in which production technology has developed (microelectronics) and individual preferences have altered (post-materialism), firms have to comply with this new 'one best way' to organize; intensified international competition leaves them no other choice. However, the efficiency argument can be challenged. It might be argued that the new power balance between employers and employees enables management to set higher goals for their workers, for as a consequence of the liberalization of international markets, power has shifted in favour of the management of multinational firms. Alternatively, it can be argued that the spread of recent management concepts is based on imitation and mimicry, a process that is fostered by faith in consultants and gurus of organizational change.

The above suggests increasing uniformity. The similar developments seem to indicate that the development of the employment relationship is no longer codetermined by the cultural context in which the firm is embedded. Yet a more detailed and close scrutiny of the employment developments indicates that cultural differences remain. For example, both in the Netherlands and in the United States firms were engaged in a process of 'downsizing', or employee reduction. However, the procedure by which this common strategic objective was realized appears to differentiate countries. While the common procedure in the United States involves an individual allowance on the basis of seniority, in the Netherlands the employer commonly negotiates with the unions a collective 'social plan' to ensure the social acceptance of the job reduction. This procedural difference is not an isolated aspect, for owing to different change procedures, the ultimate outcomes of the change processes are different. A further example is the universal emphasis on team-based forms of work organization. Although teams are fashionable in both the Netherlands and the United States, it can be argued that teamwork takes on a different meaning in the two countries. Teamwork is an 'umbrella notion' whose actual substance depends on the cultural context in which it is embedded (Benders and Hootegem, 1997). Teamwork might refer to an organization in which each team member performs the task at which he or she excels. In this case, teamwork denotes the belief that none of the team members is superior in terms of personal status. Such appears to be the meaning that is attached to teamwork in the United States. In the Netherlands, the notion of teamwork is developed in line with the so-called 'sociotechnical systems design'. In this line of thinking, teamwork has been developed as a method to enhance the flexibility of the work organization.

Through the extension of job responsibilities and skills, it is ensured that each team member is qualified to perform the various parts of the production process.

In sum, the observation that firms irrespective of national borders employ similar management rhetoric provides only a crude indication of convergence of the employment relationship. The claim for convergence needs to be based on more detailed data that illuminate the actual operation of the particular management method.

Towards a Best Pratice Model

The analysis of the strategic direction that is chosen by, respectively, the Dutch and the American corporations in the third section of Chapter 5 indicates that the American firms have adopted a different pathway from the Dutch firms. Both General Electric and Dow Chemical focused their efforts on the creation of a value-based organization in substitution of the traditional way of hierarchical organizing. In such an organization, all employees would act for the good of the company without having to wait for orders. The traditional distance between managers and workers would be reduced. In contrast, the developments at the Dutch firms, Akzo Nobel and DSM, show their ambition to increase the flexibility of the employment relationship.

The strategic objectives are no isolated events. The findings can be generalized to the broader population of Dutch and American firms. The developments at General Electric and Dow Chemical are in accordance with the general trend in the United States. Since the mid-1980s, American enterprises have experimented with new forms of work organization that de-emphasize hierarchy and emphasize collaboration and teamwork (Appelbaum and Batt, 1994). As many as 86 per cent of the American firms have introduced quality circles or some other employee involvement programme (Lawler et al., 1992). In 37 per cent of American workplaces, more than half of the workers are involved in the following new employment practices: self-directed teams, job rotation, quality circles or total quality management (Osterman, 1994).

Likewise, the employment developments in the Netherlands that are initiated by Akzo Nobel and DSM are in accordance with a general pattern. Since the 1980s, the attempt to incorporate more flexibility in the organization of the employment relationship has dominated the employment strategy of Dutch companies (Albeda and Dercksen, 1994; CBS, 1996).[1] This drive for flexibility is reflected by the increase of flexible labour contracts (Haan and De Vos, 1994), the emphasis on the employability of the employee (Gasperz and Ott, 1996) and the closer match between employment conditions and individual preferences or employee performance (Goslinga and Klandermans, 1996).

The adoption of different strategic pathways by, respectively, the American and the Dutch firms is a case of cross-cultural learning. The differential employment strategies should be explained as intentional attempts to improve on the weak features of the traditional work-related cultures of the Netherlands and the United States. To grasp this claim, recall the traditional work-related cultures of the Netherlands and the United States that were described in the second section of Chapter 5. Table 6.1 summarizes the dominant employment practices of Dutch and American firms. Moreover, it adds a third column that characterizes the best practice for each employment practice. The 'best-practice' column is based on the dominant beliefs among current management pundits.[2]

Table 6.1 Traditional American and Dutch employment practices compared with best practice as suggested by management pundits

	United States	Netherlands	Best practice
Work organization	Individual standardized jobs, narrow job content	Group work, broad job content and multi-skilling	Group work, broad job content and multi-skilling
Human resource flow	Reliance on external labour market mechanisms (flexible)	Reliance on internal labour market mechanisms (rigid)	Flexibility
Reward system	Individual-based	Collectivity-based	Individual-based
Employee participation	Little; large worker–management distance	Substantial; small worker–management distance	Small worker–management distance

According to the best-practice employment model, firms are advised to organize the work system on the basis of teamwork in which the members are multi-skilled and are given broad responsibilities. The human resource flow should be managed in a flexible manner so that the firms can respond to business demand. The design of the reward system should be focused on the individual in response to the increase in individualistic value patterns. Accordingly, individualized forms of remuneration, such as performance-based pay, should replace collective modes of payment. Finally, the management literature suggests providing ample room for employee participation. Employee commitment should be enhanced to unlock the intellectual capacity of the workers to the advantage of the firm.

From Table 6.1 it can be inferred that the dominant employment practices of the Dutch firms in the realm of work organization and employee participation are considered to be in alignment with global best practice, but the Dutch employment practices diverge from global best practice in the area of flow and reward management. In contrast, the American companies are in line with global best practice if we consider the manner in which they manage human resource flows and rewards. However, the prevailing fragmentation of job contents and antagonistic supervisor-subordinate relationships in the traditional American work organization can be evaluated as weak in view of the best-practice model. Following this argument, the developments in the United States and the Netherlands can be understood as adaptation to the best-practice standard. Since the 1980s, the need to introduce group work and to enhance the level of employee participation has been consistently emphasized in the American management literature. Notions such as corporate culture, total quality management, decentralization, teamwork and the need to drive out of fear from the workplace have been put forward as crucial elements of an employment strategy by which American firms can regain competitiveness in the global business environment (Peters and Waterman, 1982; Deming, 1986; Dertouzos et al., 1989; Pfeffer, 1994). Likewise, in the Netherlands, the need to enhance the flexibility of the employment relationship in response to intensified international competition has been consistently expressed by management consultants and government bodies alike (Bolweg and Kluytmans, 1989; SER, 1991).

In sum, the developments in both the Netherlands and the United States can be understood as attempts to improve on the flaws of the traditional model to organize the employment relationship. Dutch and American managers appear to adhere to a similar best-practice model. Differences in the strategic content of the change processes in the Netherlands and the United States are attributed to the different initial positions. This conclusion raises the question whether the manner in which the employment relationship is organized is converging towards a new global best-practice model. However, such a conclusion would seem to be premature. Although the strategic initiatives might indicate such a convergence, the emergence of global convergence needs reference to the actual outcomes. Analysis of the actual outcomes needs to prove the growing flexibility of the employment relationship in the Netherlands. Furthermore, analysis of the actual outcomes must reveal whether the introduction of a team-based work organization has indeed transformed the American workplace.

EVIDENCE FOR CONTINUING DIVERGENCE

The previous section provided evidence in favour of the convergence thesis. However, the evidence is based on the analysis of the employment strategies that were initiated by the higher management layers of the corporation. This section will argue against the convergence thesis and support the view of continuing divergence. It will do so by showing that the strategic initiatives are not converted into the actual outcomes. The reason for this disparity between strategies and actual outcomes is found in the change procedure by which the strategic initiatives are realized.

A Closer Look at the Actual Outcomes

Has the degree of flexibility of the employment relationship been substantially enhanced in the Dutch business environment? Has the introduction of empowered teams in the American context transformed the traditional American workplace relationship? Based on the findings in the third section of Chapter 5 these claims can, with good reason, be questioned.

Consider the pursuit of flexibility, the primary issue that confronts the traditional organization of the employment relationship in the Netherlands. Flexibility of the employment relationship is pursued by various means. Most notable is the emphasis on employability. Some commentators, when speaking about 'employability', imagine a perfectly flexible labour market that is populated by workers who sell their skills temporarily to an employer. In this view, the permanent labour contract that characterizes the traditional employment relation is replaced by temporal contracts. The employee is considered as a business partner who sells his or her skills to the firm. To ensure job security, workers need to ensure the 'employability' of their own skills on an individual basis. Such a perspective of the labour market is in sharp contrast with the traditional work-related culture of the Netherlands, for in this culture the use of internal labour market arrangements is emphasized. However, in actual practice it can be observed that the notion of employability has been interpreted in line with the traditional Dutch work-related culture. The application of employability in the collective labour agreements of the Dutch companies DSM and Akzo Nobel recognizes a long-term employment relationship between the firm and the employee. New employment practices that are initiated under the label of employability concern primarily the continuous training of employees. Employability refers to the mutual responsibility of the employer and employee to ensure that the employee remains of value to the firm during his or her career. In this view, employability is in line with qualitative or internal flexibility rather than with quantitative or external flexibility. The traditional reliance of Dutch companies on internal labour market mechanisms is not affected.

Similar demonstrations that the pursuit of flexibility by Dutch firms does not conflict with the traditional cultural preferences in the Netherlands are the use of labour pools, the introduction of performance-related pay and the trade-off between working time reduction and flexible working hours. Consider the use of labour pools. The instalment of employees in a labour pool whose members can be deployed on various activities across the firm is a mode of flexibility that is consistent with the Dutch work-related culture, for the employees that constitute the pool can be offered a permanent employment contract and form a part of the internal labour market of the firm. Likewise, the introduction of performance-based pay evaluation in combination with the preservation of basic salary levels cannot be considered as a deviation from Dutch work-related culture. Although the system provides employers with the flexibility to link individual performance with rewards, it leaves the collective reward system unaffected. The trade-off between working time reduction and flexible working hours provides a final illustration of the way flexibility is introduced in the Dutch employment relationship. Management is given the right to determine the working hours of employees in a more flexible manner; employees gain the right to reduce their working time from 38 to 36 hours on average a week.

In a similar way, it is claimed that the introduction of new, team-based forms of work organization in the United States has not transformed America's work-related culture. Characteristic features of this culture, such as the antagonistic supervisor–worker relationship, the prevalence of management prerogatives, the limited decision-making authority of workers and the narrow definition of individual job contents, have reappeared in the newly designed work organizations. Evidence for this claim is found in the analysis of the functioning of empowered teams at the production establishments of General Electric and the Dow Chemical Company. This analysis shows that the workforce has clung to the old rules. The antagonistic relationship between supervisors and operators has remained in place. Production supervisors at General Electric have retained the authority to make decisions. Democratic decision-making bodies, such as the Operate Plant Team at the Dow Chemical plant, are distrusted because they are thought to be manipulated by management. Traditional unwritten rules, such as 'never voice your opinion without fear of reprisal' and 'always tell management what they want to hear' have continued to characterize workplace relations.

Furthermore, although the theoretical model of empowered teams promises to broaden the job content of operators, the narrow definition of tasks is continued in actual practice. At the General Electric plant, a return to higher specialization was even observed. The operators at Dow Chemical received some multi-skilling training, but no one was assigned to other than their original production sections. Moreover, the frequency of job rotation of operators was set at 18 months. Given such a low frequency of job rotation, the operators cannot be considered to constitute a multi-skilled workforce. It appeared that management prefers specialization, because it ensures individual accountability, and that they have acted upon this preference.

Planned versus Emergent Change Procedure

It was observed above that the introduction of flexibility and team-based work systems in the Dutch and American organization of the employment relationship has not transformed their traditional work-related cultures. This section elaborates on the causal mechanism that underlies this observation. Why are original strategic objectives not converted into actual outcomes? It is argued that the deviation between the strategic management goals and their actual realization should be understood by reference to the procedure by which the changes are realized. The change procedure constitutes the link between the formulation of strategy and the way things turn out in reality. It is shown below that the procedure by which the American firms realize their employment strategies is fundamentally different from the procedure that is followed by the two Dutch companies. Owing to these different change procedures, the convergence of the organization of the employment relationship in the United States and the Netherlands to a single global standard is unlikely.

The typical procedure by which changes are realized in the United States and the Netherlands can be characterized as, respectively, 'planned' and 'emergent' (Wilson, 1992). This conclusion is based on the third section of Chapter 5, which describes the change procedure at both the higher management levels as well as the plant level. Management that follows a 'planned' change procedure assumes that the change can be planned in advance. Beforehand, the objectives of the change process are defined. The primary task of change management is implementation. The direction of change has already been established. In contrast, change can also be approached as an emergent phenomenon. In this case, the objectives of the change process are not defined in advance, but they arise in the course of the process. Management that follows an emergent change procedure may still set some future desired states, but the actual content of the change emerges during a process of interaction of the various stakeholders.

Consider the way the American firms aimed to introduce a team-based work organization into their production establishments. The change procedure can clearly be characterized as 'planned'. Management at higher hierarchical layers defined the direction of change. Moreover, management laid down the change procedures, the training manuals and the time planning of the realization of the change. The plant managers, the supervisors and the operators were confronted with the ideas of higher management: their sole responsibility was the implementation of the change. The unilaterally imposed change process has frustrated the objective of the change. The mechanistic approach to change, the lack of employee involvement and the tight time schedules have inhibited the transition from the traditional work organization to a self-directed workforce.

The change procedure by which the Dutch companies aimed to enhance the flexibility of the employment relationship can be characterized as 'emergent'. Although management initiated the search for more flexibility in the employment relationship, the actual measures resulted from intensive and lengthy interaction with the employee representatives of either the works council or the trade unions. Through regular consultation and joint study groups, management and unions have designed distinct strategies to enhance flexibility that are acceptable to both of them.

CULTURAL EXPLANATION

The previous section argued that the procedure by which the employment relationship is changed separates the Dutch from the American context. Furthermore, it is argued that these procedural differences affect the actual outcome of the development of the employment relationship. The planned change procedure that is applied by the American companies is inconsistent with their aim to transform the workplace. Similarly, the emergent change procedure that is followed by the Dutch companies is unlikely to result in the kind of flexibility that would harm the interests of the workers in a unilateral way. In other words, it is concluded that, owing to the procedural differences by which the change processes are brought about, the employment practices in the Netherlands and the United States continue to be different. However, the objective of this book is to show the causal relationship between national work-related culture and the development of the employment relationship. From this point of view, the foregoing conclusion is unsatisfactory. A final step is missing. It still needs to be demonstrated that the procedural differences are rooted in the work-related cultures of, respectively, the Netherlands and the United States. Accordingly, this section seeks to explain the procedural differences in terms of national work-related culture. This cultural explanation draws on the perspective of national work-related culture that is presented in Chapter 4. On the basis of Giddens' structuration theory, culture is defined as the cluster of nation-specific institutions that are reproduced by actors when they engage in social action. The influence of national culture on the employment relationship can be elucidated when one can show that actors in their day-to-day activities draw upon the rules that are specific to their culture. Accordingly, as a cultural explanation, it needs to be shown that the procedural differences between the Dutch and the American context are based on different cultural rules that were drawn upon by the actors who shaped the change processes.

The major point of difference between an emergent and a planned change procedure resides in the manner of interaction between management and employees. Intensive interaction is characteristic of the emergent change procedure that is found to be typical in the Netherlands. The typical American change procedure is characterized as planned. A crucial feature of such a change procedure is the limited interaction between management and workers.[3] Below, it is argued that the reliance on an emergent or a planned change procedure is firmly rooted in, respectively, the Dutch and the American work-related culture.

In the Dutch work-related culture, unions occupy a well-established position in the codetermination of employment conditions. This position is supported by formalized institutions, such as law and consultative bodies, as well as by informal institutions, such as shared norms and expectations. Management is supposed to interact intensively with representatives of national union organizations. Management cannot issue detailed employment strategies without prior consultation. National union representatives are likely to reject such guidelines that are unilaterally imposed. The cultural norm in the Netherlands is the pursuit of consensus and accommodation in the case of conflicts of interest. The case studies show that the actors that have shaped the change procedure have reproduced the cultural rules of the Netherlands. The recent developments in Dutch employment strategies, such as the trade-off between flexible working hours and working time reduction, are outcomes of a procedure that allowed for extensive interaction between national management and representatives of national trade unions. Accordingly, the recent developments can be understood as involving the reproduction of the cultural rules that guide change processes. By engaging in an interactive process to shape new employment practices, the representatives of management and unions have drawn upon and reproduced the cultural rules, such as the orientation towards consensus, the preference for equality of outcome, and the position of the unions, that characterize the Dutch work-related culture.

In contrast, the American system of industrial relations leaves no room for interaction between management and the unions at national level. Regular consultation between corporate management and national union representatives is non-existent. Generally, unions have never been considered parts of American work-related culture. The non-union industrial relations system is a chronic feature of the American system of industrial relations (Dunlop, 1993). Collective bargaining has always been a minority feature of this system.[4] Moreover, even when trade unions are acknowledged, the interaction between management and union representatives takes the form of power bargaining rather than a consultative process to accommodate the diverging interests. The preservation of management prerogatives has thus always been prominent. The case studies show the reproduction of this characteristic feature of the American work-related culture. Corporate management has unilaterally imposed detailed employment programmes on its production establishments. No prior consultation of workers' representatives was involved. Lacking a balancing influence from workers' representatives, the employment strategies reflect solely the viewpoints of management and its advisers. By following a procedure that has left no room for the views of collective labour, the representatives of the American companies have drawn upon and reproduced the cultural rules of the United States.

Likewise, the presence or absence of management prerogatives is similarly rooted in, respectively, American and Dutch workplace relations. In the American workplace, in the eyes of both the worker and the manager, the right of the manager to 'manage' is uncontested. Typical unwritten rules in this environment are 'never voice your opinion without fear of reprisal' and 'always tell management what they want to hear'. In contrast, the lack of authoritarian power of the manager is characteristic of Dutch work-related culture. To interfere in the work organization, a Dutch manager cannot make use of his hierarchical position by giving orders and imposing sanctions. This cultural 'rule' is reflected by formalized institutions, such as the position of unions and the works council. However, informal institutional 'rules', such as norms and expectations, are equally important. Workers expect to be consulted. Workers' resistance is legitimate if the manager fails to convince the worker of the need to change (Iribarne, 1989).[5] The case studies demonstrate that these cultural rules were at the root of the change processes in, respectively, the American and the Dutch production plants. Accordingly, the employment change processes at the Dutch plants can be understood as involving the reproduction of the cultural rule that workers' resistance is legitimate. Likewise, the planned nature of the change processes at the four American plants involved the reproduction of the acceptance of management's prerogatives.

Finally, it should be noted that these institutionalized differences with regard to the worker–manager relationship do not stand alone, but are reinforced by the broader institutional context of, respectively, the Netherlands and the United States. In the United States, the distance between managers and workers coincides with the divide between college-educated and non-college-educated students that results from the American education system. The Dutch educational system, in contrast, plays down the educational differences between the various actors in the production plant. The absence of large gaps in educational background is likely to underlie the relatively small distance between management and subordinates that characterizes Dutch workplace relations. Furthermore, the ballot system that determines the representation of unions in the United States reinforces the antagonistic relations between the two social groups in that country. Moreover, American labour law sanctions workers' resistance far more strongly than Dutch labour law. This institutional condition, in combination with the reality that social welfare provisions are limited in the United States, leaves workers little choice other than to accept management's prerogatives. Managers, on the other hand, as a consequence of the American system of corporate governance, are not stimulated to compromise on economic objectives in favour of employee needs. Dutch workers, in contrast, are supported in their quest for participation by labour law that allows for works councils and inhibits dismissal. Moreover, Dutch managers are appraised by a supervisory board which has a legal obligation to balance the interests of the various stakeholders of the company.

CONCLUSIONS

That there are globally common features in the nature and evolution of the employment relationship is not denied in this book. The book acknowledges the key role played by global trends as triggers of change in the employment relationship. Various global trends, such as intensified international competition, development of microelectronic technology, new management methods, the shifted balance of power that favours multinational firms and the emergence of a post-materialist value system, induce firms to adjust the employment relationship. The continuing process of globalization compels firms, irrespective of national borders, to adjust the employment relationship to the new global realities.

Yet this book demonstrates that the triggers of change should be distinguished from their effects. The various global trends operate as triggers of change and firms that operate in the competitive international business environment need to respond to the challenges imposed on them. However, the actual response of firms depends on the cultural inclinations of the actors who represent them. National culture is important if we are to understand the effects of global trends, for culture plays a role in shaping the process whereby these global trends are institutionalized. The comparative study that includes the Netherlands and the United States demonstrates that the actors that shape the employment change processes act in accordance with their cultural inclinations. A consistent finding of the study concerns the difference of the procedure in which changes are realized in the American and the Dutch context. Actors in the Dutch context rely on an emergent change process, while change processes in the American context are realized in accordance with a planned scheme. The different role that is ascribed to managers and workers in the design of the change process is at the root of this distinction. An emergent change process involves extensive interaction between management and workers; a planned change process is directed by management without employee involvement. The different role that is ascribed to workers and managers in the design of the change procedure in the United States and the Netherlands is not an isolated feature of these countries. The rules that are drawn upon by the various actors that shape the design of change procedure are firmly rooted in the work-related culture. Formal institutions such as the educational system, the labour law and the industrial relations system, but also informal institutions such as norms and expectations, reinforce the circuits of reproduction that ensure the preservation of cultural differences in the way changes in the realm of employment relations are realized.

As a result of the culturally guided process by which the global trends are institutionalized, the actual outcomes of the change processes do not converge to a single global standard of employment relations. The planned manner in which the so-called 'empowered teams' are implemented in the United States inhibits the actual transformation of the American workplace. In theory, the empowered teams promise to transcend the traditional shortcomings of the American workplace. However, this book shows that the manner in which the empowered teams operate in actual practice is in accordance with the traditional American work-related culture. Similarly, the need to enhance the flexibility of the employment relationship in the Netherlands is achieved without deviation from the traditional Dutch work-related culture. New initiatives, such as labour pools, employability and the trade-off between working time flexibility and the reduction of working hours, provide Dutch enterprises with more flexibility, while the characteristic features of the Dutch work-related culture, such as the reliance on internal labour market mechanisms, are preserved.

In sum, this book concludes that actors' responses to the global challenges vary in line with their cultural values. Culturally diverse nation states find distinct solutions to the challenges posed by the process of globalization. Consequently, this book challenges the widespread belief that global trends will lead to the homogenization of the employment relationship.

NOTES

1. The emphasis on flexibility is not restricted to the Netherlands; it has characterized employment developments across all Western European countries since the 1980s (Brewster et al., 1997).
2. It should be noted that the realism of the resulting 'best-practice model' is questionable. The best-practice model may be valid if the employment practices are regarded in isolation. However, it is doubtful whether the various best practices can be consistently combined. For example, following Lipietz (1995), it can be argued that flexibility of the human resource flow cannot be combined with the pursuit of employee involvement.
3. This observation is confirmed by Wilson: 'Planned change relies on a model of organization in which there is uncritical acceptance of the managerial role. This appears to be particularly true of North America' (Wilson, 1992, p.12).
4. Many reasons have been put forward to account for the relative lack of union power in the United States. Some observers refer to the diverse national origins of the immigrants that constituted America's workforce. It has been argued that this heterogeneity has hindered the development of working-class solidarity. Others point to the tension between unions and the American ideology. Unions are associated with a socialist ideology emphasizing solidarity and equality of outcomes. Thus unions do not fit comfortably with the American preference for individualism and control of one's own destiny. Jacoby (1991) explains the marginal role of unions by reference to the conscious use of power by American

employers to play down the role of unions.

5 Lawrence (1991, p.138) reports on an interview he once conducted with a Dutch executive manager who remarked that, in Europe when you make decisions, you are playing on three chess boards; in the USA only on one. In the Netherlands, a decision is taken in the management board. The decision is passed to the supervisory board. It is cleared with the works council and it will be communicated directly to the trade unions too.

References

Abrahamson, E. (1997), 'The emergence and prevalence of employee management rhetoric', *Academy of Management Journal*, **40**, 491–533.

Adler, N.J. (1991), *International dimensions of organizational behavior*, Boston: PWS-Kent Publishing Company.

Aglietta, M. (1979), *A theory of capitalist regulation*, London: NLB.

Albeda, W.B. and W.J. Dercksen (1994), *Arbeidsverhoudingen in Nederland*, Alphen aan den Rijn: Samson Bedrijfsinformatie.

Albert, M. (1990), *Capitalism against capitalism*, London: Whurr Publishers.

Alchian, A. (1950), 'Uncertainty, evolution and economic theory', *Journal of Political Economy*, **58**, 211-21.

Alchian, A. and H. Demsetz (1972), 'Production, information costs and economic organization', *American Economic Review*, **62**, 777–95.

Alexander, J.C. and S. Seidman (eds) (1990), *Culture and society: Contemporary debates*, Cambridge: Cambridge University Press.

Allaire, Y. and M.E. Firsirotu (1984), 'Theories of organizational culture', *Organization Studies*, **5**, 193–226.

Alvesson, M. (1993), *Cultural perspectives on organizations*, Cambridge: Cambridge University Press.

Amin, A. (1994), 'Models, fantasies and phantoms of transition', in A. Amin (ed.), *Post-Fordism: a reader*, Oxford: Blackwell Publishers.

Amit, R. and P.J.H. Schoemaker (1993), 'Strategic assets and organizational rents', *Strategic Management Journal*, **14**, 33–46.

Appelbaum, E. and R. Batt (1994), *The new American workplace: Transforming work systems in the United States*, Ithaca: Cornell University Press.

Aram, J.D. (1993), *Presumed superior: Individualism and American business*, Englewood Cliffs, NJ: Prentice-Hall.

Archer, M.S. (1995), *Realist social theory: The morphogenetic approach*, Cambridge: Cambridge University Press.

Atkinson, J. (1987), 'Flexibility or fragmentation', *Labour and Society*, **12**, 87–105.

Atleson, J.B. (1983), *Values and assumptions in American labor law*, Amherst: University of Massachusetts Press.

Badie, B. and P. Birnbaum (1983), *The sociology of the state*, Chicago: University of Chicago Press.

Bairoch, P. (1996), 'Globalization myths and realities: One century of external trade and foreign investment', in R. Boyer and D. Drache (eds), *States against markets*, London: Routledge.

Barker, J.R. (1993), 'Tightening the iron cage: Concertive control in self-managing teams', *Administrative Science Quarterly*, **38**, 408–37.

Barney, J. (1991), 'Firm resources and sustained competitive advantage', *Journal of Management*, **17**, 99–120.

Bartlett, C. and S. Ghoshal (1989), *Managing across borders: The transnational solution*, Boston: Harvard Business School Press.

Bean, R. (1985), *Comparative industrial relations*, London: Croom Helm.

Becker, G.S. (1996), *Accounting for tastes*, Cambridge, MA: Harvard University Press.

Beer, M., B. Spector, P.R. Lawrence, D.Q. Mills and R.E. Walton (1984), *Managing human assets*, New York: The Free Press.

Begin, J.P. (1992), 'Comparative human resource management: A systems perspective', *International Journal of Human Resource Management*, **3**, 379-408.

Begin, J.P. (1997), *Dynamic human resource systems*, Berlin: Walter de Gruyter.

Bellah, R.N. et al. (1985), *Habits of the heart*, Berkeley: University of California Press.

Benders, J. and G. van Hootegem (1997), 'A team is not a team: Towards a typology for comparing shopfloor teams', Unpublished paper, Nijmegen: University of Nijmegen.

Ben-Ner, A., T. Han and D.C. Jones (1996), 'The productivity effects of employee participation in control and in economic returns', in U. Pagano and R. Rowthorn (eds), *Democracy and efficiency in the economic enterprise*, London: Routledge.

Berger, P. and T. Luckmann (1966), *The social construction of reality*, Garden City: Doubleday.

Berggren, C. (1992), *The Volvo experience: Alternatives to lean production in the Swedish auto industry*, London: Macmillan.

Bhaskar, R. (1978), *A realist theory of science*, 2nd edition, Brighton: Harvester Press.

Bhaskar, R. (1983), 'Beef, structure and place', *Journal of Theory of Social Behaviour*, 81–95.

Bhaskar, R. (1989a), *The possibility of naturalism*, 2nd edition, London: Harvester Wheatsheaf.

Bhaskar, R. (1989b), *Reclaiming reality: A critical introduction to contemporary philosophy*, London: Verso.

Blair, M.M. (1995), *Ownership and control: Rethinking corporate governance for the twenty-first century*, Washington, DC: Brookings Institute.

Blau, P.M. (1971), *The structure of organizations*, New York: Basic Books.

Bloemen, E.S.A. (1988), *Scientific management in Nederland*, Amsterdam: NEHA.

Bolweg, J.F. and F. Kluytmans (eds) (1989), *De noodzaak van nieuwe verhoudingen: Beschouwingen over arbeidsverhoudingen en personeelsmanagement*, Deventer: Kluwer Bedrijfswetenschappen.

Bowles, S. and H. Gintis (1976), *Schooling in capitalist America*, London: Routledge.

Boyer, R. (1988), 'Technical change and the theory of "régulation"', in G. Dosi, et al, *Technical change and economic theory*, London: Pinter Publishers.

Boyer, R. (1995), 'Capital–labour relations in OECD countries: From the Fordist golden age to contrasted national trajectories', in J. Schor and J.I. You (eds), *Capital, the state and labour: A global perspective*, Aldershot, UK and Brookfield, US: Edward Elgar.

Boyer, R. (1996), 'The convergence hypothesis revisited: Globalization, but still the century of nations', in S. Berger and R. Dore (eds), *National diversity and global capitalism*, Ithaca: Cornell University Press.

Boyer, R. (1997), 'How does a new production system emerge?', in R. Boyer and J.P. Durand, *After Fordism*, London: Macmillan.

Boylan, T.A. and P.F. O'Gorman (1995), *Beyond rhetoric and realism in economics: towards a reformulation of economic methodology*, London: Routledge.

Braverman, H. (1974), *Labor and monopoly capital: The degradation of work in the twentieth century*, New York: Monthly Review Press.

Brewster, C. and S. Tyson (eds) (1992), *International comparisons in human resource management*, London: Pitmans.

Brewster, C. and A. Hegewisch (eds) (1994), *Policy and practice in European human resource management: The Price Waterhouse Cranfield survey*, London: Routledge.

Brewster, C., A. Hegewisch and L. Mayne (1994), 'Trends in European HRM: Signs of convergence', in P. Kirkbride (ed.), *Human resource management in Europe*, London: Routledge.

Brewster, C. (1995), 'Towards a "European" model of human resource management', *Journal of International Business Studies*, **26**, 1–21.

Brewster, C., L. Mayne and O. Tregaskis (1997), 'Flexible working in Europe: A review of the evidence', *Journal of World Business*, **32**, 133–51.

Bryant, C.G.A. (1995), *Practical sociology: Post-empiricism and the reconstruction of theory and application*, Cambridge: Polity Press.

Bryant, C.G.A. and D. Jary (1990), *Giddens' theory of structuration: A critical appreciation*, London: Routledge.

Bryant, C.G.A. and D. Jary (eds) (1997), *Anthony Giddens: Critical assessments*, London: Routledge.

Burgess, P. (1991), *European management guides: Industrial relations*, London: Institute of Personnel Management.

Bush, P.D. (1987), 'Theory of institutional change', *Journal of Economic Issues*, **21**, 1075–1116.

Campbell, J.L. and L.N. Lindberg (1991), 'The evolution of governance regimes', in J.L. Campbell, J.R. Hollingsworth and L.N. Lindberg (eds), *Governance of the American economy*, Cambridge: Cambridge University Press.

Carnevale, A.P., L.J. Gainer and J. Villet (1990), *Training in America: the organization and strategic role of training*, San Francisco: Jossey-Bass Publishers.

Cassell, P. (1993), *The Giddens reader*, Stanford: Stanford University Press.

Casson, M. (1991), *The economics of business culture*, Oxford: Clarendon Press.

CBS (1996), *Flexibilisering: het Nederlandse antwoord op internationalisering?*, Voorburg: Centraal Bureau voor de Statistiek.

CEDEFOP (1991), *Continuing training in firms and trainer development in the Netherlands*, Berlin: European Centre for the Development of Vocational Training.

Chandler, A.D. (1962), *Strategy and structure: Chapters in the history of the American industrial enterprise*, Cambridge: MIT Press.

Charkham, J.P. (1994), *Keeping good company: A study of corporate governance in five countries*, Oxford: Clarendon Press.

Child, J. (1981), 'Culture, contingency and capitalism in the cross-national study of organisations', in *Research in Organisational Behavior*, **3**, 303–56.

Church, R.L. (1976), *Education in the United States: an interpretive history*, New York: The Free Press.

Clark, J., C. Modgil and S. Modgil (eds) (1990), *Anthony Giddens: consensus and controversy*, Brighton: Falmer Press.

Clegg, S.R. et al. (1990), *Capitalism in contrasting cultures*, Berlin: Walter de Gruyter.

Coase, R.H. (1937), 'The nature of the firm', reprinted in O.E. Williamson and S.G. Winter (1993), *The nature of the firm: origins, evolution and development*, New York: Oxford University Press.

Coase, R.H. (1993), 'The nature of the firm: Influence', in O.E. Williamson and S.G. Winter, *The nature of the firm: origins, evolution and development*, New York: Oxford University Press.

Cohen, I.J. (1989), *Structuration theory: Anthony Giddens and the constitution of social life*, Cambridge: Cambridge University Press.

Collier, A. (1994), *Critical realism: An introduction to Roy Bhaskar's philosophy*, London: Verso.

Conner, K.R. (1991), 'A historical comparison of resource-based theory and five schools of thought within industrial organizational economics', *Journal of Management*, **17**, 121–54.

Craib, I. (1992), *Anthony Giddens*, London: Routledge.

Crainer, S. (1996), *Key management ideas: Thinking that changed the management world*, London: Pitman Publishing.

Crane, D. (ed.) (1994), *The sociology of culture: Emerging theoretical perspectives*, Cambridge: Blackwell Publishers.

Daniels, P.W. and W.F. Lever (1996), *The global economy in transition*, Harlow: Addison Wesley Longman Limited.

Dankbaar, B. (1997), 'Lean production: denial, confirmation or extension of sociotechnical systems design', *Human Relations*, **50**, 567–83.

Delsen, L. (1997), 'Flexibilisering van de arbeid in Europa', *Tijdschrift voor Arbeidsvraagstukken*, **13**, 23–36.

Demertzis, N. (1986), 'Cultural theory and political culture', Doctoral dissertation, Lund, Sweden.

Deming, W.E. (1986), *Out of the crisis*, Cambridge, MA: MIT Press.

Demsetz, H. (1993), 'The theory of the firm revisited', in O.E. Williamson and S.G. Winter, *The nature of the firm: origins, evolution and development*, New York: Oxford University Press.

Dertouzos, M., R.K. Lester and R. Solow (1989), *Made in America: Regaining the productive edge*, Cambridge, MA: MIT Press.

Dijk, van N. and M. Punch (1993), 'Open borders, closed circles: Management and organisation in the Netherlands', in D.J. Hickson (ed.), *Management in Western Europe*, Berlin: Walter de Gruyter.

DiMaggio, P.J. (1990), 'Cultural aspects of economic action and organisation', in R. Friedland and A.F. Robertson (eds), *Beyond the marketplace: Rethinking economy and society*, New York: Aldine de Gruyter.

DiMaggio, P.J. (1994), 'Culture and economy', in R. Smelser and R. Swedberg (eds), *The handbook of economic sociology*, Princeton: Princeton University Press.

DiMaggio, P.J. and W.W. Powell (1983), 'The iron cage revisited: Institutional isomorphism and collective rationality in organizational fields', reprinted in W.W. Powell and P.J. DiMaggio (eds) (1991), *The new institutionalism in organizational analysis*, Chicago: University of Chicago Press,

DiMaggio, P.J. and W.W. Powell (1991), 'Introduction', in W.W. Powell and P.J. DiMaggio (eds), *The new institutionalism in organisational analysis*, Chicago: University of Chicago Press.

Dirks, et al. (1994), *Culture/power/history: A reader in contemporary social theory*, Princeton: Princeton University Press.

Dobbin, F.R. (1994), 'Cultural models of economic organization: The social construction of rational organizing principles', in D. Crane (ed.), *The sociology of culture: emerging theoretical perspectives*, Cambridge, MA: Blackwell.

Doeringer, P.B. and M.J. Piore (1971), *Internal labor markets and manpower analysis*, Lexington: D.C. Heath and Co.

Dohse, K., U. Jürgens and T. Malsch (1985), 'From "fordism" to "toyotism"', *Politics and Society*, **14**, 114–46.

Dore, R. (1973), *British factory, Japanese factory: The origins of diversity in industrial relations*, Berkeley: University of California Press.

Dore, R. (1986), *Flexible rigidities: Industrial policy and structural adjustment in the Japanese economy*, Stanford: Stanford University Press.

Dore, R. (1997), 'The Asian form of capitalism', in P.H. Admiraal (ed.), *The corporate triangle: The structure and performance of corporate systems in a global economy*, Oxford: Blackwell.

Dow, G.K. (1987), 'The function of authority in transaction cost economics', *Journal of Economic Behavior and Organization*, **8**, 13–38.

Dunlop, J.T. (1958), *Industrial relations systems*, Boston: Harvard Business School Press.

Dunlop, J.T. (1993), *Industrial relations systems*, revised edition, Boston: Harvard Business School Press.

Durand, J.P. (1997), 'Is a new production system really emerging?', in R. Boyer and J.P. Durand, *After Fordism*, London: Macmillan.

Durkheim, E. (1895), *Les règles de la méthode sociologique*, reprinted in S. Lukes (1982), *The rules of sociological method and selected texts on sociology and its methods*, London: Macmillan.

Eccles, R.G. and N. Nohria (1992), *Beyond the hype*, Cambridge: Harvard Business School Press.

Eckstein, H. (1988), 'A culturalist theory of political change', *American Political Science Review*, **82**, 789–804.

Eckstein, H. (1996), 'Culture as a foundation concept for the social sciences', *Journal of Theoretical Politics*, **8**, 471–97.

Economist, The (1996), 'Le défi américain, again', **340** (7974), 21–24.

Edwards, P.K. (1979), *Contested terrain: The transformation of the workplace in the twentieth century*, London: Heinemann.

Edwards, P.K. (1994), 'A comparison of national regimes of labor regulation and the problems of the workplace', in J. Belanger, P.K. Edwards and L. Haiven (eds), *Workplace industrial relations and the global challenge*, Ithaca: Cornell University Press.

Eijnatten, F.M. van (1993), *The paradigm that changed the workplace*, Assen: Van Gorcum.

Elger, T. and C. Smith (1994), 'Global Japanization? Convergence and competition in the organization of the labour process', in T. Elger and C. Smith (eds), *Global Japanization? The transnational transformation of the labour process*, London: Routledge.

Elster, J. (1989), *The cement of society: Studies in rationality and social change*, Cambridge: Cambridge University Press.

Engbersen, G. et al. (1993), *Cultures of unemployment: A comparative look at long-term unemployment and urban poverty*, Oxford: Westview Press.

England, G.W. (1975), *The manager and his values: An international perspective from the United States, Japan, Korea, India and Australia*, Cambridge: Ballinger.

Esping-Andersen, G. (1990), *Three worlds of welfare capitalism*, Cambridge: Polity Press.

Ester, P. et al. (1994), *The individualizing society: value change in Europe and North America*, Tilburg: Tilburg University Press.

Fombrun, C. et al. (1984), *Strategic human resource management*, New York: John Wiley & Sons.

Foss, N.J. (1993), 'Theories of the firm: Contractual and competence perspectives', *Journal of Evolutionary Economics*, **3**, 127–44.

Foss, N.J. (1996a), 'Introduction: The emerging competence perspective', in N.J. Foss and C. Knudsen (eds), *Towards a competence theory of the firm*, London: Routledge.

Foss, N.J. (1996b), 'Capabilities and the theory of the firm', *Revue d'economie industrielle*, **77**, 1–20.

Foss, N.J., C. Knudsen and C.A. Montgomery (1995), 'An exploration of common ground: Integrating evolutionary and strategic theories of the firm', in C. Montgomery (ed.), *Resource-based and evolutionary theories of the firm*, Boston: Kluwer Academic Publishers.

Freeman, C. and C. Perez (1988), 'Structural crises of adjustment: Business cycles and investment behaviour', in G. Dosi (ed.), *Technical change and economic theory*, London: Pinter Publishers.

Friedman, M. (1953), 'The methodology of positive economics', in M. Friedman (ed.), *Essays in positive economics*, Chicago: Chicago University Press.

Friedman, M. (1982), *Capitalism and freedom*, Chicago: University of Chicago Press.

Gallie, D. (1978), *In search of the new working class: Automation and social integration within the capitalist enterprise*, Cambridge: Cambridge University Press.

Gasperz, J. and M. Ott (1996), *Management van employability*, Assen: Van Gorcum.

Geertz, C. (1973), *The interpretation of cultures*, New York: Basic Books.

Gelauff, G.M.M. and C. den Broeder (1996), *Governance of stakeholder relationships: The German and Dutch experience*, Den Haag: Centraal Planbureau.

Gellner, E. (1992), *Reason and culture*, Oxford: Blackwell Publishers.

Giddens, A. (1979), *Central problems in social theory*, Berkeley: University of California Press.

Giddens, A. (1984), *The constitution of society: Outline of the theory of structuration*, Berkeley: University of California Press.

Giddens, A. (1990a), 'Structuration theory and sociological analysis', in J.C. Clark, C. Modgil and S. Modgil (eds), *Anthony Giddens: Consensus and controversy*, Brighton: Falmer Press.

Giddens, A. (1990b), 'Structuration theory: Past, present and future', in C.G.A. Bryant and B. Jary (eds), *Giddens' theory of structuration: A critical appreciation*, London: Routledge.

Giddens, A. (1993), *New rules of sociological method*, 2nd edition, Cambridge:

Polity Press.

Glendon, M.A. (1992), 'Rights in twentieth century constitutions', in G.R. Stone (ed.), *The bill of rights in the modern state*, Chicago: University of Chicago Press.

Gordon Redding, S. (1994), 'Comparative management theory: Jungle, zoo or fossil bed', *Organisation Studies*, **15**, 323–59.

Goldberg, V.P. (1980), 'Bridges over contested terrain', *Journal of Economic Behavior and Organization*, 249–74.

Gordon, J., J.P. Jallade and D. Parkes (1994), *Op weg naar een beroep in Nederland, Duitsland en Frankrijk: Structuren binnen het beroepsonderwijs*, Paris, European Institute of Education and Social Policy.

Goslinga, S. and B. Klandermans (1996), 'Flexibilisering en individualisering van arbeidsvoorwaarden', *Tijdschrift voor Arbeidsvraagstukken*, 155–63.

Granovetter, M. (1985), 'Economic action and social structure: The problem of embeddedness', *American Journal of Sociology*, **91**, 481–510.

Grant, W. and W. Paterson (1994), 'The chemical industry: A study in internationalization', in J.R. Hollingsworth, P.C. Schmitter and W. Streeck (eds), *Governing capitalist economies: performance and control of economic sectors*, New York: Oxford University Press.

Groenewegen, J. and J.J. Vromen (1996), 'A case for theoretical pluralism', in J. Groenewegen (ed.), *Transaction cost economics and beyond*, Boston: Kluwer Academic Publishers.

Groenewegen, J. (1997), 'Institutions of capitalism', *Journal of Economic Issues*, **31**, 333–48.

Gronhaug, K. and O. Nordhaug (1992), 'International human resource management: An environmental perspective', *International Journal of Human Resource Management*, **3**, 1–13.

Gruchy, A.G. (1972), *Contemporary economic thought: The contribution of neo-institutional economics*, Clifton: Augustus M. Kelley Publishers.

Guillén, M.F. (1994), *Models of management: Work, authority and organization in a comparative perspective*, Chicago: University of Chicago Press.

Haak, A.T. (1994), 'Dutch sociotechnical design in practice', PhDthesis, Rijksuniversiteit Groningen.

Haan, E. and P. De Vos (1994), *Flexibiliteit van de arbeid: Op zoek naar zekerheid*, Amsterdam: NVM Welboom bladen.

Hampden-Turner, C. and F. Trompenaars (1993), *The seven cultures of capitalism*, New York: Doubleday.

Hannah, M.T. and J. Freeman (1989), *Organizational ecology*, Cambridge: Harvard University Press.

Held, D. and J.B. Thompson (ed.) (1989), *Social theory of modern societies: Anthony Giddens and his critics*, Cambridge: Cambridge University Press.

Hendry, C. and A. Pettigrew (1990), 'Human resource management: An agenda for the 1990s', *International Journal of Human Resource Management*, **1**,

17–44.

Hickson, D. and C.J. McMillan (1981), *Organisation and nation*, Westmead: Gower Publishing.

Hilmer, F.G. and L. Donaldson (1996), *Management redeemed: Debunking the fads that undermine corporate performance*, New York: The Free Press.

Hirsch, J. (1991), 'Fordism and post-Fordism: The present social crisis and its consequences', in W. Bonefeld and J. Holloway (eds), *Post-Fordism and social form*, London: Macmillan.

Hirst, P. and G. Thompson (1996), *Globalization in question: The international economy and the possibilities of governance*, Oxford: Blackwell Publishers.

Hodgson, G.M. (1988), *Economics and institutions: A manifesto for a modern institutional economics*, Cambridge: Polity Press.

Hodgson, G.M. (1993), *Economics and evolution: Bringing life back into economics*, Cambridge: Polity Press.

Hodgson, G.M. (1994), 'The return of institutional economics', in N.J. Smelser and R. Swedberg (eds), *The handbook of economic sociology*, Princeton: Princeton University Press.

Hodgson, G.M. (1995), 'The evolution of evolutionary economics', *Scottish Journal of Political Economy*, **42**, 469–88.

Hodgson, G.M. (1996), 'Evolutionary and competence-based theories of the firm', in C. Pitelis (ed.), *The economics of industrial and business strategy*

Hodgson, G.M. (1997), 'The Coasean tangle: The nature of the firm and the problem of historical specificity', in S. Medema (ed.), *Coasean economics*, Boston: Kluwer Academic Publishers.

Hofstede, G.H. (1975), 'The importance of being Dutch', *International Studies of Management and Organization*, **5**, 5–28.

Hofstede, G. (1980), *Culture's consequences: international differences in work-related values*, Beverly Hills: Sage.

Hofstede, G. (1991), *Cultures and organizations: Software of the mind*, London: McGraw-Hill.

Hofstede, G. and M. Bond (1988), 'The Confucius connection: From cultural roots to economic growth', *Organisation Dynamics*, **16** (4), 4–21.

Hollingsworth, J.R. (1991), 'The logic of coordinating American manufacturing sectors', in J.L. Campbell (ed.), *Governance of the American economy*, Cambridge: Cambridge University Press.

Hollingsworth, J.R. (1997), 'Continuities and changes in social systems of production: The cases of Japan, Germany and the United States', in J.R. Hollingsworth and R. Boyer (eds), *Contemporary capitalism: The embeddedness of institutions*, Cambridge: Cambridge University Press.

Hollingsworth, J.R., P.C. Schmitter and W. Streeck (1994), 'Capitalism, sectors, institutions and performance', in J.R. Hollingsworth, P.C. Schmitter and W. Streeck (eds), *Governing capitalist economies: Performance and control of economic sectors*, New York: Oxford University Press.

Hollingsworth, J.R. and W. Streeck (1994), 'Countries and sectors: Concluding remarks on performance, convergence and competitiveness', in J.R. Hollingsworth, P.C. Schmitter and W. Streeck (eds), *Governing capitalist economies: Performance and control of economic sectors*, New York: Oxford University Press.

Hollingsworth, J.R. and R. Boyer (1997), 'Coordination of economic actors and social systems of production', in J.R. Hollingsworth and R. Boyer (eds), *Contemporary capitalism: The embeddedness of institutions*, Cambridge: Cambridge University Press.

Hollis, M. (1994), *The philosophy of social science*, Cambridge: Cambridge University Press.

Holmstrom, B. and P. Milgrom (1991), 'Multitask principal–agent analyses: Incentive contracts, asset ownership, and job design', *Journal of Law, Economics and Organization*, **7**, 24–52.

IMF (1997), *World Economic Outlook*, Washington, DC: International Monetary Fund.

Inglehart, R. (1990), *Culture shift in advanced industrial society*, Princeton: Princeton University Press.

Iribarne, P. d' (1989), *La logique de l'honneur: gestion des enterprises et traditions nationales*, Paris: Éditions Denoël.

Iterson, A. van (1997), 'The development of national governance principles in the Netherlands', in R. Whitley and P.H. Kristensen (eds), *Governance at work*, New York: Oxford University Press.

Jacoby, S.M. (1991), 'American exceptionalism revisited: The importance of management', in S.M. Jacoby (ed.), *Masters to managers: historical and comparative perspectives on American employers*, New York: Colombia University Press.

Jackson, W.A. (1993), 'Culture, society and economic theory', *Review of Political Economy*, **5**, 453–69.

Jackson, W.A. (1996), 'Dualism, duality and the complexity of economic institutions', paper presented at EAEPE conference, Antwerp.

Jaggi, B. (1988), 'A comparative analysis of worker participation in the United States and Europe', in G. Dlugos and W. Dorow (eds), *Management under differing labour market and employment systems*, Berlin: Walter de Gruyter.

Jaikumar, R. (1986), 'Postindustrial manufacturing', *Harvard Business Review*, **64**, 69–76.

Jensen, H.E. (1987), 'Theory of human nature', *Journal of Economic Issues*, **21**, 1039–73.

Jessop, B. (1995), 'The regulation approach, governance and post-Fordism: Alternative perspectives on economic and political change', *Economy and Society*, **24**, 307–33.

Jones, E.L. (1995), 'Culture and its relationship to economic change', *Journal of Institutional and Theoretical Economics*, **151** (2).

Jones, R.J.B. (1996), *Globalisation and interdependence in the international and political economy: rhetoric and reality*, London: Pinter Publishers.

Kamoche, K. (1996), 'Strategic human resource management within a resource-capability view of the firm', *Journal of Management Studies*, **33**, 213–33.

Keenoy, T. (1990), 'Human resource management: rhetoric, reality and contradiction', *International Journal of Human Resource Management*, **1**, 363–84.

Kenney, M. and R. Florida (1993), *Beyond mass production: The Japanese system and its transfer to the US*, Oxford: Oxford University Press.

Kerr, C., J.T. Dunlop, F.H. Harbison and C.A. Myers (1960), *Industrialism and Industrial Man*, Boston: Harvard University Press.

Kerr, C., J.T. Dunlop, F.H. Harbison and C.A. Myers (1973), *Industrialism and Industrial Man*, 2nd edition, Boston: Harvard University Press.

Kerr, C. (1983), *The future of industrial societies: Convergence or continuing divergence*, Cambridge: Harvard University Press.

Kirkbride, P. (ed.) (1994), *Human resource management in Europe: Perspectives for the 1990s*, London: Routledge.

Klein, B., R. Crawford and A. Alchian (1978), 'Vertical integration, appropriable rents, and the competitive contracting process', *Journal of Law and Economics*, **21**, 297–326.

Knudsen, C. (1996), 'The competence perspective: A historical view', in N.J. Foss and C. Knudsen (eds), *Towards a competence theory of the firm*, London: Routledge.

Kochan, T.A., H.C. Katz and R.B. McKersie (1986), *The transformation of American industrial relations*, New York: Basic Books.

Korte, A.W. de and J.F. Bolweg (1995), *De nieuwe werknemer: Een verkenning naar veranderingen in werknemerswensen en de managementconsequenties daarvan*, Assen: Van Gorcum.

Kroeber, A.L. and C. Kluckhohn (1952), *Culture: A critical review of concepts and definitions*, Cambridge: Harvard University Press.

Lado, A.A. and M.C. Wilson (1994), 'Human resource systems and sustained competitive advantage: A competency-based perspective', *Academy of Management Review*, **19**, 699–727.

Lammers, C.J. and D.J. Hickson (eds) (1979), *Organisations alike and unlike: International and inter-institutional studies in the sociology of organizations*, London: Routledge and Kegan Paul.

Laurier, J. and F. Pot (1983), 'Sociaal-demokratiese arbeidersbeweging en wetenschappelijke bedrijfsvoering 1920-1940', in Braverman et al. *Taylorisme in Nederland*, Nijmegen: SUN.

Lawler, E.E., S.A. Mohrman and G. Ledford (1992), *Employee involvement and TQM: Practice and results in Fortune 5000 companies*, San Francisco: Jossey-Bass.

Lawler, E. (1994), 'From job-based to competency-based organizations',

Journal of Organizational Behavior, **15**, 3–15.

Lawrence, P. (1991), *Management in the Netherlands*, Oxford: Clarendon Press.

Lawrence, P. (1996), *Management in the United States*, London: Sage Publications.

Lawson, T. (1993), 'Realism / Philosophical', in G.M. Hodgson, W.J. Samuels and M.R. Tool (eds), *The Elgar companion to institutional and evolutionary economics*, Aldershot, UK and Brookfield, US: Edward Elgar.

Lawson, T. (1995), 'A realist perspective on contemporary economic theory', *Journal of Economic Issues*, **29**, 1–32.

Lazonick, W. (1995), 'Cooperative employment relations and Japanese economic growth', J. Schor and J.I. You (eds), *Capital, the state and labour: A global perspective*, Aldershot, UK and Brookfield, US: Edward Elgar.

Lazonick, W. (1997), 'The Anglo-Saxon corporate system', in P.H. Admiraal (ed.), *The corporate triangle: The structure and performance of corporate systems in a global economy*, Oxford: Blackwell.

Levine, D. and L. Tyson (1990), 'Participation, productivity and the firm's environment', in A.S. Blinder, *Paying for productivity*, Washington, DC: Brookings Institute.

Lijphart, A. (1968), *The politics of accommodation, pluralism and democracy in the Netherlands*, Berkeley: University of California Press.

Lijphart, A. (1989), 'From the politics of accommodation to adversarial politics in the Netherlands: A reassessment', *West European politics*, **12**, (1).

Lincoln, J.R. and A.L. Kalleberg (1990), *Culture, control and commitment: A study of work organization and work attitudes in the United States and Japan*, Cambridge: Cambridge University Press.

Linstead, S. and R. Grafton-Small (1992), 'On reading organisational culture', *Organization Studies*, **13**, 331–55.

Lipietz, A. (1995), 'Capital–labour relations at the dawn of the twenty-first century', in J. Schor and J.I. You (eds), *Capital, the state and labour: A global perspective*, Aldershot, UK and Brookfield, US: Edward Elgar

Lipset, S.M. (1990), *Continental divide: The values and institutions of the United States and Canada*, New York: Routledge.

Lipset, S.M. (1996), *American exceptionalism: A double-edged sword*, New York: Norton & Company.

Littler, C.R. (1982), *The development of the labour process in capitalist societies: A comparative study of the transformation of work organization in Britain, Japan and the USA*, London: Heinemann Educational Books.

Locke, R.R. (1996), *The collapse of the American management mystique*, New York: Oxford University Press.

Lukes, S. (1973), *Individualism*, Oxford: Basic Blackwell.

Mäki, U. (1992): 'On the method of isolation in economics', *Poznan studies in the philosophy of the sciences and the humanities*, **35**, 317–51.

Marmor, T. et al. (1990), *America's misunderstood welfare state: persistent myths, enduring realities*, New York: Basic Books.

Marginson, P. (1993), 'Power and efficiency in the firm: Understanding the employment relationship', in C. Pitelis (ed.), *Transaction costs, markets and hierarchies*, Oxford: Blackwell.

Marginson, P., P. Armstrong, P.K. Edwards and J. Purcell (1995), 'Extending beyond borders: Multinational companies and the international management of labour', *International Journal of Human Resource Management*, **6**, 702–19.

Marglin, S.A. (1974), 'What do bosses do? The origins and functions of hierarchy in capitalist production', *Review of Radical Political Economics*, **6**, 60–112.

Maurice, M., A. Sorge and M. Warner (1980), 'Societal differences in organising manufacturing units', *Organization Studies*, **1**, 59–86.

Maurice, M., F. Sellier and J.J. Silvestre (1986), *The social foundations of industrial power: A comparison of France and Germany*, Cambridge: MIT Press.

Mayhew, A. (1987), 'Culture: core concept under attack', *Journal of Economic Issues*, **21**, 587–603.

McFarlin, D.B., P.D. Sweeney and J.L. Cotton (1992), 'Attitudes toward employee participation in decision-making', *Human Resource Management*, **31**, 363–83.

Mendelsohn, S.R. (1990), *Wrongful termination litigation in the United States and its effect on the employment relationship*, Paris: OECD.

Mendoza, (1997), 'Ontological security, routine, social reproduction', in C.G.A. Bryant and D. Jary (eds), *Anthony Giddens: Critical assessments*, London: Routledge.

Meyer, J.W. and B. Rowan (1977), 'Institutionalized organizations: Formal structure as myth and ceremony', reprinted in W.W. Powell and P.J. DiMaggio (eds) (1991), *The new institutionalism in organizational analysis*, Chicago: University of Chicago Press

Meyer, J.W., J. Boli and G.M. Thomas (1987), 'Ontology and rationalization in the western cultural account', in G.M. Thomas (ed.), *Institutional structure: constituting state, society and the individual*, Beverley Hills: Sage Publications.

Miles, M.B. and A.M. Huberman (1984), *Analyzing qualitative data: A sourcebook for new methods*, Beverly Hills: Sage Publications.

Min Chen (1995), *Asian management systems: Chinese, Japanese and Korean styles of business*, London: Routledge.

Ministerie van Sociale Zaken en Werkgelegenheid (1995), *Flexibiliteit en zekerheid*, Den Haag: SDU Uitgevers.

Mitchell, C. (1983), 'Case and situation analysis', *Sociological Review*, **31**, 187–211.

Munch, R. and N.J. Smelser (eds) (1992), *Theory of culture*, Berkeley: University of California Press.

NCEE (1991), *America's choice: High skills or low wages*, Rochester: National Center on Education and Economy.

NEDO (1984), *Competence and competition: Training and education in Germany, the United States and Japan*, Washington: National Economic Development Office.

Nijs, W.F. de (1996), 'Arbeidsverhoudingen en personeelsmanagement', in A.G. Nagelkerke and W.F. de Nijs, *Regels rond arbeid*, Leiden: Stenfert Kroese.

Nelson, R.R. and S.G. Winter (1982), *An evolutionary theory of economic change*, Cambridge: Harvard University Press.

Nielsen, K. (1991), 'Towards a flexible future: Theories and politics', in B. Jessop (ed.), *The politics of flexibility*, Aldershot, UK and Brookfield, US: Edward Elgar.

Noon, M. (1992), 'HRM: A map, model or theory', in P. Blyton and P. Turnbull (eds), *Reassessing human resource management*, London: Sage Publications.

Nordhaug, O. and K. Gronhaug (1994), 'Competences as resources in firms', *International Journal of Human Resource Management*, **5**, 89–106.

OECD (1997), 'Globalisation and linkages: Macro-structural challenges and opportunities', Economics Department Working Papers (181), Paris: OECD.

Ohmae, K. (1990), *The Borderless world: Power and strategy in the interlinked economy*, London: Fontana.

Olson, W.K. (1991), *The litigation explosion*, New York: Truman Talley Books.

Osterman, P. (1988), *Employment futures: Reorganization, dislocation and public policy*, New York: Oxford University Press.

Osterman, P. (1994), 'How common is workplace transformation and how can we explain who does it?', *Industrial and Labor Relations Review*, **47**, 173–188.

Osterman, P. (1995), 'Skill, training and work organization in American establishments', *Industrial relations*, **34**, 125–46.

Outhwaite, W. (1987), *New philosophies in social science: Realism, hermeneutics and critical theory*, London, Macmillan.

Ozaki, M. (1992), 'Technological change and labour relations: An international review', in M. Ozaki (ed.), *Technological change and labour relations*, Geneva: International Labor Organization.

Parkin, F. (1982), *Max Weber*, London: Tavistock.

Peijpe, T. van (1990), *De conjunctuur van het arbeidsrecht: Rechtsontwikkeling in Nederland en andere landen, 1975–1990*, Groningen: Wolters Noordhoff.

Peláez, E. and J. Holloway (1991), 'Learning to bow: Post-Fordism and technological determinism', in W. Bonefeld and J. Holloway (eds), *Post-Fordism and social form*, London: Macmillan.

Penrose, E.T. (1952), 'Biological analogies in the theory of the firm', *American Economic Review*, **42**, 804–19.

Penrose, E.T. (1959), *The theory of the growth of the firm*, Oxford: Oxford University Press.

Perez, C. (1985), 'Microelectronics, long waves and world structural change: New perspectives for developing countries', *World Development*, **13**, 441–63.

Peteraf, M.A. (1993), 'The cornerstones of competitive advantage: A resource-based view', *Strategic Management Journal*, **14**, 179–91.

Peters, T.J. and R.H. Waterman (1982), *In search of excellence*, New York: Warner Books.

Petrella, R. (1996), 'Globalization and internationalization: The dynamics of the emerging world order', in R. Boyer and D. Drache (eds), *States against markets*, London: Routledge.

Pfeffer, J. (1994), *Competitive advantage through people*, Boston: Harvard Business School Press.

Pfeffer, J. and Y. Cohen, (1984), 'Determinants of internal labor markets in organizations' *Administrative Science Quarterly*, **29**, 550–72.

Phillips, D. (1985), *De naakte Nederlander: kritische overpeinzingen*, Amsterdam: Uitgeverij Bert Bakker.

Pieper, R. (ed.) (1990), *Human resource management: an international comparison*, Berlin: Walter de Gruyter.

Piore, M.J. and C.F. Sabel (1984), *The second industrial divide: Possibilities for prosperity*, New York: Basic Books.

Pollert, A. (1991), 'The orthodoxy of flexibility', in A. Pollert (ed.), *Farewell to flexibility*, Oxford: Basil Blackwell.

Poole, M. (1986), *Industrial relations: Origins and patterns of national diversity*, London: Routledge.

Poole, M. (1990), 'Human resource management in an international perspective', *International Journal of Human Resource Management*, **1**, 1–15.

Porter, M. E. (1980), *Competitive strategy*, New York: The Free Press.

Porter, M. (1990), *The competitive advantage of nations*, New York: Free Press.

Powell, W.W. (1991), 'Expanding the scope of institutional analysis', in W.W. Powell and P.J. DiMaggio (eds), *The new institutionalism in organizational analysis*, Chicago: University of Chicago Press.

Powell, W.W. and P.J. DiMaggio (eds) (1991), *The new institutionalism in organisational analysis*, Chicago: University of Chicago Press.

Prahalad, C.K. and G. Hamel (1990), 'The core competence of the corporation', *Harvard Business Review*, May–June, 79–91.

Pugh, D.S. (1981), 'The Aston program perspective: Retrospect and prospect', in A.H. Ven and W.F. Yoice (eds), *Perspectives on organization and behavior*, New York: John Wiley & Sons.

Pugh, D.S. and D. Hickson (1993), 'Organisational context and structure in various cultures', in T.D. Weinshall (ed.), *Societal culture and management*, Berlin: Walter de Gruyter.

Putterman, L. (1993), 'After the employment relationship: Problems on the road to enterprise democracy', in S. Bowles, H. Gintis and B. Gustafsson, *Markets and democracy: Participation, accountability and efficiency*, Cambridge:

Cambridge University Press.

Ragin, C.C. (1987), *The comparative method*, Berkeley: University of California Press.

Rebitzer, J.B. (1993), 'Radical political economy and the economics of labor markets', *Journal of Economic Literature*, **31**, 1394–1434.

Reed, R. and R. DeFillipi (1990), 'Causal ambiguity, barriers to imitation, and sustainable competitive advantage', *Academy of Management Review*, **15**, 88–102.

Reichers, A.E. and B. Schneider (1990), Climate and culture: An evolution of constructs, in B. Schneider, (ed.), *Organizational climate and culture*, San Francisco: Jossey-Bass Publishers.

Rinehart, J., C. Huxley and D. Robertson (1997), *Just another car factory: Lean production and its discontents*, Ithaca: Cornell University Press.

Ritzer, G. (1993), *The McDonaldization of society*, Thousand Oaks: Pine Forge Press.

Roberts, K.H. and N.A. Boyacigiller (1984), 'Cross-national organisational research: The grasp of the blind man', *Research in Organisational Behavior*, **6**, 423–75.

Rothman, M. and D.R. Briscoe (1993), 'The United States', in M. Rothman (ed.), *Industrial relations around the world*, Berlin: Walter de Gruyter.

Rousseau, D.M. (1990), 'Assessing organisational culture: The case for multiple methods', in B. Schneider (ed.), *Organizational climate and culture*, San Francisco: Jossey-Bass Publishers.

Rutherford, M. (1994), *Institutions in economics: The old and new institutionalism*, Cambridge: Cambridge University Press.

Sackmann, S.A. (1991), *Cultural knowledge in organisations: Exploring the corporate mind*, Beverly Hills: Sage Publications.

Sakakibara, E. (1993), *Beyond capitalism: The Japanese model of market economics*, Lanham, MD: University Press of America.

Samuels, W.J. (1995), 'The present state of institutional economics', *Cambridge Journal of Economics*, **19**, 569–90.

Sayer, A. (1992), *Method in social science: A realist approach*, 2nd edition, London: Routledge.

Schein, E. (1985), *Organizational culture and leadership*, San Francisco: Jossey-Bass Publishers.

Schein, E. (1996), 'Three cultures of management: the key to organizational learning', *Sloan Management Review*, Fall, 9–20.

Schneider, L. and C.M. Bonjean (eds) (1973), *The idea of culture in the social sciences*, Cambridge: Cambridge University Press.

Schultz, M. (1992), 'Postmodern pictures of culture: a postmodern reflection on the "modern notion" of corporate culture', *International Studies of Management & Organisation*, **22**, 15–35.

Schwandt, T.A. (1994), 'Constructivist, interpretivist approaches to human inquiry', in N.K. Denzin and Y.S. Lincoln (eds), *Handbook of qualitative research*, Thousand Oaks: Sage Publications.

Scott, W.R. (1987), 'The adolescence of institutional theory', *Administrative Science Quarterly*, **32**, 493–511.

Scott, W.R. (1992), *Organizations: Rational, natural and open systems*, 3rd edition, Englewood Cliffs: Prentice-Hall.

Segall, M. (1986), 'Culture and behavior: Psychology in global perspective', *Annual Review of Psychology*, **37**, 523–64.

Segall, M. (1990), *Human behavior in global perspective: An introduction to cross-cultural psychology*, New York: Pergamon Press.

Selznick, P. (1948), 'Foundations of the theory of organization', *American Sociological Review*, **13**, 25–35.

Sengenberger, W. (1993), 'Lean production: The way of working and producing in the future', in W. Sengenberger and D. Campbell (eds), *Lean production and beyond: Labour aspects of a new production concept*, Geneva: International Labour Organization.

Sengenberger, W. and F. Wilkinson (1995), 'Globalization and labour standards', in J. Michie and J.G. Smith (eds), *Managing the global economy*, New York: Oxford University Press.

SER (1991), *Flexibele arbeidsrelaties: Advies inzake flexibele arbeidsrelaties*, Den Haag: Sociaal-Economische Raad.

Shonen, S. and O. Renkar (1985), 'Clustering countries on attitudinal dimensions: A review and synthesis', *Academy of Management Review*, **10**, 435–54.

Sitter, U. de, J.F. den Hertog and B. Dankbaar (1997), 'From complex organizations with simple jobs to simple organizations with complex jobs', *Human Relations*, **50**, 497–534.

Skinner, W. (1985), 'The taming of lions: How manufacturing leadership evolved, 1780–1984', in K.B. Clark et al., *The uneasy alliance*, Boston: Harvard Business School.

Smircich, L. (1983), 'Concepts of culture and organisational analysis', *Administrative Science Quarterly*, **28**, 339–58.

Smith, C. and P. Meiksins (1995), 'System, society and dominance effects in cross-national organisational analysis', *Work, Employment and Society*, **9**, 241–67.

Sondergaard, M. (1994), 'Hofstede's consequences: A study of reviews, citations and replications', *Organization Studies*, **15**, 447–456.

Sorge, A. (1983), 'Cultured organization', *International Studies of Management and Organization*, **12**, 106–38.

Sorge, A. and M. Warner (1986), *Comparative factory organisation*, Aldershot: Gower Publishing Company.

Sorge, A. and W. Streeck (1988), 'Industrial relations and technnical change:

The case for an extended perspective', in R. Hyman and W. Streeck (eds), *New technology and industrial relations*, Oxford: Basic Blackwell.

Sorge, A. (1992), 'Human resource management in the Netherlands', *Employee Relations*, **14**, 71–84.

Sorge, A. (1996), 'Societal effects in cross-national organization studies: Conceptualizing diversity in actors and systems', in R. Whitley and P.H. Kristensen (eds), *The changing European firm: Limits to convergence*, London: Routledge.

Sparrow, P. and J.M. Hiltrop (1994), *European human resource management in transition*, Englewood Cliffs: Prentice-Hall.

Sparrow, P., R.S. Schuler and S.E. Jackson (1994), 'Convergence or divergence: Human resource practices and policies for competitive advantage worldwide', *The International Journal of Human Resource Management*, **5**, 267–99.

Spybey, T. (1996), *Globalization and world society*, Cambridge, MA: Polity Press.

Starkey, K. and A. McKinlay (1993), *Strategy and the human resource: Ford and the search for competitive advantage*, Oxford: Blackwell Publishers.

Stichting van de Arbeid (1996), *Nota 'Flexibiliteit en zekerheid'*, Den Haag: Stichting van de Arbeid.

Storey, J. (1995), 'Human resource management: Still marching on, or marching out?', in J. Storey (ed.), *Human resource management: a critical text*, London: Routledge.

Strauss. G. (1995), 'Is the New Deal system collapsing? With what might it be replaced?', *Industrial Relations*, **34**, 329–49.

Streeck, W. (1992), *Social institutions and economic performance*, London: Sage Publications.

Tayeb, M. (1988), *Organizations and national culture: A comparative analysis*, London: Sage Publications.

Tayeb, M. (1994), 'Organizations and national culture: Methodology considered', *Organisation Studies*, **15**, 429–46.

Taylor, C. (1989), *Sources of the self: The making of modern identity*, Cambridge, MA: Cambridge University Press.

Teece, D.J. (1988), 'Technological change and the nature of the firm', in G.C. Dosi et al., *Technical change and economic theory*, London: Pinter Publishers.

Teece, D.J. and G. Pisano (1994), 'The dynamic capabilities of firms: An introduction', *Industrial and Corporate Change*, **3**, 537–55.

Thompson, J.B. (1989), 'The theory of structuration', in D. Held and J.B. Thompson, *Social theory of modern societies: Anthony Giddens and his critics*, Cambridge, MA: Cambridge University Press.

Tichy, N. and S. Sherman (1993), *Control your destiny or someone else will*, New York: Doubleday.

Tool, M.R. (1993), 'The theory of instrumental value: Extensions, clarifications', in M.R. Tool (ed.), *Institutional economics: Theory, method, policy*, Boston: Kluwer Academic Publishers.

Towers Perrin (1992), *Priorities for gaining competitive advantage: A worldwide human resource study*, London: Towers Perrin.

Triandis, H.C. (1983), 'Dimensions of cultural variation as parameters of organisational theories', *International Studies of Management and Organisation*, **12**, 139–69.

Trompenaars, F. (1993), *Riding the wave of culture: Understanding cultural diversity in business*, London: The Economist Books.

UNCTAD, (1996), *World Investment Report 1996*, New York: United Nations.

Vickery, G. (1996), 'The globalization of investment and trade', in J. de la Mothe and G. Paquet (eds), *Evolutionary economics and the new international political economy*, London: Pinter.

Visser, J. (1992), 'The Netherlands: The end of an era and the end of a system', in A. Ferner and R. Hyman (eds), *Industrial relations in the new Europe*, Oxford: Basic Blackwell.

Vromen, J.J. (1994), *Economic evolution: An inquiry into the foundations of new institutional economics*, London: Routledge.

Waarden, F. van (1987), 'Vervlechting van staat en belangengroepen', in *Beleid en Maatschappij*, **5**, 172–84.

Waarden, F. van (1992), 'The historical institutionalization of typical national patterns in policy networks between the state and industry: a comparison of the USA and the Netherlands', *European Journal of Political Research*, **21**, 131–61.

Wade, R. (1996), 'Globalization and its limits: Reports of the death of the national economy are greatly exaggerated', in S. Berger and R. Dore (eds), *National diversity and global capitalism*, Ithaca: Cornell University Press.

Walton, R.E. (1985), 'From control to commitment: Transforming work force management in the United States', in K.B. Clark et al., *The uneasy alliance*, Boston: Harvard Business School Press.

Waters, M. (1995), *Globalization*, London: Routledge.

Watkins, J.W.N. (1968), 'Methodological individualism and social tendencies', in M. Brodbeck (ed.), *Readings in the philosophy of science*, New York: The Macmillan Company.

Weber, M. (1902), *The methodology of the social sciences*, reprinted in E.A. Shils and H.A. Finch (1949), New York: The Free Press.

Wernerfelt, B. (1984), 'A resource-based view of the firm', *Strategic Management Journal*, **5**, 171–80.

Wernerfelt, B. (1995), 'The resource-based view of the firm: Ten years after', *Strategic Management Journal*, **16**, 171–4.

Wheeler, H.N. (1993), 'Industrial relations in the United States of America', in G.J. Bamber and R.D. Lansbury (eds), *International and comparative industrial relations*, London: Routledge.

Whitley, R. (1992), *Business systems in East Asia*, London: Sage Publications.

Whitley, R. (1996), 'The social construction of economic actors', in R. Whitley and P.H. Kristensen (eds), *The changing European firm: Limits to convergence*, London: Routledge.

Whitley, R. (1997), 'The social regulation of work: Institutions, interest groups and varieties of work organization in capitalist societies', in R. Whitley and P.H. Kristensen (eds), *Governance at work*, Oxford: Oxford University Press.

Wilber, C.K. and R.S. Harrison (1978), 'The methodological basis of institutional economics: Pattern model, storytelling and holism', *Journal of Economic Issues*, **12**, 61–89.

Williams, K. et al. (1987), 'The end of mass production?', *Economy and Society*, **16**, 405–39.

Williams, K., C. Haslam, J. Williams and T. Cutler (1992), 'Against lean production', *Economy and Society*, **21**, 321–54.

Williamson, O.E. (1975), *Markets and hierarchies: Analysis and antitrust implications*, New York: The Free Press.

Williamson, O.E. (1985), *The economic institutions of capitalism: Firms, markets and relational contracting*, New York: The Free Press.

Williamson, O.E. (1993), 'The logic of economic organization', in O.E. Williamson and S.G. Winter (eds), *The nature of the firm: Origins, evolution and development*, Oxford: Oxford University Press.

Williamson, O.E. (1994), 'Transaction cost economics and organization theory', in N.J. Smelser and R. Swedberg (eds), *The handbook of economic sociology*, Princeton: Princeton University Press.

Williamson, O.E. (1996), 'Efficiency, power, authority and economic organization', in J. Groenewegen (ed.), *Transaction cost economics and beyond*, Boston: Kluwer Academic Publishers.

Williamson, O., M. Wachter and J. Harris (1975), 'Understanding the employment relation', *The Bell Journal of Economics*, **6**, 250–78.

Wilson, D. (1992), *A strategy of change: Concepts and controversies in the management of change*, London: Routledge.

Winter, S.G. (1975), 'Optimization and evolution in the theory of the firm', in R.H. Day and T. Groves (eds), *Adaptive economic models*, New York: Academic Press.

Winter, S.G. (1993), 'On Coase, competence and the corporation', in O.E. Williamson and S.G. Winter (eds), *The nature of the firm: Origins, evolution and development*, Oxford: Oxford University Press.

Womack, J.P., D.T. Jones and D. Roos (1990), *The machine that changed the world*, New York: Rawson Associates.

Wong, G.Y.Y. and P.H. Birnbaum-More (1994), 'Culture, context and structure: A test on Hong Kong banks', *Organization Studies*, **15**, 99–123.

Wood, S.J. (1991), 'Japanization and/or Toyotaism', *Work, Employment and Society*, **5**, 567–600.

Wright, P.M., G.C. McMahan and A. McWilliams (1994), 'Human resources and sustained competitive advantage: A resource-based perspective', *International Journal of Human Resource Management*, **5**, 301–26.

Wuthnow, R. (1987), *Meaning and moral order: Explorations in cultural analysis*, Berkeley: University of California Press.

Wuthnow, R. et al. (1984), *Cultural analysis*, Boston: Routledge & Kegan Paul.

Yin, (1994), *Case study research*, Thousand Oaks: Sage.

Zahn, E. (1989), *Regenten, rebellen en reformatoren: Een visie op Nederland en de Nederlanders*, Amsterdam: Contact.

Index